Positively Responsible

For co.

*In memory of Joseph Bolton (1913–2007)*
*– Inspiration and Positive Thinker*

# Positively Responsible

*How business can save the planet*

Erik Bichard and Cary L. Cooper

ELSEVIER

AMSTERDAM • BOSTON • HEIDELBERG • LONDON • NEW YORK • OXFORD
PARIS • SAN DIEGO • SAN FRANCISCO • SINGAPORE • SYDNEY • TOKYO
Butterworth Heinemann is an imprint of Elsevier

Butterworth-Heinemann is an imprint of Elsevier
Linacre House, Jordan Hill, Oxford OX2 8DP, UK
30 Corporate Drive, Suite 400, Burlington, MA 01803, USA

First Edition 2008

**British Library Cataloguing in Publication Data**
A catalogue record for this book is available from the British Library

**Library of Congress Cataloging-in-Publication Data**
A catalog record for this book is available from the Library of Congress

ISBN: 978-0-7506-8475-0

For information on all Butterworth-Heinemann publications
visit our web site at elsevierdirect.com

Printed on recycled paper

Typeset by Charon Tec Ltd (A Macmillan Company), Chennai, India
www.charontec.com

Printed and bound in Hungary

08 09 10 11 12   10 9 8 7 6 5 4 3 2 1

# Contents

Contents

# Acknowledgements

For a book like this, most of the help that we have had has come more from open discussions than from factual advice, although we had a lot of that as well. We are therefore very grateful to the following people for having the patience and wisdom to help us wrestle with the numerous aspects of the human condition, and the condition of the planet:

Ulf Andersson, Sheila Bichard, Andrew Bichard, Toby Clark, Julie Collins, Ed Deedigan, Andy Dickson, Kath Ferguson, Phil Hargreaves, Lindsey Forrester, Jason Leadbitter, Danesh Missaghian, Jonas Oldmark, Dave Picken, Jonathon Porritt, James Powell, Kjell Rosen, Chris Rose, Jason Rowley, Donna Lee, Christina Schaffer, Lord Terry Thomas, Ruth Turner, Jochen Vorfelder, Dave Wheeler, Penny Walker.

Particular thanks goes to Mark Everard.

# Professor Cary L. Cooper, CBE

Cary L. Cooper is Professor of Organizational Psychology and Health, and Pro Vice Chancellor at Lancaster University. He is the author/editor of over 100 books (on occupational stress, women at work, and industrial and organisational psychology), has written over 400 scholarly articles for academic journals, and is also a frequent contributor to national newspapers, TV and radio. He is currently Founding Editor of the *Journal of Organizational Behavior* and is a Fellow of the British Psychological Society, The Royal Society of Arts, The Royal Society of Medicine, The Royal Society of Health, British Academy of Management, and an Academician of the Academy for the Social Sciences.

Professor Cooper is past President of the British Academy of Management, is a Companion of the Chartered Management Institute, and one of the first UK-based Fellows of the (American) Academy of Management (having also won the 1998 Distinguished Service Award for his contribution to management science from the Academy of Management). In 2001, Cary was awarded a CBE in the Queen's Birthday Honours List for his contribution to occupational safety and health and, in 2007, a Lifetime Achievement Award from the Division of Occupational Psychology of the British Psychological Society.

# Professor Erik Bichard

 Erik Bichard is Professor of Regeneration and Sustainable Development at Salford University, in Greater Manchester. During his career, he has worked as a sustainable development practitioner in the public, private, third and now academic sector. Until June 2007, and for ten years, he was Chief Executive of the UK National Centre for Business & Sustainability. In addition to his role at Salford, he has his own practice: Positively Responsible. In the past he has been Co-operatives UK's sustainability advisor, and currently performs the same function for the City of Liverpool. He is a member of the UK Sustainable Development Panel, and serves on several company boards as a non-executive director including the social enterprise FRC Group, and Migrant Workers North West.

He is a frequent contributor to newspaper, TV and radio programmes covering a range of sustainability issues from recycling and renewable energy to social cohesion and responsible business issues. His most recent written work includes texts on sustainable governance, social enterprise and the recycling sector, and the relationship between health in the workplace and business reputation on sustainable development.Professor Erik Bichard

# Deniers, despairers and contrarians

*The Green Movement could not become a major political force so long as it
concerned itself primarily with natural resources rather than with the full
range of human desires. Its setbacks are yet another example of idealism being
unable to get off the ground because it has not looked broadly enough at
human aspirations in their entirety*
**Theodore Zeldin,** *An Intimate History of Humanity*

## A man of our time

Bernard could live anywhere in North America, Europe, Australia or Japan. He
could really live anywhere in the world where life is economically comfortable.
Let's put him in Dorking, a town about 30 miles south west of London. Bernard,
or Bern as his friends call him, lives with his second wife, their young son, and
her two teenage daughters from her first marriage. Their three-bedroom house
(built in 1985) lies about 1.5 miles from the town centre. Bernard's son by his
first marriage lives with his mother and her partner 70 miles away in Tonbridge,
Kent. Bern drives over to spend Sunday with him every other week.

Bern works as a facilities manager for a large construction company. His
job requires him to make sure that the buildings he manages function in a way
that ensures that the tenants don't complain. The heating and cooling machinery needs to work, the lifts and loading bays need to function properly, and the
communal areas need to be well lit and decorated. What tenants do in their own
spaces is up to them. He doesn't particularly enjoy his job, but it has its moments
and it pays the mortgage. He never really had ambitions to do anything else outside of the building trade. He stayed in school, but got a job instead of going to
university. He likes to spend time with his mates down the pub on evenings when
he doesn't get home too late.

When the talk down the pub turns to global warming, Bern is agnostic. He
understands that it is happening – the winter flowers were out even earlier this
year – but is not convinced that humans are responsible. The heavier rain and
the warmer summers are defiantly noticeable, but the claim that this is happening as a result of human activity seemed a little far fetched to him. The thing is,
even if it was, there would be very little that he could do about it. He advances
the argument that scientists have about as much of a clue as to what is going on

as the guys around the bar. He will use the fact that every week some boffin is telling us that something we've been eating for centuries is going to kill us, as a reason not to trust scientists. 'You watch these people arguing on the telly about climate change and who is to blame', he says, 'and you have no idea which of them is right.'

He is a conservative man, and scoffs at people who are changing their life-styles and adorning their houses with wind turbines and solar panels. They are either doing it to show off, or otherwise they have more money than sense. Why would you spend good money on something that won't return your investment for donkey's years, when you can buy perfectly good and cheap electricity and gas from one of dozens of power companies?

The only way that Bern would consider a micro-wind generator is if his fears are realised and gas or electricity cuts become a serious possibility. He has observed how the Russians have threatened to withhold gas supplies from their neighbours, and is resentful that Britain once had North Sea oil and gas, which it seems to have frittered away. This undermining of confidence in the govern-ment leads him to listen sympathetically to the 'small government' faction in the pub that invariably pipes up at an advanced stage in the conversation to explain that climate change is just another excuse for the government to rip us off with stealth taxes.

Bern knows deep down that the conspiracy theorists are not right about this. He feels that he pays way too much tax, but appreciates that it would be foolish to tax people for the sake of it. His opinion on green taxes is that 'they' think that they have to be seen to be doing something to respond to the green lobby, and taxation is the easy option. It only takes an announcement by the Chancellor and a wave of the pen from the Inland Revenue. Why should 'they' bother trying to talk to us if they can price us off the road and make it expensive to make our homes cosier? Mind you, if 'they' think that, then they would be wrong. Bern was asked how much he paid for his electricity by a lady with a clipboard on the high street last week, and he had to say he had no idea.

When the Prime Minister or the leader of his local council looms onto the TV, and starts talking about 'doing our bit for the environment', he does get annoyed. 'My God, listen to them', he says, 'Why can't they just take our money and leave us alone? It has to be obvious to these clowns that making us do more will not make any difference. The Chinese are building two coal-fired power stations a week.' He has read that the UK is supposed to be responsible for just 2 per cent of global carbon emissions, a figure that is going down not up because of the increase in other countries' emissions. He also recalls hearing that even if the UK gave up oil and gas tomorrow, the Chinese would replace the gap in volume that the country leaves in a matter of months. And anyway, why should we sacrifice our comfortable life when the Americans have no intention of reducing their gas-guzzling lifestyles? What about stopping the rainforests from being chopped down, or doing something about cow farts or reducing the world population? But no, they just love to have a go at hard-working people who are just trying to make a buck, and enjoy the short time that they have on this Earth.

Curiously Bern does heed the advice he took in, not from a billboard or a public information message, but which he overheard while waiting to checkout his basket of beer at the local express supermarket. Bern accepts that standby buttons and permanently plugged-in phone rechargers are a waste of electricity, and has replaced all of his incandescent light bulbs with energy-saving compact fluorescents. Well, all of them except the ones that don't fit the lamps his wife picked out to match the curtains. The idea of knowingly wasting money on energy you didn't need never made sense to him. He was not obsessed about this though. He doesn't always remember to switch off at the wall and, while he may pause halfway up the stairs on his way to bed when he remembers that he left something on, he will probably carry on up because he just can't be bothered to go back down again. He does congratulate himself on his energy conservation tendencies, and assumes that he is much better than most people living in his street.

Bern gets very angry when he hears anyone having a go at selfish, gas-guzzling SUV drivers. His good behaviour must count for the little bit of extra fuel he burns in his Range Rover. He basks in the knowledge that he is providing a safe form of transport for his family. He would be surprised to hear that urban $4 \times 4$s are involved in 25 per cent more accidents than saloon cars, and often do far more damage to both the cars and the people that they hit (Laurance, 2006). Even so, that would not make him change to a more environment or people friendly model.

Having said that he is getting fed up with his two stepdaughters complaining that arriving at school in a big $4 \times 4$ is really embarrassing. Their friends are horrified that they could be sharing a house with a planet killer. He could probably avoid this by getting the kids to walk to school, and accepts that it is a little over the top to use the car for the seven minute journey. But it often looks like rain, plus he would be late for work if he had to walk all the way back for the car, and anyway most of the time one of the girls is dawdling so they would be late if they didn't jump in the car. Then there was that kid who disappeared on his way to school last year, or was it the year before? The fact that transporting the children takes less than 5 per cent of his total drive time, and the terrific king-of-the-road feeling he gets from his elevated driving position mean he is likely to hang on to the car for a while longer.

Bern's zeal for standby switches does not mean he is consistent about energy-saving throughout the rest of the house. He did make sure that there was insulation in the loft space when they bought the house. He has not been up there since, but can confidently tell you that it is more than adequate to ensure the house does not loose heat. Bern will always buy the most energy-efficient white goods, but bought a wide-screen television that uses more energy than his old cathode ray set, which worked perfectly well until he threw it out.

He also installed double-glazed windows at considerable expense, but mainly because it annoyed him that he could hear kids on the street when he was trying to watch TV. He once picked up a leaflet about cavity-wall insulation, and being in the industry was interested enough to mention it to his wife but, faced with her horror on learning that it required holes to be punched in the side of the house, he decided to leave it for want of an easy life.

Bern leaves the holiday arrangements to his wife – she thinks about the children while he thinks about golfing and fishing. He never wins in an argument with her anyway, and ends up going along with what she and the kids want to do. The distance they need to travel to get some sun and an exotic experience (two things they do agree on) means that they almost always fly. Low cost airlines from Gatwick make this very easy and they have ended up in Florida for three of the last six years.

Once, when his eyes were glazing over as he was being told about children's entertainment in a gated village in Croatia, his eye caught an advertisement for a carbon off-setting scheme in the brochure. He had heard about this somewhere, and immediately realised that this would be a good way of impressing his step-daughters. It was only a little extra per person and so he went on-line and bought a dozen new trees in Uganda. When he told his stepdaughters they explained that off-sets were a con, and that planting trees was only carbon neutral at best, and why didn't he invest in renewable energy schemes in India instead? He has not attempted to buy a carbon off-set since.

A quick round up of Bern's other views finds that they constitute a real mixed bag. He generally separates his waste, and thinks that recycling makes sense. He has a sense of satisfaction when he quietly checks other people's bins on his walk to the paper shop, and sees that he has managed to produce more than his neighbours. He still doesn't understand why it can't all be burned though. Of course, last year he joined with others to complain about a proposal by the Council to set up a small waste transfer station on land occupied by a former car showroom.

The scheme would have meant that collected recyclate travelled a much smaller distance to be shredded and bundled ready for export to China. But Bern and his neighbours made a big fuss and the local politicians defeated the scheme.

Bern does not think much about where food comes from, as his wife does all the shopping. He thinks organic food is just another way to rip you off. However, organic cotton cloths do appeal to him, as they have a caché with his family. He likes the idea that he can wear a shirt that has not been soaked in pesticide. He would not think to ask why any of the clothes he buys are so cheap, even when stories about sweatshop conditions abound in his Sunday paper's business section. Bern bypasses these stories of corporate social responsibility on the way to check his stocks and the latest credit card offers.

Bern's employers know that sustainable development is an increasingly important part of what they do. Bern knows this too, because he is increasingly asked to help fill out pre-qualification forms and tender documents that explain the company's steadfast commitment to environmental protection and concern for people. Bern thinks that this is a bit of a game. Everyone in the built environment industry knows that winning jobs is all about the lowest bidder. He goes along with the questions about low-energy light fittings and eco-friendly cooling systems because he understands that the industry is under pressure from government, and if the client is happy to pay for expensive equipment then it is fine by him.

However, Bern does get exercised when answering questions about how his building is going to create a better society. Railing against this over lunch one day, he asks his colleagues why they should be responsible for even thinking about making life better for people who are not interested in working and who think that the taxpayer owes them a living. If they want to live in better houses, or have nice community centres, then they should work hard like everyone else and pay for it. He does not see why the building industry should bend over backwards to design in crime reduction or lower occupation costs. Couldn't this be sorted out with more police on the streets and less tax on fuel? Bern's tirade is a little too much even for his more reactionary colleagues, but when he kicks off like this, there are always a few who nod in agreement.

Bern's neighbour and friend Andy is a joiner. He owns his own business, mainly fitting out new retail units, and mostly reinforces Bern's own views. Andy thinks he does his bit. He recycles to a point, unless he is enjoying a lie-in on collection day, or his glass bin becomes full after having the boys round to watch the game. Andy recently admitted to Bern that one of his great pleasures is to put on a brand new pair of underwear every day. This means of course that he only ever wears his boxers once, and then throws them away with the packaging from the next pair. 'Fair play to you mate,' Bern tells Andy, 'you worked hard for your money, and you've got every right to enjoy it in any way you want.'

## The futility of the waggling finger

This description of the fictional Bern and his world may seem to some like a cartoon dreamed up to make a point. Others may recognise some elements of his behaviour and attitudes as similar to those displayed by the friends, family and colleagues in their world, but other aspects may seem exaggerated or invented. In fact everything that has been described in Bern's world has been observed and recorded either in polls and surveys, on television reality programmes or at first hand by the authors.

The fact is that Bern is a man of our times. He has accepted parts of the argument that requires everyone to live a more sustainable life, but he has edited out the bits that clash with his self-image as a successful citizen. He has been challenged to change the way he thinks and has responded to some, but not all, of the advice. He has absorbed some of his understanding from work, and has taken on other advice from a range of influences in the wider world. But he has also rejected some strong evidence about the way the world is being damaged, and has sought to insulate himself from being reminded of these facts by choosing company that agrees with his views. He has yet to experience any emotional link with the issues of dangerous climate change, or gross social injustice.

His rejection of the facts comes more from a state of denial than informed and rational consideration. Not really wishing to confront what Al Gore calls 'the inconvenient truth' of the way our private and corporate lives are eroding the Earth's capacity to sustain life, Bern either looks to others to solve the problem, or rails against being made a scapegoat for the sins of others. Either way he managed to do very little himself to respond to the crisis. His relative affluence, and the fact that the government likes to exhort him to change but rarely goes as far as to coerce him to do so, lets him off the hook of having to think very deeply about the changes he might make.

There is very little in the messages coming from those seeking to convert him to a sustainable citizen that says to him: what we are asking you to do will make things better for you. Instead, he screens out a series of negative instructions almost every day. They tell him to cut down his driving in favour of walking, cycling and public transport. Don't take a plane to go on holiday, stay and enjoy your own country (2007 was the wettest summer in the UK since records began). They ask whether he has read the label before buying to make sure he isn't committing an environmental or humanitarian crime, as if he had all the time in the world. They tell him he needs to recycle more rubbish, compost his vegetable scraps and turn off his lights. They say he must sacrifice his comfort and turn down his thermostats, stop running the tap when he brushes his teeth, and be prepared to become a social outcast for lighting up a propane outdoor patio heater, so he and his mates can enjoy one of the few clear nights during the summer.

## Excuses, excuses

It is hardly surprising that, faced with a sea of negativity, many people dig their heels in and resist, simply because they resent being pushed around. This bad start turns into a nightmare for the sustainable change agents if the alternative that they present appears to be unattractive at best, and downright insulting at worst, to those who are being asked to change. It makes no difference whether the rejection of these green practices is based on misinformation and ignorance, or informed scepticism; the outcome is still the same. What is worse is that they are unlikely to accept advice from the same source in the future.

Denial of humanity's role in undermining the global equilibrium that has supported us thus far is something that many commentators have identified as the prime reason for the current crisis. Most of the people living on the planet have probably seen and heard evidence of climate change and habitat destruction (of forests and fisheries in particular). They also understand that there are glaring and increasing inequalities between people living in different parts of the world. However, few are making a big enough effort to turn things around, and many are not trying at all. Denial is something that we will return to in later chapters, but it is worth describing it here in order to map out, for the absence of doubt, what humanity has to overcome.

There are many ways to describe how people tell themselves that the evidence before them is false, and that they do not have to do anything about it. In his book *Endgame*, Derrick Jensen (2006) tells the story of a Native American who is addressing an audience about the destruction of his ancestral lands, and the near extinction of the American bison in particular. He is interrupted by a white man who suggests that this would have happened anyway, even if the Europeans had not arrived, because the native people had the same tendencies.

Jensen recounts the Native American's reply as a beautiful denial cascade. Paraphrasing the encounter, the speaker starts by telling his questioner that his assumption that something or someone else is to blame 'is always the same with those who are destroying life'. He then describes a number of stages in the thinking of these 'destroyers'. The first thought is to deny the damage is happening, telling themselves that buffalo numbers may seem smaller, but are really as big as they used to be. When that does not work (because the evidence becomes too overwhelming), the argument switches to attacking the reputations of those who are delivering the message of destruction. They reply that Indians are not experts in population dynamics, and anyway they are far too emotional to be believed. When that does not work, they say that the 'damage' is not really damage, and that we really did not need all that many buffalo in the first place.

When that does not work, they switch the argument again. This time they reason that the Indians were already killing the buffalo, and that the white settlers only joined in at the end. It was natural that they would not survive, they might have said. Finally, when that does not work and they accept that they really are responsible, they then say that while they didn't really want to do it, they were compelled to kill the buffalo because the Indians would not give them some land, and they needed some way of moving them on. It was the Indian's selfishness that caused the death of the buffalo, and just to make sure that they did not take personal blame for the destructions they add that if they did not shoot the buffalo then somebody else would have come along and done it, so why should they be the ones to miss out.

Mark Lynas (2007) explains that denial (of climate change) is 'complex, involving a variety of defensive responses from the familiar "climate change is a myth" to the understandable (but ultimately no more useful) "I need my car for my job"'. He says that 'no one wants to hold a mental image of themselves as bad or evil, so immoral acts are necessarily dressed up in a cloak of intellectual self-justification'. This must be right for the people who know what they are doing is wrong, but keep on doing it anyway. The weight watcher that eats a big slice of chocolate cake will always say that one piece is not going to make a difference, knowing deep down that of course it will. But 'denial' is not as simple as this when it comes to reacting to evidence of impending environmental and social collapse.

Chris Rose (2007), who spent a large part of his career leading campaigns for Greenpeace, breaks deniers of climate change down into eight different subsets. First (and somewhat controversially), he links those that believe that it is impossible to change God's design with the simply ignorant, and calls them 'uninformed deniers'. Next are those that offer glib reactions to global warming such as 'I'm glad I don't live in Bangladesh', or 'we could do with some warmer weather'. Rose calls these people 'the indifferent'.

Next he describes 'doubters', who say that they're sceptical about whether an unequivocal climate signal has been detected'. Even though the evidence is all around them, these people still cling to the possibility that all those scientists have got it wrong. Of course the great majority of these doubters are not climate scientists, or scientists of any kind, but that does not matter.

The fourth category, according to Rose, is the 're-assigners', so called because they assign the cause of climate change to anything other than human beings. For a while they were the people talking about the effect of sun spots on the Earth's climate, and then there was the theory that explained how clouds that trapped solar warmth were generated by high levels of cosmic rays. But recent evidence published in 2007 put an end to both of these diversions. The Fourth Report by the Inter-governmental Panel on Climate Change (IPCC) stated that it was 'very likely' that global warming was due to human activity (IPCC, 2007).

Rose calls those who believe that global warming is real (and that it may well be down to human activity) but not their responsibility, the 'deflectors'. These are people who do not own a gas-guzzling SUV. Neither do they live in China, India or the USA, and are certainly not in government or running a big business. All of those people are the ones responsible for causing the problem, and they should be the ones doing something about it.

Then there are those that do take collective responsibility for climate change, but are unimpressed with any of the options that are offered to them. Rose terms these people 'feasibility sceptics'. They latch on to those that say that the solution is to close down coal-fired power stations, or to stop people flying or driving their cars. They say this will never happen, and wait for a better idea. Rose argues that they never stop to think about how a whole range of technologies changed the world, often soon after people said they would never catch on (the telephone, mobile phones and the motor car to name just three). He might also have added that at one time there was certainty that woman would never vote, that slavery would never be abolished and that the world was flat. Unfortunately, the 'feasibility sceptics' need to be sure about whether something will work before they try it, and in the meantime they continue about their unsustainable business.

The seventh category includes those that think that there is an ulterior motive for being asked to do something about climate change. These people are supporters of 'small government' and the free market, and are dubbed 'cynics and reasoned doubters' by Rose. These people believe that government is always looking for a way to intervene into people's lives and that if there was a real problem, then the market would have stepped in and sorted it out long ago.

The final group 'have bought the whole picture, accepted the reality of climate change, often been among the first to take action, and tried to do all they could'. They now sit in despair because they have tried to do things on their own and can now see the enormity of the task. They can't see how enough can be done in the time available and have downed tools. Rose does not go into detail about what these 'despairers' do instead, but one can guess that they have either stopped investing in a lower carbon life, or worse, have concluded that as we are all going to perish, they may as well live it up while there is still time, with little or no regard for the effect this will have on the planet.

Rose's categories offer a depressing, but informed picture about the way people react to the information about the current state of the world. The important point here is that people react to bad news in different ways, and even if the resulting inaction is common to all of them, the tactics to shift them into a more positive frame of mind will need to be very different.

One more attempt to describe denial is worthy of note. As a result of his observations, the economist John Llewellyn (2007) describes four different ways in which business leaders manage to avoid taking action on climate change. First there are the 'ideological contrarians'. Llewellyn says that 'if these people have an intellectual belief, it is that they are smarter than the crowd. More often to them, it is just a game of attracting attention by attacking the majority'.

He calls the second category the 'grey conservatives'. They like to appear reasonable, and say that they are neither 'pro' nor 'anti' things like climate change, but say that there is not enough evidence to support action. 'Do more research, collect more data and continue the debate,' they counsel sagely. Next are the 'non-sequiturians', who produce a range of different arguments, although all of them share a common structure. These are the same people that Rose calls the re-assigners, who highlight all possible explanations of why the Earth is warming, other than man-made influences. Llewellyn explains that they often wrap up their statement by saying 'therefore, it cannot be caused by mankind'. He says the 'therefore' is the giveaway: 'the delicious non-sequitur: just because the Earth has warmed for one reason in the past is no reason why it cannot warm for a completely different reason in the future'.

Llewellyn's last category is the 'busy executive'. He says that their argument is loftier and more pragmatic than the others. They are unmoved by the scientific evidence, preferring to wait until they know what the policy-makers are going to do. This allows these busy people to avoid the facts and simply keep a weather eye on the implications for their business. Of course, if the policy-makers get it wrong or chicken out of the tough decisions, these business leaders will probably find out all too late that it would have been better to think it through themselves. Llewellyn concludes by wondering if most of us do the same thing as he has observed in the business world. He wonders if, when we are 'confronted by a troubling issue, we seek out some territory in which we feel intellectually comfortable and are surrounded by friends'.

## Legislation, technology and market forces are not enough

The plain fact is that while there is still some disagreement about how long humanity has to stabilise the Earth, the way we exploit the natural world, consume its resources, and distribute wealth simply can't continue. In short, we are not being sustainable, which means we will not survive into the future without making changes. This book was inspired by years of working with businesses to lessen their environmental and social impacts, thereby improving their competitiveness. While the work resulted in some notable successes, ultimately the feeling was one of bemusement and frustration. Why had these businesses confined their actions to a limited number of improvements, when the evidence had shown them that a very different and more sustainable path might guarantee long-term commercial success?

For too long there has been tireless work on the part of environmental and social change advisors who have presented a vast array of evidence about the consequences of unsustainable practices. Some have reacted well to these messages, often attracted initially to the cost savings associated with lower energy and waste bills. However, even when the savings are made, they often reinvest this to increase capacity, resulting in the consumption of more energy and the production of more waste.

It seemed to be more than a little fruitless to continue with the same tactics and methods, when so many have stubbornly avoided taking the significant decisions to change manufacturing processes, rethink procurement strategies and treat their workforce and their supply chains differently. This is still resistance to something as simple as taking more responsibility for products once they have passed through the factory gates. Leasing rather than selling has still not caught on, and many continue to lobby against any move that favours secondary materials over virgin resources, even when the consumption of those resources threatens to destroy the very markets that they are so interested in capturing.

The professionals and activists that have tried to encourage businesses to both plan for and take action to achieve total sustainability need to ask themselves why they have been only moderately effective, instead of being a transforming force. Did they fail to present clear evidence? Was it difficult for their audience to believe that there is a 90 per cent certainty that the increase in global temperatures since the middle of the twentieth century is due to the increase of human greenhouse gas emissions (IPCC, 2007)? Perhaps the 10 per cent probability that this increase has been caused solely by natural climatic processes needed more explanation. Was the fact that human resource consumption is currently 20 per cent higher than the availability of land required to provide food, development and the capacity to absorb carbon emissions too hard to understand (Wackernagel et al., 2002)? Does the prediction that drought and flooding caused by climate change are likely to cause the migration of over a billion (one in seven) people over the next 50 years need to be better explained (Vidal, 2007)? Does the loss of between 5 per cent and 20 per cent of the value of the global economy due to climate change hold any mysteries (Stern, 2007)?

The reality is that few businesses are actively anti-sustainable, and most businesses can now point to something that they have done that will have a positive effect on neighbouring environmental and social conditions. The focus of attention now is all about urgency. Climate scientists have been saying for some time that we may have less than 15 years left before our world undergoes changes that will undermine every market on the planet. If we are to preserve our current way of life, we need to understand why it is that these warnings are either being ignored, or heeded at a dangerously slow pace.

Not only do we need to understand more about the human reactions to both the warnings and the advice, but we need to find a way of accelerating change. There is a resistance to change that is partly to do with a misplaced faith in technology, economic systems and the ability of government to make the necessary changes. But there is something else that stands in the way and is less well understood. What is it about human beings that allows us to consider a situation that has the potential to cause us harm, and then turn away without dealing adequately with the danger? Until we understand this, we can put forward all the evidence we want about the plight of the Earth, but it is unlikely to make much of a difference.

The good news is that there are examples of people making that connection, and reordering their lives and their businesses to accommodate the new information. This book explores these stories and draws out the lessons that can be learned by the wider global community. It also considers how these stories can

# The apparently hopeless case of sustainable behaviour

One of the biggest problems for anyone trying to motivate people to change their behaviour is to overcome the sense in many that the situation is hopeless. There are a lot of reasons why people may feel hopeless about the possibility of changing the unsustainable factors affecting the world today. These include the daunting enormity of the physical challenge to reduce levels of greenhouse gases from the atmosphere, and the aspirations of less affluent peoples around the world to have the same lifestyles and possessions enjoyed by richer nations.

Perhaps the biggest feeling of hopelessness is the one that people feel most certain about, because they think that they have first-hand knowledge of it. They think that human beings are irrational and selfish. This represents a potential brick wall for those who truly do believe that global human behaviour can be influenced in time to avert widespread and disruptive environmental and social change. Irrationality means that it is impossible to apply logic, evidence, and reasoned argument. Self-centred or selfish behaviour means that co-operation and communal effort (whether between nations or neighbours) is simply not going to work. If this were true, then it would be a disaster for humanity, for business-based sustainable initiatives in particular, as it would confirm that efforts to green the sector were always destined to fail.

# Failure is not inevitable (Part 1)

In view of the importance of this belief, it would be helpful to establish whether human beings are really as bad as all that. The range of disciplines that might know the answer includes sociologists, biologists and philosophers. In the vast hectarage of books, treatise and dissertations on the subject of the human condition, the following selection of views will suffice to test the finality of the human being as a hopeless case.

The philosopher Mary Midgley (1979) tells us that rationality is not the same as intelligence, but 'includes reference to aims as well as means, and is not far from being "sane"'. To be irrational then would be someone who was well on the way to departing from sanity. While some environmentalists may claim that we live in an insane world where we are killing our planet in pursuit of short-term gratification, this does not fit with the apparently 'sane citizens' that walk about on a sunny Saturday in the middle of towns and cities across the world, searching for a bargain.

That is not to say that the unsustainable decisions that are made by these same apparently sane folk are based on solid ground. Perhaps fatal collective screening may be a better way to describe the fact that we are shopping ourselves to destruction. The key to irrationality is to determine whether the shoppers are in possession of all the facts. Diamond (2005) explains that scientists term behaviour as rational when they 'employ correct reasoning, even when it may be morally reprehensible'. It would be difficult to argue that there were all that many people out there who purchased over-packaged goods in the full knowledge that it will lead to the disappearance of a dozen Polynesian countries under the sea.

Midgley (1979) backs this up when she says that 'if someone consistently aims at the destruction of everything, or the greatest possible degree of confusion, people will tend to call him insane, irrational or perhaps even stupid'. Irrationality, she says, describes 'something that has gone wrong with a person's system of priorities, with his sense of what is important. It suggests something wrong with the valuing system as well as the mere calculating power'.

Thinking about the people who run their lives and their businesses in an unsustainable manner, it would be hard to label them as irrational against these definitions, unless they had once held a sustainable values system and then decided to depart from it. It would certainly be irrational for anyone who was once devoted to the protection of the environment, and the preservation of social justice, to then decide that exploitation and damage were better ways of doing things. However, if that person never possessed those values in the first place, then they may be called misguided, even dangerous, but not necessarily irrational.

The designation of irrationality gets more complicated when a person only partially understands the importance of minimising environmental and social harm, but chooses to pursue an exploitative path anyway. These people would be vaguely aware that some of the things that they do are unsustainable, but choose to continue to consume in an unsustainable manner because it would be too inconvenient either to find out more, or to change their ways. Again, these people could be said to be in possession of some very lame values, or may be denying or blocking out stronger values. In contrast to people who cause wilful harm, those that are weak, or 'in denial', may be negligent but are probably not irrational.

In some ways this is good news as irrationality is a hard nut to crack. Irrational people are unlikely to respond to reasoned argument. Emotional or spiritual arguments may stand a better chance of changing the irrational to behave more sustainably, but there is no guarantee that the desired behaviour would stick. The wilful, ignorant and negligent are certainly a challenge, but given the right formula of information, argument and 'leadership by example', there will always be hope for them.

Selfishness is a more complex issue, and has exercised those who have thought about it recently, from an evolutionary perspective. However, most of the writing on this subject has come from a religious or philosophical perspective. Theodore Zeldin, in his book *An Initmate History of Humanity* (1994), lifts the lid on the attempts of religions to bend human society to embrace the broad principles of selflessness. He says that 'these sublime exhortations have had only limited effect because the majority of the faithful have obstinately narrowed them down to make the saving of their own souls the first priority, showing more interest in winning a reward in the next world in return for being compassionate, than in the act of compassion itself'.

But Zeldin sees some glimmer of hope on the horizon, as he believes that there is an increasing revulsion against cruelty, which has been brought into graphic relief through global and 24-hour news coverage. He thinks that 'compassion is a rising star, even if it is from time to time obscured in the skies. But it will only rise if they push it, and the way they can do that is by deciding whether they are content with the old style of compassion which meant helping others to clear their own conscience (and there was no need to talk to them, writing a cheque would do) or the new style which means discovering others as individuals and exchanging understanding with them'.

Zeldin's belief in a maturing global compassion may win some over, but a more serious obstacle is presented by the 'selfish gene' argument suggested by Richard Dawkins (1976). This does give those seeking global sustainable behaviour change a serious problem. Sustainable change is often (and wrongly) perceived by those in developed economies, as something that means they will have to give up the comforts and lifestyle that they see as their right, and even their duty, to enjoy in terms of giving their children a better life than they experienced. Even if this powerful perception of trading down can be overcome, there is still the requirement for living differently. If the strongest instinct of an individual is to enhance him or herself, and to exploit any opportunity for the benefit of their immediate family unit, then sustainable change will be much harder to achieve.

Midgley (2005) challenges this argument, along with the often misquoted Darwinian idea of survival of the fittest, which is thrown about by academics and bar-room debaters alike as a self-evident truth. She rejects the idea that humans are naturally programmed to look after their own interests, to the detriment of others. She starts by explaining that 'the word selfish is essentially a negative word. It means a shortage of a normal regard for others. Calling somebody self-ish simply does not mean that they are prudent or successfully self-preserving. It merely says that they are exceptional – and faulty – in having too little care for anybody else'. Clearly, by definition, it is impossible to have a majority of exceptional people, so there must be more unselfish people out there than selfish ones.

Next, Midgley (2005) turns to the argument against the ability of humanity to pull together in common cause. She rounds on Dawkins' contention that 'to build a society in which individuals co-operate generously towards a common good, you can expect little help from biological nature'. Instead she explains that selfishness, as a survival tactic, is actually surprisingly inefficient. This is because humans can be very good at protecting their own interests by being careful, or prudent, to avoid well-known dangers. The trouble is, they are very bad at doing anything about longer-term problems. Midgley says that 'when things are going well we simply don't believe in disasters. Long-term prudence, reaching beyond the accepted routine precautions of everyday life, is therefore an extraordinary feeble motive'.

Midgley advances an alternative strategy that she thinks will become more apparent as we approach 'the increasing probability of environmental disaster'. This, she explains, is the strategy of the duty to the 'enclosing whole'. She says that 'even when there is no conscious talk of duty, the people who work in any co-operative enterprise – school, firm, shop, orchestra, theatrical company, teenage gang, political party, football team – find it thoroughly natural to act as if they had a duty to that enclosing whole if it is in some way threatened'. She hopes that 'we could accept the overwhelming existing evidence of a "terrestrial emergency" without needing to be hit by a direct disaster. But whatever causes that belief to be accepted, once it becomes so, there is surely little doubt about the duty it lays upon us'.

If this sounds more than a little idealistic, then a brief look at why people vote should bring doubters back on course. Writing in *The Wisdom of Crowds*, James Surowiecki (2005) explains that some say people vote because they like to make a personal statement. He dismisses this because this selfish motive ignores the fact that no one expects their own vote to have any influence over the result. Very few people would say that any politician, even a President or a Prime Minister, had much effect on their day-to-day life. If anyone really wanted to bend others to their own interests, they would be better off taking to the stump themselves.

Instead Surowiecki says 'the more parsimonious explanation seems more likely to be true. People voted because they think they should'. He talks about the general sense of duty and the interest in having a say, regardless of how small its impact on the running of their government. Voting behaviour supports Midgley's contention that a sense of duty for the 'enclosing whole' is stronger than individual self-interest when important decisions need to be made.

There is one other word that is regularly hurled at humans to explain why they will never live sustainable lives. This is the stinging accusation that they are capable of harbouring huge reserves of 'hypocrisy'. In this context, this would be the deliberate attempt to create the false impression that one cares about environmental and social issues, while one actually has no such commitment. This would manifest itself in an individual that is highly informed, and says that they are prepared to burn less fossil fuel, and consume fewer non-renewable resources, but then consciously fails to act on these commitments.

The ability of humans to say one thing and do another is hardy a modern observation. Over 2400 years ago the Greeks gave this a name: 'akrasia'. Socrates (reported through Plato's writings) maintained that 'no one goes willingly towards the bad', and never consciously chooses to act against their better judgement. He said that a person would only undermine their own interests if they based their decision on insufficient fact or knowledge. According to Socrates, it would be impossible to act against your best interests if you had all the facts.

Aristotle disagreed with this, and thought that decisions were based on opinion rather than hard facts. He said that opinion is generated by an individual, and that it was not necessarily based on the truth. In this way, the individual could be in possession of the facts, which in turn should suggest a particular course of action. But instead of taking this action, the individual synthesises, changes or discounts the facts, and by doing so contrives to act in a different way.

The difference between Socrates and Aristotle is between making decisions using facts, and allowing the facts to dictate the decision. The theory of cognitive dissonance is apposite here. One way to resolve a conflict between facts and strongly held beliefs is for the individual to distort the facts or to fit them together in such a way that they support the overall belief system (Festinger, 1957; Coopersmith, 1967). This does not appear to be an absolute mechanism. People will hold many different beliefs. Some of these will be strong, while others will be weak. A strong belief will result in an enthusiastic search for information and opinions that support this belief. A weaker belief will not produce such a defensive reaction when challenged, and the holder is much more likely to listen to opposing views, and be convinced by them.

The Aristolian version of 'akrasia' brings in all kinds of variations on the theme of how information is treated by the individual before a consequent action, or indeed, inaction. Words like reasoning, judgement, belief, influence, bias and pre-conception could be bandied around during any discussion on the subject. Why anyone would either change or shield themselves from the facts, particularly if it was a matter of survival, is an important consideration. Some would say that in a clash between the facts and the emotional response to them, emotion will triumph every time. However, this does not really ring true. Midgley (2005) explains that whether the decision comes from the individual, or the group, preservation is the key.

However, if it is the case that people are in possession of the facts and proceed to ignore them, or at least follow them in an inconsistent manner, then we are back to selfishness. Like selfishness, hypocrisy is a show-stopper for those seeking sustainable change. However, Midgley (2005) suggests that the ability to be inconsistent, and even resistant to compelling evidence, is understandable and should be forgiven. She explains that 'during any reform, when people are beginning to recognise that something is wrong and trying to see how to alter it, some confusion and inconsistency between theory and practice is normal. It is even necessary. This is not yet hypocrisy. The kind of hypocrisy which invalidates criticism is a deliberate, chronic condition, that of somebody who has settled finally back into accepting the *status quo*. The normal confused condition is uncomfortable but transient. We can always alter practice rather than theory'.

It is enough at this stage to be able to show that there are counter-arguments to the common claims that we are on a downward spiral, and that there is nothing that we can do about it. The human frailties of an absence of rational thought, and selfishness, do of course exist, but so do other human traits that can compensate for these weaknesses in the wider population. Whether it is possible to adopt sustainable habits, and do so in a frighteningly short time period, remains to be seen. But the important thing to hold on to at this point is that is it possible.

## Failure is not inevitable (Part 2)

It is important to establish the case against the biological and philosophical inevitability of an unsustainable demise of human beings on Earth, but what about the historical record? Unfortunately, history does not have a very encouraging story to tell us. We are regularly confronted by the view that nothing will work. These pessimists, who have heard of Diamond's (2005) book *Collapse*, have the perfect apocalyptic evidence to back up this view. Diamond's book, they say, is proof that humans are incapable of maintaining a sustainable society.

This view must be an irritation for Diamond, as he says that his book is not an 'uninterrupted series of depressing stories of failure, but also includes success stories inspiring imitation and optimism'. Undeterred, the doomsayers latch onto Diamond's Easter Island account as the epitome of blinkered self-destructive behaviour. Taken in isolation, what happened on this South Pacific island is a chilling tale, but only if it is taken in isolation.

Easter Island is one of the most remote habitable places on earth. It is situated 2300 miles from the Chilean coast to the east, and is 1300 miles from Pitcairn, the nearest South Pacific island to the west. The island has an area of 66 square miles, and is 1670 feet at its highest point. Before it was inhabited, the island supported a diverse forest that probably included one of the largest palm trees in the South Pacific.

No one knows exactly what the peak population on Easter was, but Diamond reports that estimates vary between 6000 and 30 000, and considers the figure of 15 000 to be a reasonable guess. By 1864, when missionaries provided the first accurate estimate, there were just 2000 people left. The affect of kidnapping and smallpox epidemics reduced this further to 111 by 1872.

The reason for the deforestation was primarily caused by the need to transport and erect the massive stone statues that still dominate the island. There were over 100 large platform sites that featured these statues, and it has been estimated that just over 900 statues were made. The statues averaged 13 foot in height, and weighed about 10 tonnes. The assumption was that rival clans competed to commission the biggest and best statues. This would account for the fact that later statues were larger than earlier ones, and featured stone 'headdresses' that increased the height and mass even more.

Wood was required to transport the statues from the quarry to their final destination, but it was also used to cremate the dead, for heating and cooking fuel, and for canoes. Trees were also felled to make way for small agricultural plots. Deforestation commenced from the time of human arrival (about AD 900), and reached a peak around 1400. By 1722 there wasn't a single tree left. The lack of trees meant no timber for canoes, thus reducing fishing yields. A reduction in shellfish and sea birds harvests followed as these secondary sources of food were exhausted. There was little fuel for heating and cooking, and the population was reduced to burning crop waste for these purposes. Deforestation led to erosion, which reduced the already poor soil fertility of the island.

Diamond wondered what the person that cut down the last tree was thinking. Did he shout 'jobs not trees'!; or 'technology will solve our problems, never fear we'll find a substitute for wood'; or 'we don't have proof that there aren't palms somewhere else on Easter, we need more research, your proposed ban on logging is pre-mature and driven by fear-mongering'. His conclusion is that 'those seemingly nice people were neither bad nor improvident. Instead they had the misfortune to live in one of the most fragile environments, at the highest risk of deforestation of any Pacific people. The trees they cut down for political, spiritual and economic reasons just did not grow back fast enough to support their society'.

The conclusion of the pessimists is that Easter Island was a place where ecological disaster was perpetrated by its inhabitants. They died out because of their isolation, and had nowhere to go and no one to turn to for help after they undermined their eco-system. Now, they say, we have a global problem (climate change) and history will repeat itself. The whole of humanity will go the same way as the Easter Islanders. This is an understandable extrapolation of the facts. But one only has to move 160 pages further into Diamond's book to see how humans are not necessarily on an inevitably ruinous path. The antidote to the fate of the Easter Islanders is what happened on another South Pacific island.

The inhabitants of Tikopia recognised the unsustainable writing on the wall, and made completely different and sustainable decisions … and thrived. Tikopia is much smaller than Easter Island with a total area of just 1.8 square miles supporting a population of around 1200. It has been continuously occupied for nearly 3000 years. The nearest islands are 140 miles away in the Vanuatu and Solomon archipelagos. The island was originally settled around 900 BC, and evidence from waste sites shows that over the next 1000 years the islanders lived off the natural plant and animal species that lived on, around, or visited the island. Around 100 BC there was a change in their diet which showed that they were eating more cultivated foods, and there was less evidence of charcoal. This suggests that the islanders had exhausted naturally occurring foods. To save themselves from starvation, they apparently abandoned slash and burn agriculture and planted crops and trees. They also began the intensive husbandry of pigs.

Around AD 1600, the islanders turned their way of life around for the second time. They killed every pig on the island and turned to fish, shellfish and turtles as their main source of protein. They did this because the pigs became hard to manage and could not be segregated from the cultivated areas. It also became clear that pigs were an inefficient means of feeding humans. In addition, the islanders turned a marine bay into a brackish lake and stocked it with fish.

In addition to the two changes to their food sources, the Tikopians operated a different political system to the Easter Islanders. While the chiefs on Easter operated a top-down regime and competed with each other, the Tikopian chiefs were more custodians, or prime agents of the clan. Major decisions on the island were taken in consultation with other chiefs, clan elders and family members. This more collaborative method of governance is a major advantage to sustainable societies as we will see when we turn to the Swedes in Chapter 4.

The Tikopians survived because they were able to re-order their society in times of environmental threat. They co-operated even though their society was divided into separate clans. The Easter Islanders, living in more trying conditions, perpetuated divisions and produced an over-consuming socio-economic system for which they paid the ultimate price. The Tikopia story shows, in a limited yet effective way, that it is possible for humans to change their ways. It speaks to the pessimists who should curb their negativity and wait to see how the current story about the race to avert disaster pans out.

## Our survey said ...

Having made a little room for a debate about the ability for humans to change their behaviour, the next area to explore is whether this can be backed up by current attitudes to the 'terrestrial emergency'. An easy way to gauge this is by looking at the results from opinion polls and surveys. Looking at this type of data comes with the usual health warning that those polled will almost always overestimate their own performance, and underestimate the performance of other people. Hence, if asked if they would be likely to pay more or less in a pay-as-you-throw waste disposal scheme, most would say less, even though statistically that can't be the case. Mostly, people are not inflating their performance – they just don't pay enough attention to what other people do, and hence have very little to go on when comparing their own efforts to others.

Accepting this, the pollsters and survey providers have been very busy over the last few years asking people about their attitudes to issues relative to sustainable living and working. Even if the results may not be entirely accurate, they can at least confirm or deny assumptions about irrationality and selfishness. The media loves to report the fickle, feckless and conflicting responses of both individuals and businesses to questions that begin 'what are you doing about ...'. This produces mountains of material which has been collected in a variety of ways. Because of this, an exhaustive report of their findings is not possible, but by dipping into the data it is possible to get a feel for the way sustainable behaviour is being formed across the world.

People's reactions to questions about their (un)sustainable behaviour can be broken down into various blocks. First, there is the reaction to the contention that there is a looming environmental and social crisis facing the Earth. Next, there is the 'test of responsibility' – is it something that individuals should address, or should it be somebody else, or an organisation that should be fixing the problem? Then, if people believe that they might be persuaded to do something, what incentive or disincentive might spur them into action? Finally, where people do accept that individual action is required, what do they think they should do?

## Reacting to evidence

Many polls and surveys have sought to test respondents on their acceptance that there is a looming and catastrophic environmental threat to the world. The obvious assumption is that inaction on climate change must be due to a poor understanding of the causes and predicted effects of human influenced global warming. This issue has been so widely reported that it is inconceivable to believe that anyone could have failed to understand what is going on. And yet, a survey carried out by Ipsos MORI (www.ipsos-mori.com) at the end of 2006, and reported in the New Statesman in April 2007, found that 32 per cent still knew little or nothing about the threat of climate change. Of those that had heard of it, half thought that it was at least partly a natural process. Another Ipsos MORI poll, carried out in June 2007, asked how they would be personally affected if climate change was successfully tackled. A frightening 58 per cent incorrectly said that they would enjoy a cleaner atmosphere. The next largest answer was the more accurate 'less severe weather' at 30 per cent.

In the same survey, Ipsos MORI asked respondents to agree or disagree with the statement that 'human activity does not have a significant effect on the environment'. While 69 per cent disagreed, 28 per cent agreed – a surprising number considering the weight of evidence to the contrary. A survey carried out three years earlier by Brook Lyndhurst (2004) found that the exact same percentage (69 per cent) disagreed that climate change was being exaggerated, with 24 per cent agreeing that it was.

This might be explained by the answer to another question in this 2004 survey, which asked if leading experts still questioned if human activity was to blame for climate change. This time 56 per cent agreed, with just 24 per cent disagreeing. However, the positive conclusion which can be drawn from this poll is that half the people that think that human activity is to blame for climate change don't care if leading experts are still questioning this; they have made up their own minds.

More than half (53 per cent) of 1580 adults surveyed by Tickbox.net said that they would not change their lifestyles – because of confusion, a lack of time and because they did not want to be told what to do. One in five said they had no idea how to live more ethically.

## The myth of developing world self-interest

Another assumption that is often given as an excuse for inaction in mature economies is that those living in developing countries care more about living like an American, and are unconcerned about the environmental and social damage that realising such an aspiration would cause. WWF famously estimated that if everyone in the world consumed the same amount of resources as the average US citizen, we would need three more planets. These cultural differences were explored in a poll of people in 10 countries conducted by The Chicago Council on Global Affairs (www.worldpublicopinion.org). All 10 showed strong majorities that climate change was an important threat. However, the majority view that climate change was a 'critical' threat was found in South Korea, Australia, Mexico, India, Israel, Armenia, China, and Iran. The USA was not on this list.

There is not, according to this poll, much common cause between countries with mature economies. This is supported by the survey carried out by the news channel France 24 (for the television programme 'Le Talk of Paris') in January 2007 (www.newtarget.com), which asked respondents to pick their top two challenges facing the planet from a list of nine including terrorism, war and famine. Climate change featured in 54 per cent of the French answers, while just 30 per cent of Americans thought it should be in their top two. About 40 per cent of Germans, Italians and British chose climate change. A poll by The Pew Research Centre for The People and the Press in July 2006 showed that just 19 per cent of Americans were concerned 'a great deal' about global warming. This compared with 51 per cent of the Spanish, 66 per cent of the Japanese, and 65 per cent of the Indians that were questioned (www.people-press.org/reports).

## Don't look at me

Assuming that people have registered and accepted that there are both environmental and social problems in the world, the next step is to determine whether sufficient numbers of people feel that this is something that is their responsibility, or that others should do something about it. Predictably, the evidence shows that often people will say something must be done, but then point the finger at everyone else but themselves. Big business and governments are the ones most often fingered to solve the problem. In most developed economies, the domestic sector is responsible for around one-third of greenhouse gas emissions, while industrial sources rarely count for more than a quarter. However, the perception in the mind of the public is that businesses are to blame, and governments are falling down on the job of sorting them out.

The easy belief that 'personal behaviour' is insignificant, but 'company behaviour' is crucial, is a common theme in sustainable behaviour surveys. Ignoring the obvious fact for the moment that employees are also consumers, there is evidence to show that most people think that businesses should be green. A survey by Penn, Schoen and Berland in May 2007 found that 80 per cent of the UK respondents believed it was important for companies to be environmentally friendly. But when they were asked how they might demonstrate this, only 23 per cent could identify any steps a company should take to be green (www. landor.com).

The belief that businesses need to be responsible is not just confined to environmental matters. An Ipsos MORI poll in October 2006 found that 67 per cent of the general public agreed with the statement that industry and commerce do not pay enough attention to their social responsibilities, and just 10 per cent disagreed. This view is justified according to other polls that show that the ability of companies to live up to environmental and social expectations is not all that impressive. The Carbon Neutral Company showed that only 80 of the top listed companies in the FTSE 100 had identified climate change as a business risk, and just 38 had targets set out for emission reduction (The CarbonNeutral Company, 2006). When the trawl for evidence on action went to the next level (of still very large companies – the FTSE 250), there was very little evidence that any of them had considered, or had made specific plans to limit, the risks of global warming.

A survey by management consultants BearingPoint (Temko, 2007) said that British business is paying 'lip service' to green issues. It found that out of the 2.5 million company cars on the road, less than one quarter were run by firms that had travel reduction, car sharing, or route planning in place. While more had gone for lower emission vehicles, the survey found that $CO_2$ emissions were only the fifth most important issue in companies' vehicle procurement criteria.

Many companies have taken a less opaque approach to sharing their problems with the public. They explain in their sustainability reports that they have not met this or that target, but will try to do better next year. The intension to be sustainable shows that they are aware of the issues, even if they are not managing to make significant changes just yet. But if companies think that simply stating their green credentials, and waiting for the customers to roll in, is a good marketing strategy, then they should prepare for disappointment. According to a report by the business and responsibility organisation Accountability and Consumers International (whose members include The UK Consumer Council and Which?), 9 out of 10 shoppers were sceptical about the information they receive from companies and governments (Lloyd, 2007). Another survey found that 40 per cent distrusted what companies told them about global warming, and 60 per cent said they did not trust scientists on this subject (Macalister, 2007).

Worryingly, this same poll found that the colour green on packaging was enough to influence some to say the retailer had good environmental credentials. On this evidence, consumers are fast to pin the responsibility on business, but are neither clear about what they do, nor would they trust them if they said they were applying themselves to the problem. It is not hard to understand where this distrust and scepticism is coming from. There have been a string of corporate scandals from Enron, Parmalat, MCI and others that paint an unfair and untrue picture in the public mind that most corporations are soaked in greed and corruption. However, the quite legal practices of paying huge sums of money to executives (so called 'fat cat payments') and the low amount of corporation and other state taxes paid by large companies also contribute to this perception (Houlder, 2007).

Corporations are certainly not, in the view of many, organisations out for the greater good. This must be frustrating for many companies that seek to do the right thing within the strictures of their perceived wider duties of staying profitable, boosting the share price, and paying out healthy dividends to shareholders. This divergence of perceptions about the efforts that big business is making toward greater global sustainability is something that we will return to in later chapters.

The difficulty that companies face in portraying themselves as at least playing their part to reduce environmental impacts on society is neatly illustrated by the recent efforts of Tesco, Europe's second largest hypermarket chain. In 2006, it announced a stunning range of initiatives to tackle climate change including a £100 million fund to invest in renewable energy technology, and a 50 per cent reduction in energy use within its own stores by 2010. The size of the investment fund was, at the time, twice as large as the UK government pot for renewable energy grants.

This news should have been greeted with untrammelled praise, and indeed Tesco was able to quote congratulatory messages from both Greenpeace and the UK Carbon Trust (a body committed to lowering greenhouse gas emissions) in its 2006 Corporate Responsibility Review. But the move also attracted criticism. Some came from a predictable quarter. Tesco's announcement allegedly prompted the Chief Executive of rival Asda (owned by Wal-Mart) to say that Tesco's pledge to use rail instead of road to move goods was 'recycling our old news', explaining that his company had been using trains since 2003 (Finch, 2006).

While Tesco could afford to laugh off its competitor's sour grapes, a further accusation from the development charity Christian Aid was much harder to deflect. The charity accused Tesco of under-reporting its greenhouse gas emissions, by omitting to quantify indirect sources such as fuel burned by shoppers and suppliers as they drove to and from the stores. In their report (Christian Aid, 2007) the charity said that 'Tesco's existing $CO_2$ emission declaration is disappointing.' A spokesman for Christian Aid told reporters that the company's true impact on the environment could be 12 times higher than the level the supermarket admits to (Mathiason, 2007).

On one level, flak from competitors and charity groups is hardly a sensational or even a rare occurrence for a large company. However, the media love to report spats between rivals, and stories that suggest the possibility of corporate hypocrisy or greenwash. The Christian Aid attack on Tesco made the front page of the *Observer* Business & Media section and began: 'Tesco's recent attempt to present itself as a force for environmental good appears to be backfiring …'. While Tesco will always be able to defend itself, this kind of story erodes the confidence of the public that big business is really committed to saving the planet. At the very least this perception makes it easy for the less committed to say that if the main culprits (in their eyes) are doing very little, and looking after their own interests, then why should they put themselves out.

If large companies are saying that they are at least trying to become more sustainable, then the same story cannot be said for smaller ones (small and medium sized companies or SMEs). SMEs make up the vast number of all companies worldwide, and are probably responsible for between 50 and 70 per cent of environmental impacts globally. Regulators and governments find them harder to reach than larger companies, partly because they are so diverse, partly because of their sheer numbers, and partly because individually their impacts are relatively small. In any case, many are exempt from the pollution thresholds that require larger companies to comply with legislation. In the UK about 80 per cent are liable to pay a Climate Change Levy (a tax on the use of fossil fuels). However, Crichton (2006) found that 46 per cent of the small companies it polled thought that climate change was 'blown out of proportion'. Only 26 per cent thought that the phenomenon was a real threat to them.

The other body that people like to point to – when asked who should be responsible for averting environmental and social problems – is the government. When asked by Ipsos MORI in August 2007 if the government should take the lead in combating climate change, even if it means using laws to change people's behaviour, an overwhelming 70 per cent agreed and just 17 per cent disagreed. There is a majority view in favour of government intervention, even when put in a more provocative manner. Brook Lyndhurst (2004) found that 38 per cent agreed that the government has no right to make people live in an environmentally friendly manner, but 48 per cent thought that it did.

The assumption that the enthusiasm for government intervention falls off if it means agreeing to higher taxes is not entirely accurate. Brook Lyndhurst (2004) found that the majority of respondents thought it was fair for government to tax incandescent light bulbs and reduce tax on energy-saving bulbs. Lower taxes for good recyclers, and higher taxes for poor ones, was also supported. However, only 29 per cent thought that putting up tax on car fuel was fair, while 68 per cent thought it was not.

Of course, politicians themselves know full well that government cannot be the answer, or at least not all of the answer. Many commentators have talked about the impossibility of achieving sustainability via the narrow temporal bookends in which politicians work before they need to seek re-election. Bravery to take difficult and unpopular decisions is one thing, but committing political suicide by, for example, taxing travellers out of the skies is just plain foolish.

When he was Prime Minister, Tony Blair explained this problem succinctly when he said that 'often we're in a situation where it is not that governments don't want to do the right thing, but that they worry electorally about the short-term consequences of doing so' (www.number10.gov.uk/output). He is perhaps stating the obvious, but it is no less welcome for its honesty. Unfortunately, the electorate that expects solutions without any noticeable change to their habits and lifestyles gives politicians very little room for manoeuvre. This is why they have, to date, failed to deliver a sustainable future for their people.

## The mind is willing but ...

As the volume of information about the causes and implications of dangerous climate change piles up, it would be tempting to think that surveys would find more support for individuals that say they are acting decisively to lessen its impact. Unfortunately, that does not seem to be the case. The survey by Penn,

Schoen and Berland in 2007 showed how conflicted the public can be on the subject of tackling climate change (www.landor.com). While almost 70 per cent said that they wanted to take action, 70 per cent also said that global warming claims should be proved by independent parties. These people trusted scientists, environmental groups, and family or friends who were seen as being the most credible sources of advice. This classic 'I would but ...' mentality is repeated again and again. But while politicians, religious leaders and communications professionals battle to find the argument that converts the 'doubtful and the confused', the fact is that many people just don't seem to have the confidence to act, and want others to bear the burden away from them.

A poll of public attitudes carried out for the UK Environment Agency by Ipsos MORI in May 2007 found that 59 per cent were doing nothing to tackle climate change, with 22 per cent saying that they did not know what to do about the problem (www.environment-agency.gov.uk/news). Of those polled by Brook Lyndhurst (2004), 37 per cent said that changing the way they shopped would not really help protect the environment, while 46 per cent said it did.

If the Environment Agency poll is right, then at least two out of five Britons are doing something about climate change, or are they? A survey carried out by ICM for the *Observer* newspaper in October 2006 found that 64 per cent of those questioned said that they would consider switching to a green company for their gas and electricity. However, research carried out by the UK National Consumer Council (NCC, 2006) found that at the time the survey was carried out, only about 200 000 households (less than 1 per cent) had actually changed their tariff.

This gap between conviction and action is not limited to buying energy. A survey of nearly 30 000 people conducted by NOP for the UK Co-operative Group (Co-operative Group, 2004) showed that 8 out of 10 would pay a little extra for products that met higher ethical standards. Such a solid commitment should be reflected in the sales of fair trade products, the label most easily identified with ethically produced goods. The development organisation Traidcraft found that 25 European countries showed that sales have been growing at an impressive 20 per cent per year since 2000 (www.traidcraft.co.uk). UK consumers have recently overtaken the Swiss as the world's biggest fair trade consumers, yet this still accounts for less than 14 per cent of the market.

This phenomenon is manifested even in sustainably aware countries like Sweden. In a survey published in the daily newspaper *Dögens Nyheter* (DN) on 21 May 2007 readers were asked to say what they had committed to do to protect the environment, and what they would consider doing. An impressive 72 per cent said they recycled their waste, and 95 per cent said they would consider doing more. However, actual performance on other issues was less convincing. Only 33 per cent bought environmentally friendly goods, although almost everyone (93 per cent) said they would improve on their record to date. Just 26 per cent bought local goods, 11 per cent paid more for environmental products, 5 per cent owned a hybrid or bio diesel vehicle, and 14 per cent made a conscious effort to travel less.

Many people responding to questions about sustainable lifestyles know exactly what they are expected to say. The pressure is so great for some that honesty can be the casualty of the need for social acceptance. Townsend (2007), from the sustainable communications company Futerra, is interested in how to use this willingness to impress the neighbours to good effect. She says 'it is quite easy to de-status things by presenting them as un-aspirational. If a big 4 × 4 SUV is such an embarrassment that the kids don't want to be dropped off at school in it then that's a success for us. The environmental movement has always focused on news and policy-makers, and forgotten how you change what people want. You can't stop people wanting status symbols, but you can make them aspire to different ones.' This of course is a firm reinforcement of the Zelden statement about human aspirations, and is a recurring theme in our arguments about positive incentivisation.

One survey, carried out for the insurance group Norwich Union, goes some way to explain this (Clout, 2007). Over 75 per cent of the respondents said that dinner party and school gate conversations have been overtaken by one-upmanship on the issue of what one has done to save the planet. Over half said that 'unethical living' is now as much of a social taboo as drink driving. Consequently 9 out of 10 admitted to telling 'little green lies' to make it seem like they were living in a way that could be said to be environmentally friendly or ethical, even though their actions could not justify these claims.

The Tickbox.net survey found that, far from wanting to be kind to the planet, the main motivation for green or ethical consumerism was to show off. More than two-thirds (68 per cent) believed it was the new way of 'keeping up with the Joneses'. While many claimed that they were concerned about environmental and social issues, 41 per cent admitted that they were unlikely to check if clothes and food had been ethically produced, and the same number admitted to leaving their electrical appliances on standby.

While showmanship without comprehension may still get the job done in terms of sustainable living, insincerity will not, and is a real problem for those that are trying to understand whether the message is getting through to the wider population.

## Incentives and spurs

Survey work also helps to extinguish the perception that shock tactics will jolt the indecisive into action. The Tyndall Centre in the UK looked into attitudes to the way that the media was conveying the consequences of climate change in particular. The study was provocatively entitled 'Is this Climate Porn?' (Lowe, 2006). It split the respondents into three groups.

The first were shown the Hollywood film *The Day After Tomorrow*, which told the story of a world suddenly plunged into a new ice age as a result of global warming. The second group were asked to read (about 25 minutes worth of) technical and scientific papers representing 'the wider discourse' from the academic world. The third was the control group that was asked questions without being shown either the film or the literature. The respondents were then asked questions about the likelihood of sudden climate change, their level of worry about this possibility, and their attitudes to some solutions to the problem such as green taxes or more government investment.

The findings showed that the viewers of the film thought that climate change was 'a more distant threat both in location and time', thus reinforcing a growing body of climate change communication theory which suggests that negative and catastrophic depictions of climate change impacts depersonalise the problem for the public.

Lowe contrasts the effect of *The Day After Tomorrow* with the evidence-based films such as Al Gore's *An Inconvenient Truth*, or the BBC film *Are We Changing Planet Earth?* presented by Sir David Attenborough. While these films were not shown to his respondents, Lowe asserts that while the facts and images 'remain stark, Gore and Attenborough are familiar, popular and trusted messengers'. In other words, there is a more positive association with the message that they are bringing. Lowe is suggesting that while these messages are still saying 'things are bad and could get a lot worse', they are also saying 'but we are all in this together and we can work together to do something about it'.

The Gore film is now being used to motivate and illuminate the business world. For example, it has been shown to a number of smaller business gatherings in the Liverpool area, and Stuart Rose (Chief Executive of the clothing and food retailer Marks & Spencer) has shown it to his senior managers as part of his 'Plan A' sustainability strategy.

The Tyndall experiment shows that, far from being effective, doom-laden messages without a friendly guide tend to make people believe the problem will only come to a head further into the future. They make the viewers feel there is little they could do to affect the planet's future. The report concludes that 'although the public harbours deep concerns about the effect climate change is having or may have, there is a poor connection between this and the actual sacrifices they are willing to make. Popular reporting of climate change in the style of environmental "science fiction" appears not to be a catalyst for change; rather it creates a nagging concern, the solution to which is felt to be beyond the reach of the ordinary person'.

Speaking to the BBC on-line news service, Professor Mike Hulme, founding director of the Tydall Centre, said that 'not only is this not a good way of presenting climate change science, but even in trying to effect change, it's self-defeating' (Ghosh, 2007). He said the study suggested that strong messages designed to prompt people to change behaviour only seem to generate apathy.

If the presentation of stark facts cannot motivate people to change their behaviour, then perhaps disincentives might. Surveys have tried to discover whether it is possible to price people out of their bad behaviour, while others have asked 'how much is enough'. The accountancy firm MacIntyre Hudson (www.macintyrehudson.co.uk) found that just 1 in 20 people would respond to a £10 increase in air passenger duty by altering their travel plans. A £40 rise in duty would only persuade 15 per cent to significantly reduce their flying, but a rise of £80 a ticket would result in 31 per cent making 'significant alteration'. More than three in five opposed any increase in their taxes regardless of the plight of the world.

The same survey found that car use is not drastically affected by increases in fuel duty. A rise of 25p a litre would result in only 41 per cent making significant reductions to their car use. Even if petrol went up by as much as 40p a litre, 57 per cent of people said they would not reduce their driving. The survey concluded that, although the principle of green taxation is widely accepted, when questioned about specific taxes, support rapidly falls away.

However, those in favour of financial disincentives like to point to the success of the London congestion charge. This has proved so effective that the scheme has been amended to take in more of the British capital. The full story of the charge suggests that, while it may appear to be a successful negative influence on behaviour (driving in the centre of the city in this case), it was in fact a triumph of positive influencing.

An Ipsos MORI report (Downing and Ballantyne, 2007) tracked the attitude of Londoners to the congestion charge before, during and after it was put in place. The month before it was introduced in January 2003, close to 45 per cent opposed the scheme, whereas support for it was close to 35 per cent. The following summer, when it was clear that the charge had cut congestion, and improved the bus service, the figures had changed dramatically to 25 per cent opposed, and close to 60 per cent in favour. Support dipped to 40 per cent in favour and 35 per cent against during discussions to extend the scheme, but improved back to 60 per cent in favour and 25 per cent opposed the following year. The congestion charge worked because enough people were initially financially disincentivised to use their cars. This allowed the majority to see that fewer cars in the capital had a direct personal benefit to them, both in terms of greater mobility, and for its aesthetic value.

But while financial disincentives may hold back some, others may never be willing to do anything that sacrifices their perceived benefits, particularly if they think that others are taking advantage of their good will. Downing and Ballantyne (2007) found that over half of their respondents agreed that they would do more to try to stop climate change if other people did more. Of course, this is an open question. How much more would they have to do, and how many would need to do it, and who are 'they' anyway? Still, the issue of fairness, and even the spread of sacrifice, is significant for some people.

## Yes I am doing my bit – aren't I?

There are a number of things that people proudly say when quizzed about their sustainable behaviour. Top of the list is often recycling, but few would pass up a bargain, even if it was over-packaged. Many feel that they already do a lot for the environment.

However, an examination of these actions often reveals that they are far from consistent, and can have minimal impact. This does not stop people from holding the view that they are good green citizens. A good example of this is plastic bags. While many countries have used legislation to dissuade retailers from giving them out, most rely on the market place to use alternative bag distribution as a way of differentiating themselves from their competitors. If this was meant to lead to social pressure to end the use of plastic bags, it has not really worked. The Tickbox.net survey found that more than half of the respondents used new supermarket carrier bags instead of reusing old ones.

However, among those that are conscious of what their peers think, the move to be greener can have a startling affect. The desire to be seen to be green was illustrated early in 2007 when the large UK food retailer Sainsbury's brought out a durable carrier bag on which the message 'I'm not a plastic bag' was emblazoned in large letters, so that it caught the eye of passing pedestrians. The 20 000 bags sold out within hours of going on sale, even though they cost £5 each, and the plastic variety was still free. The irony of conspicuous consumption stemming from concern for the environment could not have been lost on the more sustainably aware. But this was not all. The *London Evening Standard* (Mendick, 2007) reported that 'woman stood in line from 3am to get one of the cotton bags made by leading designer Anya Hindmarch'. It allegedly transpired that they had been made in China, air-freighted to the UK, and were neither Fair Trade nor made from organic cotton.

This story suggests that picking out green or ethical products is clearly a challenge for many consumers. This also emerges from other surveys that show that people are not sure what they should be doing or buying. The reason for this, as a UK National Consumer Council (Steedman, 2005) survey showed, is because very few people are seeking out information and advice on sustainable goods and services. The NCC report 'Desperately Seeking Sustainability?' found that over 80 per cent had personally come across information or advice on how they could consume in a more sustainable way. However, only a relatively small number of consumers actively sought out this information, with just 19 per cent proactively finding information about at least one topic. This figure went down to only 8 per cent for people who researched at least five topics. This has nothing to do with a lack of proactivity, as the survey found that 75 per cent had sought information on how to live more healthily and 63 per cent had researched pensions and financial saving topics. The survey found that 18 per cent were just not interested in finding out more about sustainable consumption.

It would be easier if they were simply not offered unsustainable products in the first place. However, this is not as easy as it sounds. Apart from the complaints about intervening in, and reducing personal choice, many technologies cannot be universally deployed in every home and business. The size of some compact fluorescent bulbs, and the rarity of LED bulbs, still means that some assume that low-energy lighting is unsuitable for their homes. There are also still millions of T8 bulbs used in commercial and industrial building that could be replaced with more efficient T5s. Of course, T5s are a different length and so are expensive to fit.

The removal of goods is not a crime against shopping. No store will stock every available brand of the same product. In fact, they barely scratch the surface of the number of things they could display. This selective stocking is known as choice editing, and could be used to avoid the confusion shown in the surveys. Ultimately the solution is for shoppers to know what they are buying, and make informed choices. Meanwhile the surveys will continue to show majorities of people, that can't find, or are confused by sustainable goods and services.

While the polls and surveys point out the difficulties with sustainable consumption, there is better news from those considering new jobs. Survey evidence among new job seekers suggests that the values and reputation of a company are beginning to be as important as their terms and conditions of employment. One of the most revealing polls in recent years was a study by Stanford Graduate School of Business (2004) about attitudes among MBA graduates, a group previously assumed to have high earnings foremost on their minds. They asked MBA students in 11 countries about the importance of a number of factors influencing employer choice. The finding was that 97 per cent of job seekers said that they were 'willing to forgo financial benefits to work for an organisation with a better reputation for corporate social responsibility and ethics'.

There is one more survey result that runs counter to expectation. Brook Lyndhurst (2004) cross-referenced questions about sustainable behaviour with those of attitudes. They found that people who did not think that environmental problems were exaggerated were better recyclers and took more showers (as opposed to baths) than people who thought that these problems were exaggerated. However, both groups kept appliances off standby and bought organic food in roughly the same numbers. In a surprising turnaround, the environmental sceptics outperformed the believers 33 per cent to 27 per cent in buying energy-saving light bulbs. Clearly it is not necessary to be an eco-warrior to spot an energy-saving opportunity.

Some think that the only way that consumers will be guaranteed to buy the right things in the right amounts is to limit their capacity to harm the planet. One idea is to estimate the national share of carbon, and then divide it equally among the population in the form of a credit card (Starkey and Anderson, 2005). Every citizen would have their own annual personal quota or ration to use as they wished. This offers a degree of personal choice and avoids the need for choice editing.

It would work most easily when directly purchasing energy for transport or heating. The carbon cost of a flight is a little more complicated as it would depend on the number of passengers, the efficiency of the aircraft, and variables such as taxiing time and whether the plane was forced to circle the airport in a holding pattern. It would be even more complicated to work out the carbon cost of a multi-component item, such as a computer. However, all this is possible providing the public accept that their consumption will be capped by something other than purchasing power.

The difficulty with this idea is that the public is unlikely to view this as anything other than a reduction of existing freedoms. Like the London congestion charge, people will need to see an improvement in their quality of life in order to be convinced that this negative instrument will lead to a positive outcome for them. The promise of a statistically lesser chance of suffering a hurricane is not the same thing as enjoying fewer cars, and cannot be delivered overnight. For this idea to work, an interim benefit needs to be inserted into the equation, and this should be a materially or socially desirable reward.

## Behaviour in the context of reform

The results of these polls tell us a number of things about the state of mind of both the business community and the general public. There is clearly a real mixture of attitudes and approaches in the world today. There are some people that have completely accepted their new circumstances and have chosen to get on with what they see as their collective responsibilities. Many others are inactive, as a result of doubts and lack of confidence about what to do. A few are resisting with wilful descent, in the face of all the evidence being presented to them. We have to accept that there will always be a few people who will never believe that our current rates of consumption are destructive and that the way resources are shared is unsustainable. However, it is clear even from a cursory look at what people say when asked about these issues that there is a substantial amount of awareness, and a fair amount of theoretical good will to do something about it.

There is certainly some movement from former sceptics, who had previously either rejected the existence of the problem or refused to accept any responsibility for it. The concern about environmental issues has defiantly moved out of the 'beards and sandals' cliché and into the mainstream in certain parts of society, though certainly not most of it. Peer pressure, or at least the fear of making a social mistake, may not be the strongest reason for acting more sustainably, but it has the same impact as the actions of a committed environmentalist. The behaviour of people who wave the latest sustainable thing in the faces of others is less significant, as these people could just as easily drive up in a 3 miles to the gallon Hummer the following day.

As we shall see in the following chapters, the antidote to unsustainable behaviour is the ability to encourage the doubters to listen to, and understand, other perspectives, particularly ones that they respect. This may be the right answer, but it can't be expected to catch on without a lot more work to determine how this can be achieved. Anyone who has stood in a room full of boisterous, cynical and sarcastic sales representatives or engineers and tried to talk to them about sustainable development will know how challenging this can be. Those who haven't can probably imagine what that is like. But part of the recipe for success, as most communications professionals will tell you, is to know your audience, and then to prepare these unappetising raw ingredients into something that is not only palatable, but moreish.

We can certainly say that the blanket assumption that human beings are condemned to suffer at their own hands because they are too irrational, self-centred and hypocritical to save themselves is at least open to question – despite the apparently overwhelming evidence that this is true. In order to take the next step to believing that we have the capacity to move to a sustainable way of living and working we need to see and understand that not only is this possible, but that it has already been done by others in a way that has helped them move from something worse to something better.

# 3

# Leaders and the bolt of light

## Getting personal about sustainability

As we have seen through the work of Mary Midgley and Theodore Zeldin, it is a comfort to those working towards a more sustainable future that human beings are capable of believing that they can achieve and enjoy a more sustainable life. This is a vital step, but it is not the same as understanding how that might be achieved. In order to answer this question, we need to first find the evidence that some people have already willingly adopted sustainable lives, and created sustainable businesses. This part is relatively straightforward.

We then need to show that their choices could easily be everyone's choices, and then explain how this can be done in a relatively short period of time. This part is the great question of our time. The following three chapters consider how individual businessmen, groups of people, and whole countries managed to accept the arguments around sustainability, and how they have tried to put their beliefs into practice.

## Are business leaders bad people?

Many environmentalists and social justice campaigners rail bitterly against the current economic system that supports the worst excesses of destructive unsustainable corporate behaviour. A typical view comes from the author and activist Derrick Jensen (2006) when he says

*...each time we are left confused or hurt by the lies or other tactics of those in power – as ExxonMobil changes the climate, as Boise Cascade deforests, as Monsanto poisons the world, as BP lies about its practices – we ask...what are those in power trying to get out of what they just did? What is the ultimate benefit to them?*

Particular vitriol is reserved for the leaders of the most hated companies. Jensen goes on to ask 'How do these people (CEOs of major companies) sleep at night? Soundly, in comfortable beds in 5000 square foot homes, behind gates, with private security systems, thank you very much.'

When this view of the corporate leader as abuser or psychopath (both terms that Jensen insists are entirely justifiable) is put to individual heads of business, it is unsurprising that they refuse to recognise the description. While these are (generally) cool-headed people, they reject these accusations in guarded political language, but even they can run to the emotional at times. Writing in *The Guardian*, the sustainability campaigner Jonathon Porritt (2006) explains that *oil companies hate any analogy between themselves and tobacco companies as deal-ers in death and destruction. Indeed, they're astonished at the hypocrisy of people who enjoy the benefits of their products (in terms of driving, flying and so on), but also reckon it's the oil companies that should be held responsible for all the costs.*

It is nevertheless true that history is strewn with evidence that industry has contributed to serious environmental damage, and exploited millions of people in the name of maximising shareholder value. True, many would say, that those mistakes were made in bygone times when the evidence, the legislation, and the societal sensitivities were not developed enough to stand in the way of these actions. They would say that a statement like 'there is a reluctance to incorpo-rate climate change into their mainstream investment decisions, given the pri-mary fiduciary duty to maximise shareholder returns' is a thing of the past. Unfortunately that particular statement appeared in a report by the communica-tion firm HeadLand (2007) into asset fund managers' attitudes to climate change.

If this is true, then business leaders that run publicly owned companies and are devoted to operating in a sustainable manner will always be horribly conflicted. Those that run private firms may not have any more leeway if the owners and their financial backers do not agree with these views. Or, is it possible that some leaders can come to recognise that fiduciary responsibilities stretch further than short-term annual cycles, when sustainable thinking begins to make much more economic sense. If this realisation is possible, is there any evidence that business leaders can change from a 'risk minimisation' perspective to a lasting personal conversion, based on the absence of negative environmental and social impacts?

## Change of heart or change in fashion?

It is fair to say that recently there have been some significant and high profile business leaders who have seen the (green) light, and have announced impres-sive environmental initiatives. Some of these men represent companies not pre-viously noted for their responsible behaviour. Wal-Mart's Lee Scott described climate change as 'Katrina in slow motion' and said the hurricane had 'changed Wal-Mart forever' (Teather, 2005).

Rupert Murdoch committed News International to being carbon neutral by 2010 after seeing the devastating droughts in his native Australia (Gunther, 2007). Previous to this first-hand experience, Murdoch-owned media (including the tab-loid newpapers *The Sun* and *The New York Post*, and TV stations including Fox) had not been known for their forthright support for green issues. Stuart Rose devised the 'Plan A' strategy for Marks & Spencer saying that he was 'of a certain age' and wanted to make sure future generations were not harmed by the actions of the present. Previously, and before Rose's time, Marks & Spencer attracted heavy criticism from unions and the public for the way they dropped long-standing suppliers in a bid to produce cheaper clothes in developing countries.

Hundreds of millions of dollars in environmental investment have been announced in the wake of these decrees. What, many would have wondered, made these captains of commerce and industry turn from bad guy (or at least people who had not realised or accepted the full impact that their company was having on the Earth) to a good guy? What were their motivations?

Some campaigners may have asked whether it really matters how they came to this change of heart. It may have been a reaction to investor or customer pressure. It may have been a proactive shift, caused by a more complete understanding of how the world works, and their company's place in it. The only thing that really matters is the sincerity of a company that says it sees the 'green light'. Defensive reaction to criticism will tend to produce isolated attempts to placate the accusers, whereas a more complete understanding of the issues will result in a comprehensive set of actions without unsustainable holes.

The sincerity, motivation, or consistency of business leaders' decisions is worth more than any sales success in today's more compassionate world. If critics (including the media) even suspect that sustainable actions are cynical and devised to deflect attention away from bigger problems, then the implications are often worse than being accused of doing nothing. The 'preservation of reputation' is a constant issue for business leaders, and the erosion of it can be highly damaging.

## Reputation and corporate conformity

One example is the way Nestlé undermined its reputation as a company that cares about the 'developing world'. The company has been on the receiving end of a long running boycott: Baby Milk Action. One of its key defences was that, far from wishing to exploit the poor in developing countries, it cared deeply about these parts of the world.

This façade became more than a little dented when, in 2002, the company decided to sue the Ethiopian government for $6 million (Denny, 2002). This sum represented about one hour's turnover and a fraction of the $5.5 billion in profits the company made in the previous year. However, it was a significant sum for one of the world's poorest countries. This was at a time when the Ethiopian government was trying to cope with the worst famine to hit the country for 20 years. A perplexed public may possibly have understood that Nestlé did this as a matter of principle, because the Ethiopian's had nationalised one of their factories. However, this glimmer of understanding would have evaporated, and been replaced by astonishment, when the public learned that Nestlé had acquired the company in 1986, and the Ethiopians had nationalised it in 1975.

Nestlé explained that they were going to give the money back to Ethiopia once they had established the principle that nationalisation was theft. Unfortunately, the story broke before they could complete the plan, and they were handed a public relations disaster. No amount of explanation could retrieve their reputation. However, the hard commercial truth about gaffes like this is that the vast majority of consumers eyeing Frosted Shreddies, Munch Bunch Squashums and two-finger Kit Kats (the top selling biscuit in the UK) would have been unaware, or unconcerned, by Nestlé's actions.

Nestlé is also listed on the Dow Jones Sustainability Index, and increased its score in 2007. It is AAA rated, and ranks first among food companies on the Innovest environment, social and governance index. The company reduced its overall $CO_2$ emissions by 16.5 per cent between 2000 and 2005, and by 6 per cent between 2005 and 2006. We would imagine that running a multinational like Nestlé would not be dissimilar to running a moderately sized country, in terms of the conflicting and often difficult trade-offs that need to be made between economic productivity, and the negative environmental and social impacts caused by the activities of the company.

All this reflects directly on a man like Peter Brabeck-Letmathe, CEO and Chairman of Nestlé. He would be expected by his Board and his investors to tread the tightrope of this trade-off to minimise risk and maximise profits. The trust in him, to make a long-term and binding commitment to sustainable development, will always conflict with the unsustainable decisions he has to make in the name of shareholder value. It would be a very brave person indeed who restructures the company in the light of potential or predicted environmental problems. Braver still if this was a decision of conscience, based on moral considerations. And yet this is exactly what some business leaders have done. It begs the question: where do sustainable 'transformational decisions' originate? Are they generated by conditions in the market place, or conditions in the mind of the leader?

It is fairly clear what would have happened if Mr. Brabeck-Letmathe had experienced an internal compass shift that pointed him in a truly sustainable direction. First, he would have had to convince his Board, and then stock market analysts and key shareholders, that their conventional understanding of economic growth, based on existing rates of resource dependency (including fossil fuel), was no longer valid. He would probably be able to pull off a modest plan if profits and dividends were moving along nicely. However, as the former CEO of BP (Lord Browne) found, all of your sustainable innovation counts for very little if the company hits a bump (in his case the company's safety systems failure in the USA), and you end up carrying the can.

## Is it a conviction thing?

The question of sincerity and personal conviction has been widely debated in the formal media and the blogosphere in relation to many other corporate decisions to go green. An obvious example is Wal-Mart, which continues to be accused of poor and unsustainable practices despite a string of sustainability initiatives, including 'Sustainability 360' (www.walmartstores.com). The pressure group Human Rights Watch (2007) accused the company of routinely flouting workers rights and labour laws. It sets out evidence of harassment, forcing workers to listen to anti-union speeches, discriminating against long-term staff, and indoctrinating employees with misleading propaganda.

Grist (2005), the environmental news and commentary organisation had been regularly reporting on accusations of Clean Water Act violations in the USA, massive transport emissions, and a major contribution to urban sprawl and traffic congestion. However, the announcements by Wal-Mart divided the green lobby (Mitchell, 2006). On one side, the large distances that Wal-Mart goods cover, and its high growth strategy, could swamp any energy savings made in existing stores. On the other side, the company's sheer size could mean that Wal-Mart would catch up fast with other businesses that have been slowly working on the agenda for a while.

In a speech to employees in October 2005 Lee Scott said that the world's largest retailers would become more proactive on issues that had historically been dealt with from a defensive posture (Teather, 2005). He set out a range of initiatives that may seem modest, including the reduction of packaging on toys, selling organic food for the first time, researching ethical sourcing and promoting energy-efficient light bulbs. The company's sheer size means that it has the scope to sell 100 million bulbs by the end of 2007, saving 20 million tonnes of $CO_2$ in the process. Activists would say that if Wal-Mart has the ability to make such sweeping inroads into greenhouse gas emissions, then who really cares if Scott just did it to get the knockers off his back.

But on another level, it matters very much because 'socially responsible' investor pressure, or concerns from national and international pressure groups, may not always be so strident, particularly when there is an economic downturn. Environmental issues were high on the agenda in the late 1980s, but were overtaken by globalisation, and had to wait almost a decade before the predictions of climate scientists thrust it back onto Boardroom agendas.

The fear is that if sustainable change is not rooted in a deep conviction by the chief executive, then it will always be vulnerable to a reversal when these innovations stop making financial or communication sense. However, if the change in strategy comes as a result of a personal conversion, then it is likely to remain (despite commercial pressures) for at least as long as that business leader holds his or her position. If the leader either hands power to a protégée, or manages to embed the change into the culture of the company, then the change has a chance of continuing long after its instigator departs.

The division now is between business leaders that are susceptible to positively responsible conversion, and those that feel constrained by conventional financial imperatives. While polls show that almost any business leader would now say that acting in a sustainable manner was important to the business, there are few that have gone on record to say that environmental enhancement and social justice should be the basis for every decision.

An examination of three such leaders – Lord Terry Thomas (of the Co-operative Bank), Ray Anderson (of Interface Flor), and Yvon Chouinard (of Patagonia) – reveals a fascinating insight into how leaders come to believe in and convert their companies to be 'sustainable development exemplars'. Each has been chosen for this book, because they have created or recreated commercial organisations known for a decade or more for both outstanding environmental and social commitment, and for business success. The stories of their businesses are fairly well known, but the stories of their personal motivations are key to understanding how positive influences drove them to their achievements.

## Individual conviction: Terry Thomas

Terry Thomas (now Lord Thomas of Macclesfield) was born in modest circumstances in the small town of Carmarthen in Wales, and rose to become Chief Executive of the Co-operative Bank in the UK. Thomas took the job when the bank was at a low ebb in 1987. By the time he retired 10 years later, it had returned record profits every year and gained a reputation for being one of the most 'ethical and sustainable' businesses in the world.

Founded in 1872 as the Loan and Deposit Department of the Co-operative Wholesale Society, the bank was created to serve the growing family of co-operative retail businesses. Now serving the general market the bank's ethical policy was introduced in 1992. It set criteria standards that would govern the way it traded. This included the requirement for prospective customers to conform to those ethics. If customers did not meet the criteria, then they were politely asked to look for another bank. Investment decisions were subject to the same ethical tests. When looking to determine what ethics to use, it was necessary to consider whose ethics to choose. The bank chose to base its ethical policy on the concerns of its customers, on the basis that it is generally their money that is being used.

In 1996, the bank produced its ecological mission statement, based on the ideas of Karl-Henrik Robèrt (Robèrt et al., 1995) and his model for sustainability known as The Natural Step. Robèrt thought that one of the reasons why more people were not acting sustainably was because there was no consensus about what it meant to be sustainable. He said that 'in a democracy, public policy cannot rise above the understanding of the average voter. Consequently, the sharing of knowledge is at least as critical for democracy as the distribution of income'. In order to share the knowledge he needed to find consensus across the whole of society. Living and working in Sweden, his next stop was the Swedish scientific community. He challenged them to come up with a simple but unarguable set of rules that everyone could understand and follow. The requirements for these rules included the need for them to be scientifically supportable, and applicable to any scale. On the human level, the model had to be easily disseminated, should not require individuals to act against their self-interest, or require large-scale societal changes. He was particularly insistent that businesses, political parties and the public should be able to use the model as a practical tool.

Incredibly, Robèrt got his consensus, and the support of the Swedish King. The Natural Step is now an international movement and has been adopted by many companies. In the end there were only four rules. Three of them covered the rate of extraction of materials from the Earth's crust, the rate of emissions of man-made substances, and the rate of destruction of biodiversity. The fourth concerned the fair and efficient use of the Earth's resources throughout the world. The Co-operative bank was the first financial institution to adopt The Natural Step but, more importantly, the approach was one of the most radical and ambitious attempts to link economic success to sustainable performance that had ever been seen in the corporate world.

A year later, the bank released its first 'partnership report'. This attempted an open and transparent statement about the social, financial and environmental impacts of the company in one report, and set the trend for what are now known as 'sustainability reports'. The report cited seven partners (often referred to now as 'stakeholders' in the jargon of corporate social responsibility) that were directly or indirectly affected by the bank's activities. One of these was 'leaders, managers, staff and their families' – still to this day among the most expansive interpretation of the staff stakeholder group.

The bank has published a partnership report every year since 1997. In 2004, it started publishing a joint sustainability report with the Co-operative Insurance Society or CIS, under the merger name of Co-operative Financial Services (CFS). The last separate CFS Report was published following year, and subsequent reports will be issued under the parent Co-operative Group banner. The Group is primarily a food retail co-operative, but includes non-food businesses including travel agents, funeral director businesses and the financial service co-operatives.

The Co-operative Bank has always understood the need to be accountable to its stakeholders or, in other words, those that matter most to the business. 'Evidence', through targets, and 'open communication' are two of the main tools used to show accountability to stakeholders. The provision of measurable targets, trends over time, and indicators (benchmarked against relevant sources) have been a feature of the bank's annual reporting strategy for almost a decade.

Anyone reading the full account of this transformation, and the plaudits and awards that followed, would naturally be impressed, but would then become interested in how this change came about. The bank became a benchmark for other organisations wishing to produce a similar result. The enquiries for assistance became so frequent that Thomas approached all four Universities in the Greater Manchester area (the heartland of the Co-operative Movement), and set up a non-profit consultancy called the National Centre for Business & Sustainability (NCBS). Inquiring companies were directed to the five-way partnership for guidance and advice, on subjects including the formation of sustainability indicators and measurement techniques, and innovative and creative ways for Boards to envisage and plan for a sustainable future.

These practical questions could easily be answered, but the way that Thomas created the conditions and the leadership for such a change was less obvious. The answer to this more personal question requires an understanding of two key days that diverted Terry Thomas' path away from a skilled, yet ordinarily motivated, banking career towards becoming a sustainable business icon. The first was a Welsh history lesson when he was 13 years old. The second was a meeting with the inspirational Swedish founder of The Natural Step soon after he became head of the Co-operative Bank.

The Welsh history lesson told of the life and times of the industrialist and social reformer Robert Owen. The son of a saddler, Owen came from the Welsh village of Newtown, but left at the age of 10 in 1781 to join his brother (also a saddler) in London. At the age of 21, he became a manager in the first mill in Manchester to spin thread using a rotary steam engine. During this period Owen became a founder member of the Manchester Board of Health, which helped to bring about the earliest legislation to protect factory workers in 1802.

Owen went to Scotland to manage New Lanark mills in 1800, and set about improving conditions for the workers because, as he would write later in 1814, a 'living mechanism is improved by being trained to strength and activity, and that it is true economy to supply it regularly with sufficient, wholesome food, to keep it neat and clean, to treat it with kindness that it may not experience mental friction…'. Owen believed that people's behaviours were formed out of the environment in which they had to live (Birchall, 1994). The centrepiece of his efforts was the building of an Institute for the Formation of Character, which included a nursery, school rooms, public halls and community rooms for use by the mill workers. He also improved sanitary conditions, raised the child labour age, and attempted to show the workers how to self-govern.

By today's standards, Owen was a philanthropist. But his beliefs had a hard commercial side which Thomas never forgot. A better educated workforce was able to manage manufacturing methods and materials that would command premium prices. Sea Island cotton, one of the finest types of cloth available at the time, was expensive to buy and difficult to work with. A less skilled and less healthy workforce would cause wastage that could not be afforded. Owen ensured that the cloth was made efficiently, and with minimal wastage, by investing in his workforce, thus ensuring a good return. Towards the end of his time at Lanark, he and his partners were making a 25 per cent return on their investment.

The worldwide co-operative community still looks upon Owen as the father of the movement. He applied his philosophy of toleration, co-operation and respect, and the creation of non-competitive environments with conviction. And while his ideas were not always successful, they inspired others to create businesses that were not dependent on the exploitative tendencies that mainstream capitalism displayed at the time. For the young Terry Thomas this was a powerful and inspiring concept, but he had to wait a considerable time before he could put it into practice.

Thomas' early career in banking in the 1960s was with one of the main high street clearing banks, National Westminster (now part of the Royal Bank of Scotland Group). Frustrated at his employer's hierarchical structure, Thomas sought to fast-track his career by enrolling at Bath School of Management. Nat West was less than supportive of this move, although they did later award him with a scholarship for the course, but the damage was done.

He responded to the advertisement for a post at the much smaller Co-operative Bank, partly on the basis that he felt an affinity with the co-operative movement, which he assumed would run a much more supportive and caring business. On joining he found that sadly this was not the case. As a middle manager in the fledgling marketing department, he found an old-fashioned and backward-looking business that was relying on the past glories of the movement and the loyalty of a fading working class customer base. This was 1973.

By 1979, and the election of Margaret Thatcher as Prime Minister, the societal class stratification of Britain would be blown apart, severely challenging institutions like the co-operative movement, which relied on working people shopping and banking in places that represented their interests. The acceleration of social mobility, and the erosion of the identification with working class roots, undermined the affinity to the co-op brand, and it reacted by trying to imitate its private sector rivals, including the adoption of the very practices that it was originally created to avoid.

Thomas saw that some innovations were needed straight away. One of his ideas was to introduce 'free banking' for current accounts in credit. Many customers today probably don't realise that this has not always been standard practice in the banking world and that it had its origins in the Co-operative Bank. Ironically, this is now threatened, in the UK at least, by a challenge to the banking practice that levies high charges for those who are not in credit. However, it is unlikely that customers will give up Thomas' innovation without a fight.

By 1982, Thomas was Director of Group Development during which time he was asked to help the trade union movement set up its own financial bank (Unity Trust Bank). When the time came to appoint a new Managing Director of the bank in 1987, Terry was a natural choice. But he inherited some tough problems. The bank was making less than one million pounds a year. Morale was very low, and Thomas understood that staff would rarely admit to working for the bank unless pressed, such was the embarrassment of working for such an outmoded and unfashionable business. While the bank was not failing, it was not moving forward either, and was vulnerable to any kind of unexpected market upheaval.

His first task was to change the bank from being asset driven (loans and over-drafts) to deposit based. This would give the bank a more secure basis from which to do business. But rather than dive into the normal marketing approach of developing products that would compete on his competitor's terms, Thomas decided to go back to first principles.

His first task was to set up a small committee of inquiry that asked how the bank could increase its longevity. This was grounded in the understanding that profitability was going to be partly dependent on stretching lending periods. Lending on a one-year renewable basis was uneconomic because of the market-ing and administration costs, and Thomas was determined to give the business a more stable and profitable footing.

The realisation was that a longer-lived bank would need a strategy that kept pace with customers who would be reacting to, and changing with, the world around them. If that was the case, the bank would need a mechanism to both understand these changes and transmit its own values and messages. This would make sure that customers knew that their bank was in step with their own per-sonal values set at any given time. It would prove to be a project that would take time, but one that would also bear fruit.

At the same time, other commentators, but not other businesses, arrived at the same conclusions. Books such as *Built to Last* (Collins and Porras, 1997) and the Royal Society of Art's *Tomorrow's Company Inquiry* were saying that busi-nesses should involve a wider spectrum of people who are important to them, if they wanted to remain successful. A Co-operative Bank case study written later, quoted Thomas as saying that

*in order to build a successful and long-lived business, the Board of a company should regard themselves, not simply as beholden to generate short-term profit and share-holder value, but also as trustees charged with the responsibility of balancing the needs and aspirations of each partner against the others and across time.*

(www.co-operativebankcasestudy.org.uk)

Thomas articulated this approach by explaining that

*in dealing with our partners, we have adopted a very simple philosophy: That an important key to business success – and business longevity – is to deliver value to all our partners in a balanced fashion over time. 'Balanced over time' because we don't expect each partner to gain equal benefit from each decision we make – in delivering value to one partner we may, at times, work against the interests of another.*

This far-sighted view is now taken by many (thought not all) larger businesses as self-evident, and would be enough for most business leaders, but not Thomas. Now, two other influences from his earlier life came into play. The first shaped his method of weaving this message of 'partnership' into a workable strategy. It is one thing to have the insight to extend the radar of a company to those whose views were not previously considered important or relevant. It was quite another to put the 'listening' into practice.

Here, Thomas recalled his childhood. Son of a Catholic mother and a Protestant father, and living in a community where religion was an important social factor, Thomas learned how divisions could be wasteful and destructive. As youth groups and family activities were organised by the churches in Carmarthen, and the young Thomas was not solidly of one faith or the other, he had first-hand experience of what it meant to be excluded. This made him determined in later life to ensure that different perspectives were considered, and that all interests were incorporated for the good of the whole organisation.

His other passion was to commit his business, and later the whole of the North West of England, to do everything it could to ensure that its environmental impacts were understood and minimised. This was directly influenced by Robert Owen and his work to clean up and improve the working environment for his employees and the wider community. Later, he was to persuade key business leaders and regional public sector bodies to set up Sustainability Northwest (SNW), the first public–private partnership in Europe to promote sustainable development in a regional context. In 2001, SNW and the National Centre for Sustainability would come together to provide both the persuasion and the solutions needed to accelerate sustainable change.

It was while searching for inspirational ideas on how business and the environment should interact that he came across the writings of Karl-Henrik Robèrt. Some time later he found himself in Robèrt's house on the outskirts of Stockholm. The two men sat down with a cup of coffee and, when they concluded their discussion, they realised that they had been sitting in Robèrt's kitchen for the whole day. Thomas was completely won over by the argument that a company that wanted to last into the future had to play by the same rules that kept the planet going.

Other authors, including Fritjof Capra, helped to reinforce the message that Thomas brought away with him from Sweden, and soon he was putting the whole forward strategy together. The main pieces of the puzzle included:

- the belief in low impact, or 'beneficial' business, which he took from Owen;
- the understanding of how to stitch a sustainability roadmap into standard business practice, which comes from The Natural Step;
- the 'Built to Last' message that widening the listening/speaking radar beyond conventional stakeholders will lead to longer lasting business partnerships; and
- the people skills that helped him to navigate through difficult religious waters in his youth.

Thomas still had to carry the staff, and many who did not agree or understand his strategy, left the bank. The Board was often uncomfortable with his departure from standard banking practice. This Thomas combated by playing the co-operative card, which held that the co-operative principles were something that needed to be revived in the business, and that his new policies were completely in tune with the co-operative ideal. While not entirely accurate in terms of all the sources that he drew upon, few could argue against that contention and Thomas got his way.

Thomas would later become chairman of Red Rose Forest (a community forest), was the first Chair of North West England's regional economic development agency. He returned to Sustainability Northwest as its President in 2006. His elevation to the House of Lords was seen by many as just reward for a brave and innovative career.

## Individual conviction: Ray Anderson

Another often cited inspirational business leader, who was transformed by his experiences, is Ray Anderson, founder of the floor covering company Interface. Interface, in the words of its own website, has now 'diversified and globalized its businesses, with sales in more than 100 countries, and manufacturing facilities on four continents. In addition to carpet tiles and broadloom carpet marketed under several brands, Interface also manufactures commercial panel and upholstery fabrics'.

Now known as InterfaceFLOR, the company, under Anderson's stewardship, travelled from the manufacture and sales of carpet tiles for commercial premises, to one of the world's leading eco-product manufacturers. A visit to the company's website (www.interfaceinc.com) reveals a vision statement that says InterfaceFLOR wants to be

*the first company that, by its deeds, shows the entire industrial world what sustainability is in all its dimensions: People, process, product, place and profits – by 2020 – and in doing so we will become restorative through the power of influence.*

The company's promise to the planet, Mission Zero (this was 13 years before 'Plan A' at Marks & Spencer), is that 'every creative, manufacturing and building decision we make will move us closer to our goal of eliminating any negative impact our flooring and fabric companies may have on the environment by the year 2020'. Note the absence of the usual wriggle words in this statement, such as 'work towards' or 'doing everything we can' or 'committed to' or 'in time'. The promise is to eliminate any negative impact.

These are bold statements now, but Ray Anderson started talking about shaping his company towards the current goals in 1994. There were the usual moves to eliminate waste, and harness renewable energy in subsequent years, but what really caught the public's eye was the idea that products could be made and passed on to the customer without the need to continually exploit new resources. Interface decided to try to source the raw material it needed by harvesting recycled carpet and other petrochemical products, instead of buying virgin material made from oil and newly mined minerals.

The key to this strategy was to stop selling their product, and to start leasing it. As raw materials, and non-renewable ones in particular, become scarce, they will be more keenly sought after by many growing economies. Inevitably, the market will place a higher price on these commodities. Anderson's sustainable thinking was ahead of the physical constraints which are now affecting metals, wood and cement, mainly as a direct result of China's prolonged double digit growth at the start of the twenty-first century. Anderson believed that if Interface, a petrointensive company in 1994, could take back its property (borrowed for a price by its customers), then not only would he never have to take another drop of oil from the Earth, but he would also secure vital resources to keep his company going.

Like Terry Thomas and the Co-operative Bank story, the feelings of admiration for Anderson's deeds are followed by the inevitable question, why did he do it? In his autobiography, *Mid-Course Correction* (Anderson, 1998) he admits that

*for the first 21 years of our company's existence, I for one never gave one thought to what we were taking from the earth or doing to the earth except to be sure we were in compliance and keeping ourselves clean in a regulatory sense… We had very little environmental awareness until August 1994.*

Yet in only a few years, Anderson was recognised as one of the world's most environmentally progressive leaders on sustainable commerce, and served as co-chairman of the President's Council on Sustainable Development during the Clinton administration. So what happened at that time to make a man who had been in business for over two decades totally change his perspective and remould his company into the exemplar that it is today?

To understand the full implications of this personal conversion, it is necessary to study Anderson's life prior to his sustainable epiphany. He graduated from the Georgia Institute of Technology in 1956 as an industrial engineer, and learned the carpet and textile businesses with companies such as Deering-Milliken and Callaway Mills.

He first saw carpet tiles in 1969, during a trip to Kidderminster, England. Now known as 'modular soft-surfaced floor coverings', this was a very new idea at the time, and the experience would shape the rest of his commercial life. In 1973 he developed a partnership with Britain's Carpets International Plc., and established a manufacturing site in LaGrange, Georgia. Ten years later, Interface took over Carpets International and went on to dominate the global modular carpet market, as well as becoming a major producer of broadloom carpet and commercial fabrics.

The deep feelings for the environment all started for Anderson when a few customers began to ask about Interface's environmental policies, and the company found that it did not have adequate answers. A worldwide committee was formed, but it wanted a steer from the top, and asked Anderson to give the group 'an environmental vision'. Anderson (1998) recounts 'frankly, I didn't have a vision except obey the law and comply, comply, comply'. He resisted the invitation to speak because 'the idea that, while in compliance, we might be hurting the environment simply hadn't occurred to me'.

At this very moment, Anderson was given a copy of Paul Hawken's book *The Ecology of Commerce*. The book went on to be the recommended text on business and the environment at many business schools. Hawken, a lifelong entrepreneur, journalist and author, now based in California, had a profound affect on Anderson. In his biography, he explains that the book 'changed my life…hit me right between the eyes…was like a spear in the chest that is still there…'.

Anderson was particularly troubled by Hawken's examples of resource depletion and mass extinction caused by damage to natural habitats. This was written before the full extent of man's influence on the climate was realised, which makes the predicted mass extinction rate even more shocking. Hawken's phrase 'the death of birth' deeply and emotionally affected Anderson.

Sometime later, when he came to analyse his reaction to *The Ecology of Commerce* (Hawken, 1994), Anderson offers a number of insights into how and why Hawken's book had such a profound affect on him. He was 60 when he read the book, and later realised that subconsciously he was thinking about his legacy on leaving the company. He thought that he was searching, not just for what the company would become, but for its ultimate purpose. Clearly this thought would probably occur more often to someone who had started a company themselves rather than to a business leader hired to lead an enterprise which had been someone else's idea. Legacy is also a predominantly male aspiration. However, the feeling that one has to 'put back at least as much as one has taken' is common enough judging by the range of Foundations (Gates, Skoll, Susan Thompson Buffett, etc.) that are in evidence around the world.

Anderson said that halfway through Hawken's book he had already formulated his vision, not just for his speech, but for the whole company. When he came to make that speech he said he 'gave that task force a kick-off that frankly surprised me, stunned them, and then galvanized all of us into action'. The vision he offered was 'Interface, the first name in industrial ecology, worldwide, through substance not words.'

But it was not enough that his company should become truly sustainable. Anderson wanted it to be 'restorative', meaning that in the process of manufacturing and supplying products the company would actually put back more than it takes, and to do 'good to the Earth, not just no harm'.

The initial result of Anderson's revelation was a two-pronged initiative. The first was a programme to reduce waste, which Interface defined as any inefficiency. This involved a search for all types of waste, from heat and power to solid waste, and inventory issues right down to administrative inefficiencies. This took 40 per cent (or $67 million) off their costs in the first three and a half years that the programme was set up.

The other initiative was to begin to work out what we would now call sustainable trade-offs. A typical trade-off question would be whether to use PVC or wood. While PVC contains chlorine (dangerous and toxic if used or disposed of improperly) and oil, it is also extremely durable and can be recycled again and again. Wood is a renewable resource, although only if it is grown and harvested in a responsible manner. It also has to be replaced regularly with associated material and energy costs. To date, life cycle assessment studies have oscillated between saying which one is more sustainable. Anderson asked his people to apply what he called EcoMeterics to these issues, in an attempt to find and use the most sustainable materials. They added SocioMeterics to measure social impacts in 2000.

However, it was the thinking behind carpet leasing that was to make Anderson's reputation. The opportunity to develop the idea started with collaboration between Interface and the Southern California Gas Company (SCGC). The energy company wanted to construct a state-of-the-art eco-building to house the headquarters of the Energy Resource Centre, the name it gave to its new sustainable buildings and services advisory business. Completed in the spring of 1995, the Centre (in Downey Los Angeles) was the first building in California to be LEED rated. LEED is The Leadership in Energy and Environmental Design, a certificated green building rating system administered by the USA Green Building Council. This project was the reason that Anderson had been sent Hawken's book. Interface had originally failed to impress the environmental advisor to ERC, and the book was seen as a source to accelerate the company's awareness of the issues.

SCGC needed best-in-class exemplars for its building and its seminars, and following their re-think, Interface delivered on both of these requirements. The disposal of carpets is a major problem for waste disposal authorities. It represents about 2 per cent (by volume) of the domestic waste streams in the USA and Europe, and probably a similar amount for the private sector. It is difficult to collect and recycle, due to its bulk and its composite material structure. According to the USA EPA, the United States threw away about 2.4 million tonnes of carpet in 2002.

The Evergreen Lease product was developed by Interface as a revolutionary way of meeting customer needs without selling the resource, thereby avoiding any future disposal to landfill (Interface, 2002). Interface customers were invited to lease carpet through a monthly, quarterly or annual payment. They could choose carpet for warmth, comfort, design, colour, noise reduction, insulation and other properties, and could change the design over the period of the lease agreement.

Under the terms of the contract, Interface rotated the tiles from high use to low use (underneath desks for example) to prolong tile life. Customers could choose recycled or dematerialised product from the outset, or could buy tiles made from virgin materials. Later, the company would off-set the carbon required in the manufacture of any of their products under the 'Cool Carpet' brand. The company has also devised innovative manufacturing processes, such as methods that make recycling easier, and an adhesive system that is many times more resource-efficient than the industry standard method.

The Evergreen idea that Interface came up with was remarkable for the mid-1990s. However, by 2006 Interface was still leading the market, reclaiming 58 400 tonnes of carpet since it started the Evergreen service, and averaging over 8000 tonnes per year. The company currently recycles 85 per cent of this material into new products.

Anderson's vision was that this method of providing products to the market would not only apply to carpet tiles, but to virtually any commodity that can be recycled. The National Centre for Business & Sustainability (NCBS) once worked with a quarry company that supplied ballast (the rock chips that surround railway lines) to the UK rail network. They were genuinely taken aback when it was suggested that they retain ownership of their product, and take it back when it needed to be replaced due to wear and tear, perhaps decades after it was laid down. One reason that this idea does not fit with the prevailing view of commerce is that the accounting processes discount value over time. The problem with this is that depreciation of many materials does not make sense in real terms. A rock, even after millions of years, is still a rock.

Another anti-sustainable practice laid at the feet of the accountants is the practice of sub-dividing costs. Returning to carpet tiles, the cost of buying and fitting, maintaining and replacing, of disposal and renewal are often split between multiple budgets held by different people in different departments. It is difficult to convince buyers responsible for one part of the whole-life cost of carpeting to part with money that they view as part of someone else's budget.

In addition, the whole-life cost of a service or product often needs to be calculated over a time period that stretches well beyond the usual annual or three-year budget horizon. These problems have delayed Anderson's material revolution over the past few years. The (slow) increase in the understanding of sustainable consumption and production theory, and practical measures such as the introduction of sustainable criteria for procurement and maintenance contracts in companies and public sector organisations, will improve matters. However, until managers run the 'sustainability rule' over the whole of their organisation, good ideas will always become mired in unfashionable, yet vital sections like the procurement team.

One other observation by Anderson is worthy of mention. Influenced by Fritjof Capra's 'Turning Point' (via the film *Mind Walk*), Anderson grasped the idea that everything was interconnected. He called those that needed to understand and be understood, 'constituencies' or 'stakeholders', while Terry Thomas called them 'partners', but the idea is very similar. Anderson's understanding led to his view that there were seven steps to sustainability. These were:

- the elimination of waste
- the elimination of harmful emissions
- the exclusive use of renewable energy
- the adoption of closed-loop processes
- the utilisation of resource-efficient transportation
- the redesigning of commerce so that a service is sold that allows the company to retain ownership of the product and to maximise productivity, and
- the energising of stakeholders around the vision.

This active commitment to all stakeholders is very different to the more defensive understanding of the need to communicate with the outside world that many business people hold to this day. Market research and, for larger companies, reports aimed more at stock market analysts than the wider public is about as far as it goes for many.

Anderson and Thomas thought that the only way they could really take advantage of the benefits of making contact with people who mattered to their businesses was through actual and meaningful two-way discussion. Anderson was particularly interested in having a dialogue with his workforce. All Interface employees were required to undertake a two-day training course. The course covered The Natural Step framework, and related this back to the whole of the company's activities, from procurement and manufacturing through to sales. The management teams also receive in-depth tutoring to help them understand why the vision and mission is important to the financial sustainability of the company. The relatively complex Evergreen leasing system (compared to the one-off sale of product) covers the whole-life costs of the carpet, as well as the carbon and social consequences of doing things differently. This requires knowledge of sustainable consumption and production and (what Paul Hawken calls) natural capitalism. These issues are revisited during continual education programmes.

Anderson knew that in order to succeed, he needed to bring his message to all corners of the company and beyond. However, in a laudable candid section right at the end of his autobiography, he reveals that he may not have been able to do this by himself. Anderson was reliant on his chief operating officer, Charlie Eital, who he describes in the book as 'the most emotionally intelligent person I know'.

In 1997, the company gathered for its 24th birthday celebration. The themes they covered included global poverty, the role of human beings on the Earth, and the impending environmental crisis. People were encouraged to talk about their feelings. It had a profound effect on the company. Anderson comes to the conclusion that the 'soft side' of business, or 'spirituality in business' is essential to success. These are dangerous words to many that feel that these are personal issues, and are best left for individuals to consider outside of the workplace.

But Anderson criticises a male-dominated, macho business culture, driven by 'analytical objective, numbers orientated factual result-driven thinking'. He admits that he would not have been open to Hawken's message, and all of the environmental innovation that followed, if his more impersonal mentality had not been reconciled with his own emotional intelligence and a business partner that was predisposed to this way of thinking.

The Ray Anderson story tells us quite a lot about the conditions under which business leaders can be turned on to the power of sustainable thinking. There was evidence that he was certainly ready for, and more open to an accommodation between the Earth's needs and his company's needs, through his need to establish a legacy and the acceptance that he had a spiritual side that he had hitherto ignored.

He, like Thomas, understood the need to reach out to groups of people that mattered most to the company, and staff in particular. He also needed a spark or catalyst to ignite the sustainable tinder that was obviously waiting to catch fire. This was provided by Hawken's book, but then he kept on reading and talking, stoking that fire which to this day has continued to burn.

## Individual conviction: Yvon Chouinard

The subtitle in Yvon Chouinard's (2005) autobiography *Let My People Go Surfing* is 'the education of a reluctant businessman', and it is significant. For a man that just wanted to pursue what we now call 'extreme' or 'adventure' sports, the founder and owner of the outdoor equipment and apparel company Patagonia has done very well indeed. In 2006, Patagonia turned over $267 million, and employed around 1300 people.

Much of the company is based on catalogue orders, but it does operate retail outlets in the USA, Japan, Korea and Europe. The company now caters for hikers and trekkers, skiers, climbers and anglers. Its carries a full range of clothes and has pioneered the practice of layering (as opposed to fewer, heavier clothes), and worked hard with suppliers to produce wicking – fast drying fabrics that are accepted as the norm today.

Patagonia is renowned for its quality and innovative nature of its products, but also for its remarkable commitment to sustainable business and environmental causes. Like Terry Thomas' Co-operative Bank and Ray Anderson's Interface,

Chouinard's Patagonia is an icon of a values-led business. Anyone picking up a Patagonia catalogue could not fail to understand the direction from which the company comes. However, it would be less apparent to those purchasing the clothes through dealers and intermediaries.

Many mainstream business people would view Chouinard as an eccentric who uses an excellent first-hand understanding of his market, and an intolerance of things that do not work properly, to indulge his commitment to the environment. While this may result in a grudging respect in some quarters, many others do not take well to his fervour. Michael Hiltzik (Barton, 2007) said that Chouinard is 'someone who is perfectly right in principle, but an insufferable person'. His friend and supporter, the former NBC News anchor man Tom Brokaw said of Chouinard, that 'he walks the walk more than anyone else I know in American business'.

Chouinard himself explains (Patagonia, 2007) that 'what we want to do – the reason we are in business – is to inspire and implement solutions to the environmental crises'. The Mission Statement encompasses quality, advocacy and care for the environment when it says that the company will 'make the best product, do no unnecessary harm, use business to inspire and implement solutions to the environmental crises'.

Chouinard calls the five guidelines that motivate and drive Patagonia his 'business philosophy' and, like the products he sells, it is simple yet highly effective at communicating his view of what a business is created to achieve. The five guidelines are:

1. *Lead an examined life* – Know the consequences of our actions. Much of the damage to the environment is done either unintentionally, or through ignorance, or by wilfully ignoring the chain decisions that lead to bad results.
2. *Clean up our act* – Once we understand the results of our actions, change them.
3. *Do our penance* – No matter how much we clean up our act, all of us are still polluters. So give back.
4. *Support civil democracy* – When we give back we support activist groups working on the front lines. They are the most effective agents of change in our democracy.
5. *Influence other companies* – Lead by example.

Note the absence of any reference to money. Chouinard (2005) is clear about the generation of profit and the rate of growth. He says that 'its OK to be eccentric as long as you are rich, otherwise you are just crazy'. The motivation to be profitable comes from an interest in producing products that have low environmental impact, help activists, yet reap a reward for this stance in the market place. The attitude is closer to a social enterprise (a business that produces surplus to invest in righting a social wrong) than a conventional manufacturer.

Much of this thinking came out of a company crisis in 1991, when Patagonia had to lay off 20 per cent of its workforce (over 120 people). The problem came from a decline in sales, coupled with an assumption that rapid growth would continue unabated. It made Chouinard and his wife Malinda question the assumptions behind the business, and made them ask themselves why they were in business in the first place. In the process, this opened up everything they were doing for discussion with senior managers. Typically, Chouinard took them to the windswept mountains of Patagonia in Argentina to do this. This was the region that inspired the name of the company after all, and when they came back they put together a new values statement. The first part of the statement reveals the true nature and depth of the culture that runs through Patagonia:

*We begin with the premise that all life on Earth is facing a critical time, during which survivability will be the issue that increasingly dominates public concern. Where survivability is not the issue, the quality of the human experience of life may be, as well as the decline in the health of the natural world as reflected in the loss of biodiversity, cultural diversity, and the planet's life support systems.*

*The root causes of this situation include basic values embodied in our economic system, including the values of the corporate world. Primary among the problematic corporate values are the primacy of expansion and short-term profit over other considerations such as quality, sustainability, environmental and human health and environmental conditions.*

*The fundamental goal of this corporation is to operate in such a manner that we are fully aware of the above conditions, and attempt to re-order the hierarchy of corporate values, while producing products that enhance both human and environmental conditions.*

These values, guidelines and mission statement produced an impressive, and often trailblazing, range of initiatives. Patagonia questions everything they do, and it applies life cycle assessments and whole-life costing techniques to the whole process and the supply chain. Since 1993, the company has recycled over 92 million plastic drinks bottles into fleeces and other clothing. They estimate that 150 jackets save 42 (USA) gallons of crude oil.

After analysing the impact of commercial cotton, they found that it is responsible for the spread of 25 per cent of global insecticide production, and 10 per cent of the world's pesticides, while occupying less than 3 per cent of the farmed land area. In 1994, they decided to change to organic cotton, even though it was up to twice as expensive, and cotton goods represented 20 per cent of company revenue. By 1996, they had switched their 66 cotton products and achieved their goal. The shift ensured that Patagonia almost single-handedly created an organic cotton agriculture sector in southern California, and put more organic cotton clothes on the market than had ever been seen before.

It took a further decade, but today the organic cotton market is blossoming, with the UK market set to expand by 50 per cent in 2007. Sales in the UK will reach $120 million and the global sales are expected to top $2.6 billion by the end of 2008 (Soil Association, 2007; Organic Exchange, 2007).

Patagonia's efforts also ran to replacing toxic dies. The company has invested in solar panels, bought wind farm electricity, recycled large amounts of its own waste, and built an award-winning warehouse in Reno Nevada, only the second distribution centre in the whole of the USA to be given a gold level LEED certificate. They dropped the plastic wallets and cardboard sleeves used to package underwear and hung them loose on racks. Having been warned that sales would drop, they found they actually increased by 28 per cent (customers were able to feel the quality), and saved $150 000 and 12 tons of packaging year on year.

Another of Patagonia's achievements of note is '1 per cent for the Planet', an alliance of businesses pledging to donate 1 per cent of their sales towards active efforts to restore the natural environment. Co-founded with Blue Ribbon Flies during a fishing trip, 1 per cent FTP avoids fair-weather corporate donations by sourcing the money from sales and not profits. This means that members give whether they have a good year or a bad year. Membership reached nearly 500 businesses in 2006, with a combined contribution of over $6 million. Patagonia has, to date, given over $29 million in grants and in-kind donations to more than 1000 organisations.

Even by the yardstick of companies that have tried to stand out as sustainable exemplars, the Patagonia story is remarkable. Simply the sheer volume of achievements, juxtaposed with commercial success, makes it a tale that is almost, but not quite, too good to be true. If Chouinard is a one-off, then it would be difficult for aspiring sustainable businesses to draw any lessons from his story.

However, an examination of how he started, and his early inspirations, could easily have affected almost anyone.

Yvon Chouinard was born in Maine in 1938, but moved to southern California when he was eight. During the trip he saw his mother give the family's entire supply of preserved corn to a Hopi woman, to feed her hungry children. His father was French Canadian and a blacksmith by trade. He did not fare well at school. He was small, did not speak English very well, and had a 'girl's' name. His grades did not improve even when he transferred to another school, and he became a loner. He found solace by finding isolated places to fish, and hunted rabbits with a bow and arrow. High School was not much better and he was often in trouble. He was athletic, but did not like performing in front of a crowd, and so continued to find his better times on his own in the ocean, or the hills surrounding Los Angeles.

His lifelong love of rock climbing came from his membership of the Southern California Falconry Club. In the spring, eggs were taken from hawk nests and young birds banded. He learned to abseil down the cliff faces, and was amazed one day to find a climber coming up the other way. In order to pursue his interest in climbing, he decided to employ the knowledge gained from his father to manufacture pitons, and started selling them to other climbers. Pitons are metal spikes that were hammered into the rock as an anchor point for the climbing ropes. He started his small business (Chouinard Equipment Co.) in 1964, and by 1970 he was the largest supplier of climbing gear in the USA. Previously all the equipment had been imported from Europe, but it was Chouinard's simple elegant and lighter design that caught the eye of the climbers.

It was after ascending The Nose, on El Capitan, one of the more challenging faces in Yosemite National Park, that he noticed that pitons were damaging the mountain. He decided to phase out the spikes, and adapt a chock and cable method he had heard that the British were using. This design used a lump of metal, often shaped like a nut (the kind that fits a bolt) that can be wedged into cracks and then pulled out when the climber is higher on the face. Chouinard produced his catalogue in 1972 with a 14-page editorial essay explaining the damage that ordinary pitons were doing, and showing how to use the new equipment, which he said would result in 'clean climbing'. Within months Chouinard was selling his new chocks faster than he could make them.

It was soon after this that Chouinard got his idea for making clothing. First, he remembered an old corduroy mill he had seen in England that made durable work clothes before denim was made, and had them send him the cloth to be made into climbing trousers. In 1970, during a trip to Scotland, he was impressed with the tough fabric that went into rugby jerseys, and the overbuilt collar in particular, which he could fold up to protect his neck from his hardware slings. He brought one back and found that all his friends wanted one. An order from Umbro sold out and soon he was ordering shirts from wherever rugby was played in the world. By 1974, he commissioned a factory to make his own in Hong Kong.

Yvon Chouinard was never interested in the day-to-day running of his company, and always tried to hire chief executives to manage the businesses. He saw himself as the research and development arm, travelling to far-flung parts of the world, climbing, fishing and surfing, but keeping his eyes open for new ideas, and trying out prototype clothes and equipment. Between the mid-1980s and mid-1990s, Patagonia grew its sales from $30 million to $100 million. Yet within this whirlwind success story there is a recurring theme that defines Chouinard's character, and is generally a positive driver in his life. Whether it is Patagonia's support for environmental campaigns, the efforts that go into recruitment and staff support, or the work that has gone into customer communications, there is a consistent belief that 'the individual' is the starting point for sustainable change.

As Chouinard travelled the world, he saw first hand the environmental destruction that was going on. He saw the felling of rainforests and the hunting of bush meat in Africa, and the industrial pollution in wilderness areas of Russia. Closer to home he witnessed the urbanisation of California, and the reduction of salmon in Wyoming rivers due to excessive damming. But while this made him feel sad and angry, it did not really come home to him that he could do much about it until something happened on his doorstep.

The clothing and equipment factory was located in Ventura near the ocean (handy for surfing). The city wanted to channel the Ventura River, so that the flood plain around it could be developed. The authority argued that there was very little wildlife remaining in the estuary, and that it would not affect the surf break. Chouinard attended the city council meeting, where a young graduate student called Mark Capelli gave a photographic slide show that demonstrated that there was life in the river, including spawning fish. The plan was defeated, and Chouinard sponsored Capelli with office space and a small donation to help him keep up the fight for the river. In time, the water quality and flow of the river improved, and with it came more fish and wildlife.

The experience taught Chouinard that grassroots efforts really do succeed. But he also saw that he could make a difference by the support he gave to activists. He was greatly encouraged that environmental protection work was not just a vain attempt to stop progress, but that it could actually lead to improvements.

These paths led him, via many different schemes, to founding the '1 per cent For the Planet' group.

Back in the workplace, Chouinard and Malinda were also concentrating on the individual. In 1984, a new office building gave the company the opportunity to provide a staff child-care facility (one of only 150 in the whole of the USA at the time) and a staff cafeteria that sold healthy food. Management and training meetings were conducted where possible in natural settings, and later a staff committee was set up, elected from fellow employees, to award environmental grants.

The 'Let My People Go Surfing' initiative was a flexitime scheme, which allowed employees to be able to leave work at short notice to take advantage of the weather or the surf, or simply to enable them to order their family life in a more accommodating way. Chouinard justifies the policy by saying that 'it allows us to keep valuable employees who love their freedom and sports too much to settle for the constraints of a more regimented work environment'. His view on employing different kinds of people is explained when he says that

*hiring people with diverse backgrounds brings in a flexibility of thought and openness to new ways of doing things, as opposed to hiring clones from business schools who have been taught in a codified way of doing business.*

In 2004 and 2005, Patagonia made the top 25 medium sized companies (250–1000 employees) in the Great Place to Work awards.

Chouinard is of the opinion that employees should either be committed to the values of the company, or at least should not mind working with a lot of people that live by these values. Over the years, the company has tried to hire people by word of mouth on personal recommendation to retain this cultural continuity. The same has applied to the hiring of management. Chouinard says that 'finding a dyed-in-the-wool business person to take up climbing or river running is a lot more difficult than teaching a person with a ready passion for the outdoors how to do the job'.

This idea of hiring for affinity, or attitude or value set, is still very alien to the business world. However, while skills and experience can still remain the prime reason for getting a job, it is hard to see how a culture of sustainable action can be fostered without a values set that employees can believe in. This is a serious flaw when attempting to encourage the adherence to internal procedures, but a potential disaster when the unconvinced employees come face-to-face with the customer.

Hiring for attitude is rare, but certainly not unique to Patagonia. South West Airlines (SWA) love to tell the story of how they embed their culture in their workforce. SWA was the pioneer of the no-frills airline. Anyone travelling with them will be aware, painfully or joyously, of the quirky nature of the carrier. The Hawaiian shirts worn by the crew (including the pilots), flying killer whale paint jobs, and the singing announcements from the cabin crew, leave passengers with few doubts about who they are flying with today. The founders (Rolllin King and Herb Kellaher) decided that 'if you get your passengers to their destinations when they want to get there, on time, at the lowest possible fares, and make darn sure they have a good time doing it, people will fly your airline' (www.southwest. com/about_swa). The statistics bear them out. Since 1987, the airline has consistently had very low customer complaints.

One of the SWA secrets is that they hire for attitude and not skills. On a visit to their Oakland base they told a group of social entrepreneurs from England that the interview process is geared to understand potential employees' personality and approach to life. They said that a few do get through the net, but as soon as they show signs of disaffection they are encouraged to find another job. They added almost as an aside that while it was not a common occurrence, they had a pilot on their books that joined as a baggage handler. Once the laughs died down, and the unlikely fact sank in, it was a very powerful statement. SWA were also very proud to recount that after 9/11, when the aviation industry suffered a dramatic fall in passenger numbers, there were widespread lay-offs across the industry but not at SWA, where the workforce agreed to take a pay cut to keep the company going. They said that over that period, nobody was laid off.

These are impressive, even emotional stories, and while many businesses may not choose to emulate SWA, whether it is for sector or cultural reasons, the 'employee care' concept holds. It is surprising, however, that many more businesses do not choose to invest more in their workforce.

The final application of Yvon Chouinard's faith in the individual can be seen in his regular attempts to engage the customer. Chouinard learned very early, when he redesigned and sold his replacement pitons, that if you have a good design and combine this with a good argument, the product will do well. Since that time he always assumed that the individual will be able to understand and act upon the information that Patagonia is offering to them. Essays on environmental issues are commissioned and printed in the catalogues, and display space is given over in retail stores to current campaigns. This helps their customers understand their stance on various issues.

Again, confiding to this degree in your customer base is rare, but others have tried a similar approach. In the UK, the medium sized Mid-Counties Co-operative has helped customers in their supermarkets understand issues including fairtrade foods, the importance of supporting local farmers, and climate change. The messages are conveyed on plasma screens as shoppers move around the stores. They found that when they began these messages, there was a marked increase in the sale of fairtrade bananas, chocolate, tea and coffee. The Body Shop, under guidance of its late founder Anita Roddick, was also keen to explain why the business took so much care to ensure that the materials they bought from developing countries were obtained in an ethical manner. When The Body Shop suffered a dip in sales, the harder commercial management team that replaced Roddick and her husband toned down the campaigning elements of the company. Since its sale to L'Oreal, the social and environmental profile of The Body Shop has, to some extent, been revived.

Informing customer awareness about social and environmental campaigns and strategies does not always have to be overt. Ben & Jerry's, the ice cream makers, have for many years tried to make their product with the minimum social and environmental impact. Their policy on flavour suppliers is that they buy goods and services from 'producers and supplies that share our values' (www. benjerry.co.uk). Those values include using business as a tool for social and environmental change. Jerry Greenfield explains that 'nobody wants to buy something that was made by exploiting somebody else'. The fact that, unwittingly, many people do this every day does not diminish the aspiration. The interesting thing is that this sustainability message is not widely understood outside the USA. Most people in Europe have no idea that Ben & Jerry's buy from flavour manufacturers that help to rehabilitate offenders, or are owned by ethnic minority entrepreneurs. And, unlike The Body Shop, the sustainable stance has not been toned down since the company's takeover by Unilever.

There is a point here that brings us back to the Patagonia experience. Yvon Chouinard understands that being sustainable is not a winning formula in itself. The business also has to be successful. Chouinard's businesses are successful because of his fascination for improving the function of a product, and using the best materials and the simplest designs. Ben Cohen once said that he thought that between 20 and 30 per cent of sales were influenced by their ethical approach to business, but that would count for nothing if they didn't make great ice cream.

Whether a business believes in influencing its customer base or not, it is a fact that Chouinard has never appeared to loose his faith in the ability of the individual to make a difference. It is this faith that continues to encourage him to bring his message to his customers and anyone else that will listen, regardless of how insufferable he may appear to others. It is his contention that 'somewhere along the line individuals caused this whole mess, and it is up to us to fix it'.

## Isolated stories or a recipe for global success?

Looking for patterns in the stories of these three men is not as clear-cut as one might imagine. Thomas ran a co-operative financial institution. He gained some, but not all, of his sustainable philosophy early in life. He then had to wait many years before he completed the picture and got the opportunity to put it all into practice. Anderson founded his own manufacturing company which is now listed on the NASDAQ stock exchange. He also introduced sustainability strategies towards the end of his time as head of the company. However, all of Anderson's sustainable inspiration came to him late in his career. Yvon Chouinard also founded his own manufacturing company, but realised fairly early that he was in business to influence sustainable behaviour in his customer base and in his competitors. His company remains wholly owned by his family.

Each of the three men were motivated in different ways, but ended up working to very similar goals:

- a minimal negative environmental impact and a maximum beneficial social impact from their company's activities;
- a determination to educate their customers about sustainable products and issues; and
- a willingness to try to create a dialogue both inside and beyond the boundaries of their company.

All of them maintain a solid and passionate commitment to their values and beliefs, and worked hard to help their employees understand why this was important to the whole business.

For all three, the experience of keeping a business profitable while staying true to these beliefs had many difficult moments. But when you listen to them speak, or read the accounts of their deeds, there is one overriding feeling that exudes from them all: they all felt extremely positive about what they were doing.

# 4

# Working together: boycotts, campaigns and the feelgood factor

## Who's talking, and who's listening?

In Chapter 2 we saw how some people were convinced about the environmental and social problems threatening the Earth, while others were not prepared to believe that this was the case. Chapter 2 also showed that there was a far larger number of people who were confused about the implications of the situation, and did not feel informed enough to act on the information that they received. Those working to move these people from unsure to actively sustainable will need to unlock the potential of the confused and get them to listen again to the scope of the problem, and enthuse them with the solutions.

Is there any reason to think that there is that potential in the population? Midgley (2005) thinks there is, and says that

*in spite of recent influences, direct concern about the destruction of the natural world is still a natural spontaneous feeling in us, and one that we no longer have any good reason to suppress. Most people, hearing about the wanton destruction of forests and oceans find it shocking …*

She thinks that while this shock is the 'energy-source' that makes change possible, it has not yet been properly tapped. She concludes that while it may take a few more disasters to bring the importance of change home to people 'the feeling is there and it is surely already becoming stronger and more vocal'.

Concern about the future, without the understanding or belief that something can be done to avert the danger, is a very unhealthy way to live. Well before the actual threat to life or livelihoods occurs, those who worry (and feel they have no control) are vulnerable to all sorts of potential ill health effects. Humans, like most animals, need to engage with 'fight or flight' behaviour when they feel that they are being threatened. Waiting for dangerous climate change to crash over them is the animal world equivalent of a rat rooting itself to the spot while the cobra winds up for the deadly bite.

## The door to the burning building

Solitaire Townsend and her Futerra team helped the UK government to understand that it is pointless and dangerous to inject fear into the population without offering them agency (Futerra, 2005). In other words, by all means help them to understand the building is burning, but make sure you point them towards the door. Townsend also observes that 'people want to be good, important and useful'.

While some may only feel confident enough to make tea for the firefighters, others may be emboldened to volunteer to man the hose. However, Townsend says that everyone needs to 'understand and trust that they are making a difference'.

One of the ways that people feel they can do something is to withdraw their support from those that they identify as being part of the problem. During election time this is done by voting for 'the other lot', or not voting at all. The problem with this is that representative democracy offers us about 70 minutes throughout our entire lives to actively influence the democratic process. This is the average amount of time people spend in the act of voting, and represents about one-third of an average day in front of the television (Ginsborg, 2005). There are other ways to get involved in the democratic process but, with a few notable exceptions such as the Swedes, many people are disaffected with politics.

A more accessible way to withdraw support is to withhold money. Some have tried withholding part or all of their tax from the government in order to protest, for example, against the waging of war. This is generally not very effective unless the campaign has widespread, and probably majority, support from the population. The State tends to feel very threatened by the possibility of running out of money, and is likely to take action against citizens or single interest groups that are breaking the law.

A notable exception was the campaign against the poll tax in the UK in 1989 and 1990. The campaign, which included a mass refusal to pay, was effective because of the feeling of gross injustice the tax generated. It was a uniform sum that was required to be paid by every adult in the land, regardless of how much they earned. Active opposition to social injustice traditionally falls to those on the left of the political spectrum, but the boycott spread to all parts of the population and the tax was withdrawn.

The tactic of 'boycotts' has been most effective when applied to a product or commodity. It is associated with an everyday activity, and the 'activists' that withdraw their support from the supplier can do so completely anonymously if they wish to participate quietly. When boycotts work they can be very effective. The tax on tea in the American colonies led to a refusal to buy the product, and the grievance was the subject of a certain 'tea party' in Boston harbour in 1773 that hastened the beginning of the American War of Independence. Mahatma Ghandi asked Indians not to buy imported cloth from Lancashire. He wanted to save the Indian handloom industry which had suffered from a protectionist tax and import restrictions set by the British.

The authors, growing up in the United States in the 1960s, have clear memories of two boycotts that interrupted their childhood eating pleasures. One was sparked by the Vietnam War. In the late 1960s and early 1970s, the anti-war campaign was constantly looking for new ways to influence the withdrawal of military forces from South-East Asia. It targeted companies that were known to support the Republican government. One of these companies was Hostess, makers of, among other things, the Twinkie. The Twinkie was a highly processed sweet cream cake, undoubtedly packed with trans-fats and wrapped in plastic. Kids often found them in their lunch boxes, or wolfed them down as a snack after getting home from school. It was a big disappointment for those kids living in politicised households to learn that they were off the menu, but it certainly got their attention.

If this wasn't bad enough, at about the same time, table grapes and iceberg lettuce were also crossed off the shopping list because of concerns about the poor conditions of migrant workers in the fields of California and Florida. The boycotts highlighted both the low wages and the health risks that the workers were exposed to as a result of the heavy use of pesticides. By the late 1960s there was a good understanding about the environmental implications of the widespread use of pesticides thanks to Rachel Carson's exposé of the effect of DDT in her landmark book *Silent Spring*. While the migrant agricultural workers' plight was originally brought to the attention of the world in 1960 by Edward R Murrow's documentary *Harvest of Shame*, it took strike action almost a decade later to motivate sections of the American public to boycott their employers.

## Rallying around the Spar

One of the most dramatic boycotts of recent times centred on the battle over an obsolete North Sea oil platform in the spring of 1995. The structure assumed an importance far beyond its physical implications, and showed how collective action in support of the environment can engage many people very quickly. The subject of the confrontation was a 14000 tonne oil storage buoy called the Brent Spar. In 1994, Greenpeace had discovered that the oil industry was seeking to test out a loophole in the rules on dumping at sea. The plan was to tow the obsolete platform from its site on the North Sea border between the UK and Norway to deep waters off western Scotland and then sink it.

Shell happened to be the first company to own a platform that would qualify for this method of disposal. Shell had considered a range of other solutions and concluded that for both health and safety reasons (risks to the deconstruction team) and environmental reasons (spills and land contamination) it would be far better to deal with the platform off-shore. What is more, Shell sought and received the agreement of the UK government that this was the best solution.

Greenpeace became interested in Brent Spar when a Dutch activist brought word of the discussions about the Spar to the attention of his German colleagues. Jochen Vorfelder was Head of Media at Greenpeace Germany at that time. He was a professional journalist, not an activist, although he was of course highly sympathetic to the organisation's goals. He had previously worked very effectively on the Greenpeace campaign to stop 'clear felling' during the Clayoquot Sound campaign on Vancouver Island. He had learned in Canada that a successful campaign could not rely on the weight of scientific evidence alone, and that something more was needed to stir the emotions of the public. In particular, he was convinced that the power of images was a vital part of a successful campaign.

The Brent Spar incident fitted very well with the long-term commitment by Greenpeace to stop dumping at sea. They had previously opposed the marine disposal of nuclear waste, old nuclear submarines, industrial waste, the incineration of waste at sea, and the dumping of sewage sludge. For Greenpeace, Brent Spar was a campaign waiting to happen but Vorfelder and others needed to first convince their colleagues that it was a fight worth waging. When the head of the Greenpeace International Marine Division agreed, a team was assembled. The Germans would supply the money and the action team, the UK would do the research, and Greenpeace International would co-ordinate the communications.

It was known that the sinking of Brent Spar was due to occur sometime between May and October 1995. The Greenpeace objections did not stop the licence to dump at sea being issued. In April, Greenpeace sent its first boarding party to occupy the deserted platform. The key piece of equipment that they brought on the trip was a satellite dish that they managed to rent from an independent German communications company. Initially they only had enough money to use it for two weeks. If Shell had decided to ignore the protests, then there would have been very little of interest to broadcast, and the occupation would have lost its main weapon. Fortunately for Greenpeace, Shell played into their hands and sent in the eviction teams. Dozens of occupiers were forcibly removed by Shell, and their boats were harassed and sprayed with water cannon. The pictures that were beamed across Europe produced bemused, and later angry, reactions among the viewing public.

By coincidence, the battle for the Spar coincided with the Kirchentag conference in Stuttgart. The Kirchentag came into being just after the Second World War. Its purpose was to draw together the Protestant Germans in order to strengthen their belief and to remain within the community of worldwide Christianity (www.kirchentag.org.uk). It has met since 1954 and is attended by tens of thousands of German Christians. Politically it is a must for those political parties that have a link to the Christian community, and for the powerful Christian Democrats in particular.

Greenpeace had regularly manned a stand at the Kirchentag, as they often do at any large convention or conference. They seized the opportunity to bring the events that were unfolding in the North Sea to the Kirchentag organiser's attention, more in hope than expectation. To their amazement, it featured in a keynote address, and was immediately taken up by subsequent speakers. It is unclear who first thought that a boycott was a good way of showing Shell how displeased people were about its actions, but the idea did not come from Greenpeace.

Greenpeace had been suspicious about using boycotts as a tactic for two reasons. First, it is often difficult to call a new boycott after one has failed. People are wary about associating themselves with something that turns out to be rejected by the majority. Once you have lost the confidence of the boycotting public, it is hard to get them back again. The Greenpeace view was that the tactic should not be used unless it was going to be a guaranteed success. Greenpeace was convinced that Brent Spar was worth fighting for, but not that the public would identify with it to the extent that they would take action themselves. The second reason is that once unleashed, a successful boycott is very difficult to control. They were wrong on the first count, but right on the second.

The politicians were probably responsible for whipping up most of the enthusiasm for the boycott during Kirchentag. It was an easy and obvious cause with which to be associated, even for the conservative Christian Democrats. However, the Green Party was in its element and its leader Joschka Fischer (later a German Foreign Minister) gave full vent to his opinion that Shell was committing an unforgivable act.

Next it was the turn of the media. The German press, through the magazine Focus, had already been invited by Greenpeace onto the Spar for an exclusive story on the occupation. Now others saw that the story would sell and reported the campaign on front pages, culminating in a full article in the influential Der Spiegel. One regional newspaper, the daily *Rheinische Post*, printed postcards (after seeking help with the wording from Greenpeace) that readers could send to Shell, demanding that they stop their plans to sink the platform.

The boycott spread like wildfire. There was no need for Greenpeace, or any other organisation, to co-ordinate the action. It was later reported that sales of fuel from Shell Germany filling stations dropped by 40 per cent within a matter of days. Then things started to get out of hand. Shots were fired through the window of a Shell station in Hamburg, another station was firebombed, and the language of the boycotters, who were ordinary people, was getting angrier by the day. Improbably, Vorfelder and his counterpart at Shell collaborated to see if the situation in Germany could be defused. In separate but co-ordinated messages, both Shell and Greenpeace called for calm.

Between April and June 1995, and encouraged by the public reaction, Greenpeace reboarded the platform. They were removed, but mounted a third occupation. By this time Brent Spar was an almost daily news story across Europe, and the lobbying for Shell to relent became intense. The pressure that mattered came from two different directions. The first came from other parts of the Shell organisation – the Netherlands, Germany and Austria in particular – who were angry with their UK colleagues. It appeared that internal communications within Shell Europe had not been very inclusive. This was in contrast to Greenpeace which had set up almost daily e-mail discussions across all of their European centres to ensure that they knew what was going on. Towards the end of the battle, Shell executives and country managers began to break ranks, and openly criticised their British colleagues for embarking on an ill-conceived plan.

Shell UK realised that they were in a very difficult situation by now. They were under intense pressure from the UK government to stick to their original plan and sink the platform in the sea. The government, having backed Shell to sink Brent Spar, was concerned that they would lose face if the company changed its mind. The anger generated in government ranks continued for years. In 1999, four years after the matter had been resolved, former Conservative Party ministers who had been voted out of power in 1997 were still chipping away at Greenpeace for claiming that Brent Spar contained large amounts of toxic material. Finally, Greenpeace were forced to apologise for overstating the case, and even the BBC had to apologise for repeating the Greenpeace claims. Later, Chris Rose the UK Greenpeace co-ordinator would say that the level and volume of the contamination was an unnecessary distraction, and that technical arguments about the nature and extent of the environmental threats should always play second fiddle to the primary principle that dumping anything at sea is wrong, whatever it is.

While these high-level arguments raged, the second front opened up. The Germans had a particular commercial problem. The loss of income from the boycott of Shell filling stations was insignificant to the multinational company, but the margins on the sales of petrol and diesel for the station operators meant that they could not sustain the loss of income for much longer before going under. The pressure to do something to get their customers back was a consuming problem for Shell in Germany, and added strength to their voice and the pressure they were putting on the British.

On 20 June, close to the sinking ground, Shell gave in and agreed to drag the platform back to the Norwegian shore where it had been fabricated, and where it would be broken up in a dry dock. Chris Rose's opinion was that this particular victory against marine dumping was effective partly because it moved beyond the technical merits of dumping at sea, and onto the moral issue of using a common resource to dispose of one company's problem.

However, there were other theories. Some thought that people began to wonder why all this fuss was being made, and were interested in discussing whether the government was trying to hide something more sinister. This view was confirmed when Rose asked the former German MEP Benny Haerlin why the boycott of Shell took off so effectively in Germany. Haerlin said that Brent Spar was 'a drama and there was uncertainly about how it would end'. Effectively, Brent Spar had turned into a soap opera, and everyone wanted to tune in for the next exciting instalment.

Jochen Vorfelder's analysis is that it is impossible to pinpoint a single reason as to why the boycott attracted so many people, or why it generated such strength of feeling in the German public. He thinks that it needed a critical mass of public imagination, political support and a media in full voice to tip the balance from concern to full blown civil action. While this is very likely to be true, it does not completely explain why the Germans were so exercised about Brent Spar, and why many other countries were not.

While there were some consumer protests in the Netherlands and Sweden, they did not react with the same outrage as the Germans, even though they are also traditionally sympathetic to the support of environmental causes. There was also no boycott in the UK, even though this was the country that was at the heart of the dispute. The British are historically quite prepared to take to the streets in support of a cause, as the large anti-Iraq war demonstrations can testify, but Brent Spar did not generate this level of activism.

Jochen Vorfelder has a theory about why the Germans care so much. His view is that Germans elevate the North Sea from a minor extension of the Atlantic to a romantic entity. This stems from a general tendency of Germans to idolise nature, but they also have a specific interest in the sea, and the North Sea in particular. Germany is almost alone amongst northern European countries in that it has a relatively small coastline in relation to its size. Vorfelder explains that 90 per cent of Germans have very little contact with the sea, and this leads to a greater sense of appreciation and very positive feelings when they do have a chance to come down to the coast. He speculates that this love of the sea may be associated with childhood memories. It may also be influenced by a large body of German romantic poetry and literature. Heinrich Heine's *Heimkehrcycle, Die Nordee* (or *North Sea Cycles*) is a prime example of this. Vorfelder thinks he understands, as a German as much as an environmentalist, why the public was so outraged by Shell's intentions over Brent Spar.

German public opposition may also have been motivated to oppose the sinking of Brent Spar simply because of the belief that it is bad manners to litter in a public space; or some may have rejoiced in the opportunity to hit back at what was perceived as greedy and cavalier big business. However, whatever the motivation of those that decided to act, they all did so because they felt compelled to act.

These German boycotters did not have to be motivated, exhorted or cajoled. Neither did they need to pore over the technical details that rumbled on for years about how much toxic material was contained in the platform, or exactly how it would affect the sea bed if it leaked out. They got on with it because it felt like the right thing to do. They were moving from something bad (their feelings of anger and injustice, and above all helplessness) to something better, which involved active challenge and the satisfaction that they were depriving the object of their dissatisfaction of their custom. Whether they thought that their own particular action would make a difference is hard to say, although all of them must have hoped that it would. The main thing was that they were doing something about it, and that is a more positive place to be than harbouring feelings of impotency, resenting the fact that nothing was done (by an individual or society) to avert the perpetration of an injustice.

Reflecting on the whole affair, Cor Herkstroter, then CEO of Shell International, said

*we have listened very closely to our customers. We have listened very closely to our government and to our staff. They, after all, were the institutions we had always dealt with. Of course, we also dealt with environmental groups … In essence we were somewhat slow in understanding that these groups were tending to acquire authority. Meanwhile those institutions we were used to dealing with were tending to lose authority.*

(Grayson and Hodges, 2001)

The comments show that Shell's understanding at that time was still flawed. The company failed to understand the attitudes of a significant section of their customer base.

## The search for a little respect

Many boycotts and campaigns are motivated by concern over the erosion of a way of life or a sense of place. While some of this can be motivated by conservatism, there is often a real worry about losing the identifying features of a place to the 'any town, anywhere' look of so many places in Europe and North America. Examples of community opposition to new development can be found in almost any country in the world. Often this is motivated by fear of the unknown or unwillingness to countenance change. Sometimes this is dubbed NIMBYism – opposition for the sake of ensuring that new development is 'not in my back yard'. Politicians can join in to support communities because of a genuine conviction that the proposal is wrong, or for more cynical electoral reasons of currying favour with voters. This latter reason has been referred to as a NIMTO response or 'not in my term of office'.

Another motivation for opposing new development may be a way of venting frustration at an existing situation. In the late 1980s and early 1990s cheaper and more reliable gas was becoming readily available from the North Sea, and some companies were taking advantage by building combined heat and power plants in the UK and Northern Europe. These used the gas to generate energy and then used the waste steam for industrial processes. One such proposal was planned by the British chemicals giant ICI at its existing site near Middlesbrough in the North East of England.

The CHP plant was a fairly benign affair compared to the forest of chemical plants that had been operating on the site for decades. But when asked for their opinion, the local people in the village of Lazenby (the closest concentration of housing to the proposed new plant) made it known that they would strongly object to the application.

ICI had asked the ill-fated Enron Corporation to build and operate the plant for them, and the Texans descended on the little village expecting to win them over. What they had not appreciated was that ICI had been upsetting the locals for a long time. Their large nylon plant and other petrochemical facilities adjacent to the CHP site had been allowed to flare volatile gases on a 24-hour basis for many years. When a surplus of these gases needed to be emitted, the effect on the surrounding area was spectacular, particularly in the middle of the night. The modest flame at the top of the tower would grow to the extent that night became day. This was accompanied by a thunderous noise that could last many minutes. There was absolutely nothing that the locals could do about this apart from complain. But they had learned long ago that ICI was perfectly within its rights to do this, so the complaints had tailed off long ago.

Now a group of Americans was trying to get them to agree to yet another facility, but everyone knew that ICI was behind the plans. The public meeting to win over the locals was a fiasco. The Enron team was advised to park their vehicles well away from the hall to preserve property and aid a quick getaway. Speaker after speaker was shouted down by a hostile crowd that was in no mood for compromise and Enron, ICI and the city officials that were backing the scheme left to catcalls and boos.

Inevitably, the application was rejected as local politicians gauged the strength of feeling from Lazenby and other adjacent villages. However, the story had a twist at the end. A matter of weeks later, the council planning committee reconvened and accepted the application. Soon after, work started on a brand new community facility in Lazenby, and the CHP plant was completed a few years later.

In this case, the ability to be heard and appreciated was clearly the driving motive of the collective action. The size of the public meeting and the strength of feeling were clear evidence that this was not a weak issue that had been whipped up by a few activists. The fact that the people of Lazenby appeared to be placated by a new community facility shows that collective action does not always mean outright opposition, but can be motivated by the simple desire for respect and the sense of fairness that comes from being compensated for being put at a disadvantage.

Writing about the anti-globalisation movement, Paul Kingsnorth (2003) tells another feel-good story about the time he spent with a group in small-town California called Citizens Concerned about Corporations. This group managed to pass a bye-law by a 60 to 40 majority. The bye-law required a series of meetings, committees, policies and programmes to

*ensure democratic control over corporations conducting business within the city of Arcata in whatever ways are necessary to ensure the health and well-being of our community and its environment.*

One result of the proposals was to limit the establishment of new restaurant chains in the city. Kingsnorth reports that the talk in the town, for a time, was all about the referendum, and whether large corporations were a force for good or ill. Crucially, local politicians saw that there was enough popular support, at least to see the referendum to its conclusion, and they supported the campaign. Later, many other groups from other towns across the USA would seek advice on how Arcata managed to gain popular support for its stance, and then emulate the campaign in their own areas.

A more common motivation for activists is the goal of outright victory to remove, deflect, or block the arrival of the offending object of the campaign.

Halting the march of chain stores into small towns and cities is a recent example of a single issue that has been taken up in a variety of ways by local activists. The group Tescopoly exists to block, or at least hinder, the expansion of the UK's largest chain: Tesco. The group's strap line – 'every little hurts' – is a mockery of Tesco's own 'every little helps' catchphrase. While issues on the website include the effect of Tesco on farming, the environment and employees, the main focus is on local shops. The site highlights the House of Commons All Party report that gloomily concluded that independent convenience shops are unlikely to survive in the UK beyond 2015 (House of Commons, 2006). Tescopoly reports that by the middle of 2005, butchers, bakers, fishmongers and newsagents were closing at a rate of around 175 a month (www.tescopoly.org). This concern is mirrored in the USA by groups targeting Wal-Mart and Carrefour in mainland Europe.

Taking these examples together it is clear that remedying perceived injustice is a very powerful motivational influence on those that choose to boycott and campaign. While the preservation of place is important to those that oppose new development, it is the unfairness associated with putting small businesses to the competitive sword that rankles most with activists. The arguments about whether local is more sustainable than global is not entirely cut and dried. Economies of scale can bring efficiencies, and large retailers are quick to point out that the chaos and pollution created by hundreds of local deliveries have a much bigger impact than a single delivery by one large lorry.

Of course, this ignores the gross inefficiencies and unsustainable excesses associated with shipping goods to and from distribution depots, the methods and conditions of production, and the distances that imported goods travel. All of these issues are swept aside by the large retailer with the simple answer that if the public did not like the products, then they would not buy them. Stories that unmask the conditions under which cheap clothing is produced are starting to appear, and labels showing how far food has travelled are being trialled. But mass boycotts of intercontinental food and clothes produced in sweatshop conditions are some way off. At present, the tangible threat of a superstore coming to your area, or the prospect of an oil platform being dropped in the sea, are much easier targets for sustainability campaigners.

## Dissecting effective campaigns

With so many committed people, and so many sound causes, it is worth pausing to ask why the environmental and social justice movements have not prevailed and changed the world. Of course there have been some significant turning points and victories. It took over 60 years, but those who fought for the abolition of slavery won their fight. Women have the vote. The ozone layer was saved, and hundreds of thousands of kids no longer work in filthy conditions when they should be in school. Greenpeace, of course, did stop the Brent Spar from sinking beneath the waves.

But look a little further and you can see that hundreds of thousands of people are living as slaves today. Woman may have the vote almost everywhere, but they are far from equal citizens almost anywhere. The ozone layer was saved, but is now threatened by an explosion of people buying fridges in places where it is still permissible to use ozone depleting gases. There appears to be no way back for those interested in dumping things into the sea. However, waste plastic can be found floating on the surface of every ocean and sea. So, have the boycotts and campaigns really been that effective?

Chris Rose (2005) has a theory. He thinks that the environmental and social movement has been unachieving because it has never had heroes that could unify, perpetuate and build on the movement's fleeting successes. He singles out the environmentalist and campaigner John Muir as a prime example. Muir probably did more than most to protect the environment, and yet he has not really been recognised as a world leader even within his own environmental movement.

Muir emigrated with his family from Scotland to the USA in 1849 when he was 11. He had his moment of conversion under a black locust tree at university in Wisconsin. A fellow student explained how the giant tree was related to the humble straggling pea plant. This simple fact astounded him, and started him off on a lifelong passion for natural history. He went on to found the environmental organisation, the Sierra Club, in 1892. Over a century later it has more than 1.5 million members.

In 1903, while travelling with Theodore Roosevelt, he got the President to agree to establish the Yosemite Valley as a national park. This was later extended through the efforts of the Sierra Club. One of Muir's twin legacies was to show how independent environmental membership groups (now called 'non-government organisations') can be effective in working to protect the environment. The other was to establish the principle of State-protected areas for land that has intrinsic natural beauty.

Rose believes that such an important figure should have had more impact on the movement, but argues that in its eyes he was doubly disadvantaged. First, he was interested in mass communication and writing for the popular press in particular. By favouring this method, he set himself out as a maverick because mainstream campaigners have always focused on the power held by politicians or big business. Muir was less interested in courting important people, and even fell out with his own Sierra Club committee over a row about a proposed new dam (he was against it and they weren't). He just did not endear himself to those in charge, whether they were politicians, businessmen, or the committee members of the environmental movement.

If this was not bad enough, Rose observes that 'the dominant form of campaign communication [in the environment movement] stresses the economic, the political, the scientific and the rational realms rather than the psychological and the emotional'. This statement is challengeable, particularly for those who equate environmental campaigns with 'something must be done' tactics based on alarming statistics and images of despoiled landscapes and injured or cute animals. The fear factor, and the sympathy reaction, are certainly aimed at an emotional response from the target audience. But Rose believes that the environmental movement has been fairly one-track for a long time: always focusing on the facts of the issues, rarely relying on a motivation reaction other than shame or fear.

Rose thinks that the environment movement is much weaker for its lack of heroes. In yet another link back to Zelden's observation about the failure of the environmental movement, he thinks that to be a hero you need to be truly revered, respected and followed by society. In order to do this you have to engage people's emotions, speak to their psyche and appeal to their hopes and dreams. Rose seems to be saying that you can pitch your cause to the crowd using factual and rational means but, while this might be interesting, it will not be exciting or inspirational.

The lack of environmental and social justice 'heroes' may have more to do with the perception of the public that heroes sacrifice everything for a noble cause. Most people would probably respect and laud those that battle poachers to save the tiger or the panda, but the lad who dives into the mud in front of a bulldozer to delay a new road or runway is probably going to miss out on the sympathy vote, never mind become a hero. Historical heroes were leaders of dazzling military campaigns. Modern heroes save people from burning buildings or reach the pinnacle of sporting success. And yet, these deeds pale into insignificance compared with those who sacrifice time and energy to ensure that humanity is able to survive into the next century by opposing the continued and profligate burning of fossil fuel.

But it is even worse than that. We may well admire the 'derring do' of the campaigner that shins up Nelson's column, or chains himself to a platform in the middle of the North Sea. It is dramatic and plucky, regardless of the disparaging comments about 'bearded weirdies' from the boys in the pub. But now consider the reaction to those that are committed to help people conserve more energy by installing an extra layer of loft insulation. You really would be wasting your money investing in a tight suit and cape for that cause. Is it a bird, is it a plane? Nah, it's just that guy trying to get us to buy draft excluders again. Saving energy is an emotional non-starter in most places, unless you have serious fuel poverty issues.

Rose started to think about why some campaigns were effective while others fell flat. One of the things he realised was that the size of the issue was important. If it was too small, then no one would care about it. If it was too big, then people would feel that there was very little that they could do about it. Either way there would be little support for the cause. If an issue like climate change (Rose's example) is considered to be too big, then it needs to be broken down into smaller, understandable or identifiable elements. The campaign team could then home in on the one that is representative or symbolic of the wider issue, and would be more likely to catch the imagination of the public. This is why Greenpeace has targeted individual companies like Exxon, or products like urban four-wheel drive vehicles, even though proportionately many other companies and products are more guilty of causing significant environmental impacts.

This makes sense in campaigning terms, but it has the potential to remove the ability of people to understand the reality of complex global issues. An explanation of the link between fossil fuel and climate change is a good example of where the problem lies. One cannot say that more greenhouse gases directly affect weather systems. However, one can say that if the trend towards warmer climate continues, we can expect more severe weather. This is confusing for many people and it sounds like splitting hairs. It would be so much easier to say, 'look, every time you drive your car you stand a greater chance of coming home to find that your roof has blown off, and your ground floor is under a metre of water'. Cause and effect is a great persuader, but it can't always be brought into play when explaining things like climate change. On the other hand, if we had all paid a little more attention at school when we were told how the Earth works, or had the access and the cultural affinity to lifelong learning, then perhaps we would not be so reliant on simple cause and effect arguments.

At the other end of the scale, a small issue like garbage can rear up and become very controversial indeed. It is true that when burning (incineration) and burying (landfilling) our waste was assumed to be best practice, then all public authorities needed to do was exercise the out-of-sight-out-of-mind rule and everyone was happy. Occasionally, a gross abuse of the trust placed in public authorities came to light, such as the Love Canal scandal in the USA (buried toxic waste), or when a nasty accident brought a hazard into focus such as Seveso in Italy (a spillage of dioxins). When these things happened, legislation was changed and life continued.

Then came doubts about the environmental wisdom of burying or burning, and a new determination to reuse or recycle resources began to be discussed. All of a sudden the public's easy life was interrupted by requests to separate their rubbish. This in turn gave rise to higher taxes and fees to dispose of waste, and the threat of fines if new regulations were transgressed. The frustration with rubbish collection and disposal now comes from two distinct directions.

One is from those people that would like to do more to help the environment. They would happily segregate and recycle the waste they produce, and would stop buying over-packaged products to avoid producing it in the first place if they could. These people cannot understand why their concern is not backed up by an equal and proportionate effort by their public authorities. Local authorities would be expected to say in their defence that it is expensive to provide recycling services, particularly to more remote settlements. They say that even when recyclate is collected, there is no market for it and it ends up in large container ships being sent to places where the labour to sift and sort it is cheap, and working conditions are appalling. They may be right, but it cuts no ice with those that are thwarted from doing their bit.

The other type of disgruntlement is from people who feel that the drive to be more environmentally friendly is just another excuse to extract more taxes. This is as true for businesses as it is for individual householders. Even worse, in the UK public authorities are so short of funds that they are trying to pay for recycling services by cutting the general refuse collection service from once a week to every two weeks. Outraged communities that have not come to terms with separating out their paper, plastic, and food waste, in particular, find that their bins are overflowing for days before collection time, and have started to resort to hiring private collection services to get around their plight. This may have been a small issue at one time, but sustainable resource consumption has well and truly migrated from academic theory to political hot potato within a few short years. Of course, the answer to this problem is to incentivise the public by paying them to recycle, and we discuss this and other positive motivation ideas later in the book.

## Why boycotts and campaigns are a positive force for change

In the final analysis, boycotts and campaigns have varying degrees of success. While it is instructive to examine the outcomes of these campaigns, it is more helpful to understand why the activists were motivated to work so enthusiastically for the cause. Some people exhibit dogged determination with little regard for their own comfort or safety. Often associated with selflessness, committed campaigners are just as likely to be motivated to act because of their own feelings. In particular, the boycotters will feel better because they are taking action, rather than worse because they are passively witnessing the perpetration of what they perceive as an injustice.

Commitment to a cause is not a trait particular to environmental and social justice campaigners. The movement in the North East of Britain that was passionate about keeping imperial pounds and ounces in opposition to the switch to the European metric system was just as committed to what it believed in. And many thousands of people spend their time opposing sustainable development proposals like wind farms. But there is something about the qualities of those fighting for environmental and social justice that seems to set them apart.

Midgley (2005) would say that there is a part of all of us that wants to preserve the beauty of the world, and stamp out exploitation and cruelty. However, environmental campaigners are characterised by their obsessive concentration on what they see as their compelling 'duty to act', and the way that they filter the world through the cause that they are fighting for. You could not imagine the Baby Milk Action people being able to let a friend reach out and pluck a box of Cheerios (a Nestlé brand) off the supermarket shelf without some kind of comment passing their lips.

However, the key component in an effective campaigner is not their obsessiveness, although that helps. It is their heightened sense of awareness, and a consistent reaction to unsustainable behaviour. Imagine if everyone that grabbed a shopping trolley and started off down the aisle knew the damage that food flown thousands of kilometres across the globe did to the Earth, just so people could eat the product out of season. The awareness of 'food miles' would mean that they would make sure they checked labels for country of origin. Their consistency would mean that they would not cave in if the recipe that they were cooking for friends arriving in an hour demanded fresh vanilla pods. Many people would fly out the door, probably into their cars, and snatch the Madagascan product off the shelf. But the sustainably aware would not compromise. And they would do this, not because of guilt or fear that the 'carbon police' would fine them, but because they had understood the issue and felt good that they were able to rein in a former tendency. Instead of 'buy and be damned' they would chalk one up for the planet instead.

Campaigners like these are rarely smug, and don't have the luxury of feeling good about the way they behave. When they are not agitating about the latest crime against the Earth, they are being consistently outflanked, ignored or ridiculed. They feel best when they are working with others for something that all the scientific and sociological evidence tells them is right. What is more, it is something that many, many other people also know is right but, for various reasons, have not been able to break habitual behaviours. Imagine a planet full of people that had been able to adopt both the awareness and the consistency of action. The world may well avoid the dreaded 3°C increase but, perhaps just as important, it would be full of more content people.

Paul Hawken (2007) has tried to explain how he feels about all those people that give up varying amounts of their time to try to do something about making the world more sustainable. Speaking about this group, which he calls the 'unnamed movement', he says that

*when asked at colleges if I am pessimistic or optimistic about the future, my answer is always the same: If you look at the science that describes what is happening on earth today and aren't pessimistic, you don't have the correct data. If you meet the people in this unnamed movement and aren't optimistic, you haven't got a heart. What I see are ordinary and some not-so-ordinary individuals willing to confront despair, power and incalculable odds in an attempt to restore some semblance of grace, justice and beauty to this world.*

## The making of a reputation

Ask many throughout the world which country cares most about the environment, while also being devoted to a fair and just society, and the answer is almost always Sweden. And the Swedes know this, although their natural, almost pathological, modesty makes it difficult for them to crow about it. However, just occasionally it sneaks out. In 2006, Sweden announced that it intended to end its reliance on oil. The opening paragraphs of the groundbreaking policy document 'Making Sweden an Oil Free Society' state that '...the phase out of oil can further strengthen our position as one of the world's leading nations in sustainable development'.

The Swedish Commission on Oil Independence reported that the motivation to phase out the country's dependency on oil came from a desire to reduce climate impact, while securing long-term energy supplies by using and developing Sweden's 'green gold': it's forests and fields. This was coupled with the expectation that the signal this gave to the market would strengthen international competitiveness in general, and enable the country to be 'a leading nation in the development of new technology in the areas of sustainable energy generation and efficiency', relying on a history of engineering innovation exemplified by companies such as ABB, Ericsson and Aga.

While this is a sensible policy, it is hardly unique among European nations. However, it was the detail and the timetable that impressed. The objectives stated in the Commission's report explained that Sweden would end its dependence on oil in 2020 by ensuring that:

- the consumption of oil in road transport will be reduced by 40–50 per cent;
- no oil will be used for heating residential or commercial buildings; and
- industry will cut consumption by 25–40 per cent.

The major challenge for Sweden is the transport, construction and agriculture sectors, which are reliant on petrol and diesel. But even here, over a quarter of the ethanol used in Swedish vehicles comes from home-grown wheat, and the plan is to scale this up in the coming years.

Critics, and there are always critics, say that while the oil-free commitment looks brave and bold, the country had been quietly at work cutting it's dependence on oil since the 1970s, so that at the time of the announcement just over 30 per cent of end-use energy was reliant on fossil fuel. Over 70 per cent of space heating comes from bio fuels (less than 10 per cent of homes are heated by any kind of fossil fuel) and just 11 per cent of industry energy comes from oil.

This type of criticism comes from the same people who responded negatively to British pride that the country will be one of the few signatories that will meet its Kyoto agreement target by 2012. They point out that British success is not the result of a marvellous commitment to a sustainable society. Rather, it has only been possible because of the closure of the coal industry, a reduction in manufacturing capacity, and the reliance on North Sea gas.

Sceptics of the Swedish programme express doubts about the sincerity of making ambitious promises that have medium or long-term delivery dates. Lars Lindblad, then an opposition environment spokesman for the Moderate Party said 'the Swedish government is very fond of setting targets but it has problems with delivery' (Cowell, 2006).

The key to understanding why Sweden is likely to succeed in its plan may be found in the foreword to the Commission's report by the then Prime Minister Göran Persson. In it, he said that

*the changes required will not be realised solely by political decisions, nor by market forces in industry alone, nor by individual farmers or forest farmers who see future opportunities for profit. Not until all the positive forces in society aim for the same goals can Sweden achieve independence from oil.*

While the statement suggests that this commonality is no foregone conclusion, such faith in collective 'positive forces' singles Sweden out for investigation.

And if the Swedes are capable of such actions, then could this positive and optimistic outlook be passed on to other, more pessimistic or less enlightened countries? But before we can explore how to transfer a whole cultural outlook, it is necessary to explore a number of key questions, including whether the Swedes really do think of themselves as environmentally and socially conscious. In short, does Sweden deserve its international accolade as one of the most sustainable nations and, if it does, what is it doing that is so different from everybody else?

## Do they mean us?

The *Special Eurobarometer* report (European Commission, 2005) published by the European Union asked people in all 25 EU countries, and seven other

European countries, whether they felt that they had 'a duty to protect nature, even if it means limiting human progress'. An impressive 98 per cent of Swedish people agreed with this statement. Denmark and Norway were next with 96 per cent. The UK (80 per cent), Ireland (78 per cent) and Malta (78 per cent) were last on the list of those polled. The average result was 89 per cent.

However, when asked to agree that 'we have a right to exploit nature for the sake of human well-being', opinion was much more divided. Hungary (10 per cent) was the least enthusiastic about exploiting nature. The Swedish answer to the exploitation question was 62 per cent, the fifth highest answer behind the most enthusiastic, the Slovakians (73 per cent). Taken together it would be the Germans, the Austrians and the Hungarians that wanted to protect nature the most, and exploit it the least.

Swedes generally did not support the statement that 'exploiting nature may be unavoidable if humankind is to progress'. Only 37 per cent agreed with this, although they were some way from the most dissenting opinion which was Austria at 22 per cent. The country most in agreement with the unavoidability of exploitation for human progress was Lithuania at 76 per cent. The average number supporting the statement across the 25 states was 51 per cent.

The Swedes (89 per cent) thought that passing on a sound environment to the next generation was very important, although seven other countries were within two percentage points of them, and the table was topped by the Dutch (91 per cent). The Swedes had relatively low numbers that would never agree to genetically modified crops (31 per cent) compared with Cyprus (56 per cent) and Greece (54 per cent). These survey returns show a society in tune with nature, but also a very practical people.

The Swedes are also an ordered society, and have a predisposition for systems. Sweden has the most enthusiastic take up of formal environmental management systems such as the international environmental management standard ISO14001. Most countries employ these management systems in commerce and industry, but in Sweden these systems have also been adopted by local authorities and NGOs. It has also become popular in Sweden to associate an eco-label with events that will ensure carbon neutrality, local food and the use of video links for speakers based in places remote from the event.

Swedish local authorities came up against the same difficulties as other bodies when attempting to implement sustainable procurement criteria. The EU procurement rules can, if interpreted in a certain way, mean that the buyer cannot exclude less sustainable competitors from bidding for contracts. The Swedes developed what they call 'technical change procurement' that allows the buyer to specify goods and services that have limited environmental and social impacts without breaking European anti-competitiveness rules.

On social issues, the Swedes (with the Greeks) are most in agreement with the need to give more democratic powers to people about matters that affect them at home and at work, but among the least supportive of giving people more say in government decisions. The Swedes are also among the most tolerant people in Europe, with half agreeing that it was very important to integrate minorities and other cultures into their society. This was the second highest answer of the 25 EU countries; Spain was highest with 55 per cent. Interestingly, of the other European countries polled, it was Turkey with 63 per cent that showed most support for integration.

Save the Children (2007) reported that Sweden was the top ranked country (out of 41 developed countries) for the treatment of both mothers and women, and ranked fourth for the treatment of children. It was fifth out of 177 countries in the UN Human Development Index (www.hdrstats.undp.org), which is a basket of indicators including life expectancy, literacy attainment and standard of living. The country was seventh out of 121 countries in the Global Peace index (www.visionofhumanity.com). Sweden also has had the most number of women holding parliamentary seats (47 per cent in 2006).

The Swedes' ability to marry business interests with ethical and sustainability issues was confirmed by a study in 2006 by the international social responsibility organisation 'AccountAbility' and its partners. Sweden came first out of 108 countries in AccountAbility's 'Responsible Competitiveness Index'. The Index compares 21 different social, governance, environmental and ethical business indicators (Accountability, 2007).

As we saw in Chapter 2, the Swedes are not immune to the problem of inaction getting the better of intention. At least Swedes can say that they are probably no worse that anyone else in 'following through' with their sustainable beliefs. However, this may fall short of the high expectations reserved for one of the leading sustainable countries in the world. The Swedes would also have very worthy competitors for the title of most sustainable country. The Dutch, with their obvious passion for land preservation in the face of flooding by the sea, would be one. The Germans have been operating advanced recycling schemes for years and, as we saw in Chapter 4, have a romantic and strong affinity to nature. The Belgian region of Flanders recycled more than anyone in Europe in 2006, and New Zealand was the first country to declare a zero-waste policy. But while this is all undoubtedly true, it is the total package that Swedish society presents that tends to raise their reputation above all others.

## Sustainability as a cultural characteristic

Pan Yue, the deputy director of China's State Environmental Protection Administration (SEPA), explains that environmental protection should be considered a cultural issue in China (Pan, 2007). He says that

*one of the core principles of traditional Chinese culture is that of harmony between man and nature. Different philosophies all emphasise the political wisdom of a balanced environment. Whether it is the Confucian idea of man and nature becoming one, the Daoist view of the Dao reflecting nature, or the Buddhist belief that all living things are equal, Chinese philosophy has helped our culture to survive for thousands of years. It can be a powerful weapon in preventing an environmental crisis and building a harmonious society.*

If this permeates the majority of Chinese citizens, then there is certainly hope for the world's most populous country.

However, until recently China has not been known for its environmental protection record. In fact, rapid economic growth has meant that the country has an unsustainable thirst for both non-renewable resources, including minerals and metals, and is burning brown coal at rates that are causing severe air quality problems in many major cities. Increasing car ownership is exacerbating this problem. They are also consuming renewable resources, and timber in particular, at rates that the world is finding hard to replenish. This has created what the Worldwatch Institute calls an 'ecological implosion' (Turner and Lu, 2006). The Institute says that environmental degradation is costing China nearly 9 per cent of its annual gross domestic product.

In 2007, China overtook the USA as the largest emitter of greenhouse gases. In the same year it suffered one of the worst bouts of sustained storms in its history. Over 700 people died and more than 7 million suffered interruption to their water supply due to flooding (Reuters, 2007) and another 7.5 million suffered from a severe drought. And yet China refuses to accept mandatory caps on the emission of carbon. In a worrying statement, the Chinese Foreign Minister Yang Jiechi said that greenhouse gas emissions by developing countries were 'emissions for survival and development'.

It is understandable that a country like China needs to allow its population to feel that it can aspire to all of the comforts that they see on their television screens. To deny them this is to court social unrest further down the road. However, the Chinese leadership must have registered that the environmental chaos that is affecting the country is bad for their development plans. Where Pan Yue's cultural and spiritual affinity to environmental protection fits in all of this is hard to see. Those working to achieve global sustainable behaviour will hope that the will to protect nature in China will win through, but all the signs are that the affinity he talks about is not strong enough on its own to halt the dash towards unsustainable development.

## Do Swedes live it?

While the image of the Swedes as the overall leader in sustainable thought and deed endures, it is not very useful to any other culture unless it can be explained in their own terms. The detail, and the context of their commitment to sustainable principles, needs to be widely understood if there is any chance that it can be adopted or adapted by others.

One way for an outsider to understand why Sweden is associated with sustainability would be to ask insiders – Swedish professionals working in the field of sustainable development who are informed about the issues, yet objective and realistic in their views of the performance of the country. Our sample included academics, officials with the national environmental regulator, and the head of The Natural Step, effectively the head office of the Swedish founded international sustainable change organisation. The questions they were asked included:

- Do Swedes deserve the reputation as the world's leading sustainable nation?
- If so, is there any evidence that proves this view?
- What is it about Swedish culture that links it with nature and responsible behaviour?

The answer to the first question, with all the provisos about the dangers of generalising an entire national population, was a careful and reserved 'yes we do deserve our reputation'. The caution over saying that Swedes are better than anyone else needs to be explained and, in a fascinating twist, is also part of why Swedes behave in the way that they do.

The Swedes are culturally modest people who admire collaboration, team play and co-operation over extreme behaviour and individualism. They are governed by tendencies of *lagom*, which means 'just enough, in balance or in moderation'. Another phrase they use in a positive context is *mellanmjölk*, literally 'middle milk', meaning not full fat but not skimmed. However, there is a difference between saying they are the best, and actually believing this to be true. The reality is that Swedes don't really think about their performance in comparison with others, but when confronted they would not be surprised to find that in this area they are one of the top performing countries. While modesty is generally an admirable trait, this is not necessarily helpful. If the Swedes have the answer to a sustainable future, the rest of the world needs to hear about it.

There are a few other drawbacks to the *mellanmjölk* world of the Swedes, particularly when considering the need for urgent behavioural change in the face of the current rapid deterioration in global environmental and social conditions. One is the 'I will if you will' principle, where the comfort zone for Swedes would be to wait until there is global consensus before acting. However, the Swedish policy commitment to make the country oil-free does tend to counter-act this concern. A more practical example of *lagom* is the apparent near unanimous agreement by industry that sustainable change is a good thing (wanting to conform to a societal aspiration), which is later found to be more intention than solid commitment. But if this is the case, it is hardly unique to Sweden.

Mass communication about the environment has also played a part in the Swedes' civic attitude toward their impact on nature. Most municipal authorities have a local newsletter and, while nationwide referenda are not very frequent (compared with those that favour them, such as Switzerland), most local elections will include an invitation to vote on a locally important issue. A recent example was a vote for those living in Stockholm on whether they would support a congestion charge to drive in the city. Even here, the Swedes felt the need to pilot the idea first before canvassing opinion. The vote was in favour of the charge, albeit by a narrow majority.

The 'Keep Sweden Clean' campaign in the mid-1960s stuck in the minds of many, when asked to recall particular examples of national civic initiatives. The campaign did not simply rely on messages through the media. It involved awards given out by each municipality to neighbourhoods that showed the most commitment. It also engaged schools, and started a tradition that all school children should devote one day a year to activities that improve local areas.

This is particularly notable, in that Swedes do not subscribe to social philanthropy, and there is very little staff volunteering or charity work for those in need of social support. Swedes believe that the State should deal with these issues and that this should be funded through the tax system. The willingness to override this tendency emphasises the strong feelings that Swedes have for environmental protection. Another mass communication example was the initiative by

Karl-Henrik Robèrt, originator of The Natural Step (Det Naturliga Steget). His efforts resulted in widespread support (including the King of Sweden, Carl XVI Gustaf) to send a pack about sustainability to every household in Sweden.

The answer to the second question – whether the evidence supports Sweden's sustainability reputation – drew mainly personal, rather than statistical evidence from interviewees. Most talked about the strong commitment to teaching children about the natural world from the time they start pre-school, right through to the most senior years. This is built into the national curriculum, and reinforced by considerable investment and support by other bodies including materials developed by the Swedish Environmental Protection Agency (Natur Vårds Verket), the Swedish Energy Agency (Energimyndigheten), and private industry.

Parents are culturally primed to ensure that children understand the value of nature. It would be almost unthinkable for parents to avoid taking their children out into the countryside to pick berries, flowers or mushrooms. The majority of Swedes own small summerhouses (often modest wood frame structures) in the countryside, and stay there at weekends and for extended periods in the summer. Even those that don't have access to a summerhouse can reach the countryside in minutes, even from the centre of Stockholm, using public transport. There is also a tradition of summer camps for children.

As Sweden was urbanised relatively recently compared to other more industrialised countries such as Britain, Germany or France, many Swedes can say that they personally know someone who still makes their living from the land. While the days of staying on an active farm may have begun to disappear, links with extended family, and those living and working around summerhouses, mean that Swedes still retain their link to the land.

## Sustainable talk

Another major element of the Swedish affinity for sustainable behaviour comes from their belief that issues need to be discussed and agreed in the most consensual manner possible. It is easy to find examples of this, particularly for situations where land is either threatened or needs rehabilitation.

One example of this took place in the municipality of Danderyd, a suburb in the northern part of Stockholm. It concerned a proposal to expand the green space around a lake called Ekebysjön. An exhibition was mounted locally and a number of options were put forward. These ranged from a modest green fringe around the water through to a substantial extension of green space that linked with more urbanised areas.

Extended green space is being considered in many European cities, and is referred to as green infrastructure in the UK. This proposes that green space should form a continuous connection from the countryside on the urban fringe, right through to the centre of urbanised areas, in the same way that roads connect the periphery to the core for traffic.

Following the consultation period, the politicians decided that the best option was a small green fringe around the lake. This was not acceptable to many people, and resulted in the formation of a coalition of bodies (at least 11) that set out to challenge this decision. The coalition (Ekebysjöns Vanner, or friends of the Ekebysjön) was a combination of associations specific to that area, and the local branches of national organisations. The strength of feeling from the coalition was so strong that it reopened the debate.

Another well-known story in Sweden concerns the fate of wetlands in the south of the country. The land surrounding the southern town of Kristianstad lies almost three metres below sea level, and regularly experiences problems of inundation and flooding. The municipal authority faced a decision: should they invest in flood defences and technology, or should they opt to create wetlands? Early in the debate the authorities were favouring the technological approach. One of the reasons they were wary about the wetlands option was that there was no clear understanding of how to manage the wetlands, or how it would benefit the municipality.

The area in question is known as the Vattenrike, which translates as 'rich wetlands'. It covers the catchment area of the River Helge å, and the coastal stretches of the large bay known as Hanöbukten. The area also holds the largest groundwater reserve in northern Europe. Kristianstad itself is a thriving town of approximately 23 000 inhabitants. The usual methods used to establish land management involve an initial land use and ecological survey. Then come the appointment of publicly funded officials, the establishment of boundaries and rules, and time limited funding packages. This can produce a well-administered nature reserve, but a top-down approach can also alienate local land owners, and fail to gain the support of the local population.

The Vattenrike experience was different (Schultz et al., 2007). The ecological inventories were carried out alongside a social-ecological survey that concentrated on the skills and interests of the people that lived near the area. Dozens of people and associations were interviewed. They were asked to provide information about what they did in the area, why they enjoyed this activity, and what their expectations of the creation of a wetland park might be should it be created.

They were all asked about their associations and voluntary groups including how they started, how they are able to continue, and what the future held for them.

There was a belief behind the survey that new conservation areas are much more likely to satisfy potentially conflicting interests of farmers, municipal authorities, conservationists, and local people if they are created through the self-organising capacity of local stewards. The end result was the creation of an 'ecomuseum', which states on its website that it is

*an example of cooperation between local government, authorities, organisations, companies and, of course, the landowners themselves, are also key partners (www. vattenriket.kristianstad.se).*

The ecomuseum and the surrounding park comply with the UNESCO World Network of Biosphere Reserves criteria. The museum co-ordinates activities which come under the direct supervision of the chairman of the local municipal executive committee. The early concern by the municipal government has now been replaced by acceptance, and the new logo for the administrative area features wetland symbols.

The key to all of this was the co-ordinator who was chosen as a result of the initial eco-social survey. This person needed to be a member of many different associations and groups, and was therefore able to understand and link the interests of a large number of other local actors.

## Consensus as a nature-based thing

Asked why it was that Swedes liked to solve their problems by talking them through together, some said it had a lot to do with the environment. Because land used to be passed on equally to the owner's children, Sweden traditionally had a large number of smallholdings. Although this had been reversed in modern times, like every modern economic country, while this persisted it resulted in the need for co-operation. Because the growing season is so short in Sweden, and the winters descend so quickly, farmers needed to gauge the moment when crops had to be gathered with some precision, or risk losing everything. The speed at which the crop had to be taken from the land and brought under cover was therefore of the essence. This was a real challenge if you were doing it yourself, and thus led to a keen inter-reliance between neighbours who would gather on each other's land to speed the process and beat the weather. This has, in effect, made Swedes team players.

## Understanding more about nature as Swedish social context

These accounts are not merely anecdotal remembrances from a small section of Swedish society. Dahl (1998) explains these tendencies within the context of what it means to be Swedish. An anthropologist at Stockholm University, Dahl says that there are two strong themes in Swedish culture. The first is the sense of freedom, and the other is the power of nature. The two, Dahl explains, are interlinked in 'two contexts: one is the celebration of summer in public ritual and popular ballads, and the other, discourse on the allemansrätt, or the Swedish Law of the Commons'.

The celebration of midsummer is, for most Swedes, more important than Christmas. While Christianity is widely practised in Sweden it is largely a secular country, and there are very few examples of religious exuberance such as those found in evangelical denominations. Indeed, this is another example of Swedish distaste for behaviour that stands out from the crowd. While originally based on the feast of St John, the religious aspects of midsummer have now been lost.

Typical activities at this time would be the raising of, and dancing around, a maypole accompanied by folk music. Traditional and regional dress, ring dances and games may also be part of the festivities. While this is often put on for the children, the evenings are taken up by barn dances for the adults. The period in the year is marked by images of common meadow flowers on posters, emblems and window dressing. It is considered a quintessential Swedish experience, even though all other European countries have both the season and the flora. A bunch of flowers, Dahl writes, 'becomes the condensed symbol of the country where the national flag serves that purpose in many other countries'.

The actual flag, and nationalism in general, is associated in Swedish culture as something that is negative and even destructive. This can be traced back to a very strong belief that social harmony can only be achieved through co-operation. Revering ones own State above those of your neighbours goes against this belief. A good example of how strongly this is felt is the decision to maintain neutral status during the Second World War. Swedes were appalled as they watched Europe descend into chaos and killing because of the appropriation of national-ism by factions that used this to steer populations into conflict.

The love of summer, and what it brings, can be explained as the behaviour of those that have to suffer long cold and dark winters. Once the chill goes out of the air, it is understandable that the population reacts in a surge of collective celebration and relief. This in itself is not much to go on as many countries have harsh seasons that last for months. However, Dahl explains that if this exuberant celebration of nature is coupled with a passionate commitment to the freedom to roam free in the countryside, then it all starts to make sense.

*Allemansrätt* literally means 'every man's right', but in practice equates to 'public right of access'. This deep-seated belief in the right of access is taken for granted by the Swedes, but is rare in other countries. By comparison, this has only relatively recently been extended in the UK under the Countryside and Rights of Way Act 2000, and is generally referred to as the 'right to roam'. The fairly limited public footpath system in Britain was established only after a mass trespass in the English Peak District in 1932. This was led by working people (and miners in particular) who valued their time above ground, and objected to being barred from private upland for the sake of the protection of a few grouse that were shot by the wealthy. However, they needed to wait nearly 70 years for the kind of access the Swedes enjoy.

In Sweden, anyone is allowed to walk at will on any farmland, forest, lake or coastal area. Swedes would expect to be allowed to gather wild berries, mushrooms, flowers or fallen branches. They would not expect to remove stones, moss or wood on the trees. This even extends to the right to camp on anyone's land without consent, but usually only for a night or two.

This startling freedom could not have persisted without some very strong social norms being in place. Dahl calls these unwritten rules 'admonitions and exhortations'. While some of these were codified in 1991, the details of what Swedes think of as the *Allemansrätt* are not in the constitution. Broadly speaking, Swedes understand that there can be no freedom without responsibility. Dahl's opinion is that the overriding feeling of Swedes seems to be that one does not impose oneself on nature. She says that this extends to people as well. This seems to be a strong basis for what ecologists call 'living lightly on the land'.

In her conclusion, Dahl says that the Swedish right to roam is considered by Swedes as a human right, and that it symbolises the values of freedom and equality. These are basic human desires and as such it becomes much clearer how the denial of access to nature, either by fences or because it has been ravaged by pollution or climate change, becomes not just regret, but a major self-identity crisis. For Swedes it's personal.

## Can the Swedish experience be translated?

In a newspaper interview in 2006 (Cowell, 2006), the then Prime Minister Göran Persson acknowledged that his land of 9 million people, with its vast empty spaces reaching far to the Arctic north, is scarcely a perfect exemplar for America. However, perhaps Mr Persson is underestimating the influence of his fellow countrymen.

The combined elements that shape the Swede's behaviour are worth considering, either in the same form, or in ways that could be reinterpreted by other cultures. The themes are:

- commitment to consensus in society;
- the reinforcement of the value of nature through regular and unobstructed access;
- the keen focus on active enjoyment of nature following long harsh winters;
- a faith and a history in innovation leading to less resistance to change;
- the potential for solitude in nature;
- trust in politicians; and
- cross societal responsibility (parents, schools, government, industry) for the protection and enhancement of nature.

Each one of these factors is a positive influence on the Swedish population. The key to emulating their affinity to a more sustainable society is to inject these positive influences into the veins of every culture so that is seems as if the influences came from within rather than from outside.

# 6

# Why sustainable change works better at work

## Workers' sustainability time

When people are asked to explain what they are doing to improve the environment, the questioner almost always want to know what they are doing in their personal lives – at home, with their cars, or on holiday. They are rarely asked about what they do at work. This is because questions about corporate actions and behaviour are presented to officials and representatives, and not ordinary employees. Consequently, it is difficult to gauge how people feel about their employer's treatment of environmental or social issues, and some may not consider that it is really any of their business.

Given this emphasis, it is hardly surprising that much of the literature about influencing people to change the way they think and act on sustainability issues comes from either environmental pressure groups, or the growing number of marketing and advertising professionals that are specialising in environmental communications. The majority of information that is directed at companies comes from publicly funded business advice bodies, or single issues campaigns concentrating on things like energy efficiency or waste minimisation. The focus here is almost exclusively on the economic benefits of environmental improvement.

The actual job of changing employee attitude and behaviour has been mainly left to individual employers, who may or may not take up the challenge. From a public policy perspective, this is a curious tactic. While it may be easy to get a mass communication message over to homeowners (through a public information message via television or billboard, for example), it is much more difficult to monitor its success, and impossible to have meaningful dialogue with the recipients. On-line reaction to blogs and articles get closer to an exchange of views, but the participants are self-selecting and the contributions are unmanaged. Exhortations to be more sustainable will hang in the ether rather more in hope than expectation.

There are some notable exceptions to this, particularly from the world of reality TV. Recent programmes in the UK such as Channel 4's *Dumped* and the BBC programmes *No Waste Like Home* and *Outrageous Wasters*, either pick improbably wasteful individuals, or cast ordinary people into challenging environments to see how they react to our unsustainable society. The subjects of the shows are introduced as people that can't possibly live life without converting their entire house into a Turkish bath, or boil washing their entire collection of clothing every single day. They are unmasked as being hopelessly ignorant about how society deals with resources, with one participant in *Dumped* admitting that he had no idea where his waste went after it was collected from the front of his house, and had never heard of a landfill. They always start by saying they could not survive five minutes without conducting their lives with the help of a whole range of wasteful practices, and mostly finish the programme by confessing that they now see that a more sustainable life is not only cheaper, but much more enjoyable.

This is all very well, but there are two reasons why using mass media is unlikely to influence the majority of people to be more sustainable. First, viewers seldom think that their behaviour is as bad as the TV people. Second, like the endless cooking and do-it-yourself shows reveal, being entertained on the screen is one thing, putting it into practice is quite another.

Fortunately, the home is not the only place where sustainable behaviour can be discussed and performed. Most people spend more waking time at work than at home, and there is good scope for improving attitudes and opinions about the environment and social matters in the workplace.

At work employees are expected to conform to a corporate value set, or at least a set of written and unwritten rules. If a company instructs its staff to do things in a certain way, then they will generally do it, even if it may not be the way they would conduct their lives at home. People behave differently when they are away from work, and there are no guarantees that they will respond to the same kind of instructions or suggestions from authority, unless ignoring them will result in some kind of sanction. Of course employees can and do bring sustainable habits and ideas from their private lives into the workplace. Organisations such as Global Action Plan (www.globalactionplan.org.uk) have also shown that sustainability ideas to recycle waste, save energy and travel more responsibly, can be learned at work and practised at home.

Inspired employees can influence organisations that are 'culturally ready' to take on these challenges and perhaps just lacked the ideas or the champion. But, however successful this may turn out to be, a 'tail-wagging the dog' approach to policy formation within an organisation is just too haphazard when considering the potentially business-ending prospect of unsustainable practices. This is even more serious if the leadership and culture is still in denial, or remains doubtful about the changes that need to be made right now. It is highly unlikely that employees who do as much as they can to reduce their environmental impact at home will give up this behaviour after working for a company that does not support their actions. They are more likely to quit and find a job with a company that better fits their values set.

The prevailing case in the business world is not dominated by dinosaurs or management teams with their heads in the sand. This is not to say that everyone is rushing headlong to embrace sustainable change, because they certainly are not. However, the predisposition is to do more, provided that it makes business sense, and this presents an opportunity to accelerate sustainable change. Any management change, and particularly a comprehensive sustainable change programme, needs to take its workforce with it in order to be successful.

One of the heaviest obstacles in the way of a more sustainable future is intransigence and inertia, and most of the time this can't be altered by manual or diktat. Leaders need to bring their people with them by giving them the information and the time and space to come to the same conclusions as management. The first step in understanding how this can be achieved is to confirm that changing attitudes through persuasion in the workplace is possible and desirable, and then to consider whether this is going to be effective for a subject like sustainability.

## Can attitudes about sustainability be changed at work?

Attitudes are more complicated than they seem at first sight (Arnold et al., 2005). Different components, some of which fit together but others that don't, mean that changing attitudes is difficult, but not impossible. The psychology of the workplace may even be the key that unlocks wholesale change in the rest of society, but only if there is a better understanding of how and why employees can come to work with particular views about the world and then go home having been persuaded in another direction.

Secord and Backman (1969) define attitudes as 'certain regularities of an individual's feelings, thoughts and predispositions to act toward some aspect of his environment'. Unpacking this, there are three components of an attitude including an emotional or 'affective' part, a thoughtful or 'cognitive' part, and willingness to act or 'behavioural' part. However, an attitude should not be confused with a guarantee that the individual will act upon it. If someone is emotionally and intellectually committed enough to form an attitude about something, but is unlikely to demonstrate this through specific behaviour, then it could be argued that attitudes don't really matter at all. We have already shown, in Chapter 2, that there is a disconnect between people's attitudes toward things like climate change and recycling, and their behaviour to do something about it. If someone likes their work, it does not follow that they will work any harder.

But attitudes do matter. If they are shared, encouraged, and confirmed by others they often result in positive action. This was shown in the work of Ajzen and

Fishbein (1980) who explained the relationship between attitudes and behaviour. Refined later into the theory of 'planned behaviour' (Ajzen and Madden, 1986) it showed that in order to behave in a certain way, an individual needed to form the intention to act, based on a belief that the action was going to be effective. In other words, there is a calculation before acting that works out whether the individual is in control of the situation. However, the intention itself is formed from two other factors. The first is the attitude, borne from the mix of emotions, thought and a predisposition to do something about it. But the other factor is a concern about how other people will react to their beliefs or actions.

An example would be the current emotive issue of the citizen's duty to segregate their rubbish into different recycling receptacles. Assume an individual had the attitude, as many do, that the taxes he or she pays to the municipal authority should mean that the authority will take on the responsibility of separating out the bottles and paper from the kitchen scraps. The result is a reluctance to participate in kerbside recycling schemes. However, if everyone else in the street were fastidious recyclers, and the individual was concerned about their opinions, then they would recycle against their attitudinal convictions. The difference between linking attitude and behaviour would therefore depend on the balance of tension between the concern about what other people thought, and the strength of one's attitude about the issue.

While this general rule can be applied to the way attitudes and behaviours work, it can't be applied to individuals, because each issue creates a different tension. People may feel it isn't worth standing out from the crowd on some issues, but feel so strongly about others that they are oblivious to other people's opinions or the consequences to their social standing as a result of their actions.

The concern about social rejection is not always real, and for some is largely imagined. This is a real problem for businesses that have employees who harbour good sustainability ideas but are afraid to voice them. Not only will the company miss out on potentially profit-boosting contributions, but it makes for miserable and frustrated people who are unlikely to live up to their productive potential.

In more general terms, those rejecting the opportunity to perform in front of others for fear of making a mistake is a typical example. Excluding paying audiences that expect excellence from professionals, most audiences, gathering for example to hear the reading of children's poems or original songs performed by members of a folk club or an amateur dramatic production, would be very forgiving if any of the participants made a mistake. However, the fear for many prospective performers would be that their mistake would be a mortifying experience that they could not accept. This potential but unfounded fear of the loss of self-esteem puts paid to many people even attempting to perform in front of an audience. If those with a predisposition to act had a more accurate understanding of how their opinions and behaviour would be received, then it is probable that many more 'intentions' would be converted into 'actions'.

If attitudes towards acting more sustainably are being confounded by the fear, real or otherwise, that their colleagues would mock or ostracise them for their suggestions, then that would be a disaster for both the company and for society at large. But without exploring attitudes to sustainability with the whole of the workforce, companies are leaving sustainable innovation to a small number of senior or specialist people.

James Surowiecki (2004) in his book *The Power of Crowds* tells the story of the company Innocentive, a spin-off from Eli Lily. It set up an experimental market to test whether their employees could distinguish between drugs that were likely to be approved by the authorities, and those that were likely to be rejected. The diverse mix of employees quickly identified the winners. These 'decision markets' could only function in a culture that was supportive of both a range of ideas, and the belief that anyone is capable of good judgement.

## Attitude change through persuasion

Innovation such as decision markets would work a lot better for companies if everyone was rowing to the same beat. Unfortunately, this is rarely the case when it comes to the commitment to sustainable change. The commitment from the leader of a company can sometimes be enough, as we saw when we talked about iconic sustainable business leaders, but this needs to be coupled with effective communication. But even this is not always enough. Attempts to change people's attitudes to something they experience personally and often (such as work), solely through verbal persuasion, are unlikely to be successful (Arnold et al., 2005).

Before accepting a whole range of ways to help a workforce come to a collectively positive view about sustainability (which we will explore in later chapters), business leaders first need to accept that investment in persuasion and motivation initiatives are both valid and achievable. The first and basic point to understand is that the credibility of a communicator rests partly on their expertness and trustworthiness, as perceived by the person on the receiving end of the communication (Hovland and Weiss, 1951). A trustworthy source needs to be accepted as honest (Eagly et al., 1978). Thus an audience will only be open to persuasion if the communicator seems to know what they are talking about, has no axe to grind, and/or is open about the position they are taking in the argument.

Once the communicator is accepted, then the tactics of the delivery come into play. On an issue like sustainability, and the need to save energy in particular, it would be easy for management to play the green card, only for it to be discounted as another penny-pinching extra demand on the workforce. If the energy supplier is wheeled on to give the same message, then suspicion could easily be fostered about their motives.

The better way of engaging people to consider change is to present both sides of the story (Hovland et al., 1949). Of course, the idea is to make sure that one will appear more convincing than the other, but a two-sided presentation offers the opportunity for the audience to make up their own minds, whereas a one-sided argument foments thoughts that the whole story is not being told.

Robert Cialdini (RSA, 2007) describes an experiment where two different sets of letters of recommendation about a prospective candidate were sent to Fortune 500 companies around the United States. Half of the letters were uniformly positive and glowing about the abilities of the candidate. The other half first mentioned a weakness in the candidate, and then ended with positive and praiseworthy information. Amazingly, the letters that mentioned the weakness produced significantly more requests for an interview than the letters that had no flaw assigned to the candidate.

Cialdini explains that it would be easy but wrong to look at these results and conclude that US companies like to recruit people who have a weakness. Instead he thinks that the admission of weakness, the revealing of the other side of the story, enabled the source of the positive information to be more deeply processed and believed. He says that everyone knows that every recommendation, proposal and programme has strengths and weaknesses.

Understanding this is only half of the advantage gained by those standing in front of employees and asking them to believe in a new sustainability programme. The other half requires knowledge of when to play the honesty card. Cialdini says that the temptation is to talk first about all of the positives (especially the strongest features), and then to do the honest thing and explain about the drawbacks. But that is the wrong way around. The key moment to persuade is just after the persuader opens up to the receiver and reveals a weakness.

An example of this is the Co-operative Bank's early attempts in the mid-1990s to project its reputation for honesty and trustworthiness through its sustainability reporting. The bank's specific selling point is social justice and environmental responsibility, but it is a bank, and so trust is a key customer attractor. When explaining about the responsible way it treated its staff, it first talked about how it has failed to attract black and minority people in numbers that reflected the surrounding community. The rest of the talk included figures that explained how the bank had very low staff turnover rates, and how they consistently got very high staff approval percentages. None of this information was given disingenuously, but by admitting a weakness at the start, and following that with a positive story, the bank gained more respect and admiration than if they had done it the other way around.

There are a number of other learning points about persuasion in the workplace that leaders should understand. First, as we have already mentioned, scare tactics rarely work, and can backfire. High amounts of fear immobilise people (Jepson and Chaiken, 1990). A leader could say that 'if we don't reduce our energy consumption by 30 per cent in the next five years, this company will fail and you will lose your job'. Without an energy plan, delegation of duties and an incremental set of targets, the result is more likely to be higher than average resignations or time off sick, not lower energy consumption.

This brings us to the wider question of what kind of a leader is required to get the right message across. The assumption is that because the consequences of dangerous climate change and global demands for equal human rights are so dramatic, only a leader with passion and charisma could do the issues justice. However, that is not the case. Arnold et al. (2005) explain that leaders can adopt one of two approaches. 'Transactional' leaders motivate their workforce by 'observing their performance, identifying the rewards they desire, and distributing rewards for appropriate behaviour'. 'Transformational' leaders operate by 'inspiring and challenging the intellects of followers in order to go beyond self-interest in the service of a higher collective purpose, mission or vision'.

Intuitively, the expectation would be that the transformational leader will be more successful at getting workforces to accept that unsustainable behaviour is wrong, and to adopt sustainable behaviour for the greater good. However, there is no reason why inspiring leadership cannot be reinforced by 'contingent reward', meaning that the two approaches are not mutually exclusive (Bryman, 1992).

There are also a number of drawbacks to strong leadership, and Arnold et al. (2005) list some of the problems that might arise from a leader that shows 'evangelical zeal'. They may tend towards authoritarianism, stifling democratic discussion of the issues. The lead-from-the-front mentality may send the organisation down the wrong path, even if the leaders have the right understanding, because they have the wrong vision or method of operation. Over-strong leadership may undermine efforts of other members of staff to contribute effectively. Finally, there are certain situations where a charismatic leader can undermine the process of sustainable change. This is particularly true if values and attitudes need to be changed before the job of transforming the company can take place.

This is also true where the strategy relies on people taking personal responsibility for sustainable change. Gemmill and Oakley (1992) say that as individuals we may try to transfer tasks to leaders that it would be better to do ourselves. These observations about leadership suggest that there is certainly a role for inspirational motivation, and a reward system for appropriate behaviour. However, it does not follow that the leader has to be all things to all employees; only that these elements should be part of the persuasion strategy.

Another element to understand about persuasion is that intentions get translated into action more consistently if the commitment is made in public (Kiesler, 1971). This has to do with the need for social confirmation, or not reneging on a promise. However, there is also something very affirming about voicing a commitment, even if it is to just one other person.

This can be shown in another of Robert Cialdini's stories, this time about a restaurateur in Chicago who got fed up with people booking tables and then not showing up on the night (RSA, 2007). He asked his receptionist to change two words when she was dealing with people calling to book a table. Instead of saying 'please call if you have to change or cancel your reservation' she said, 'will you please call if you have to change or cancel your reservation?' and then she paused. The pause caused the caller to voice the commitment that they would of course call if they were not able to get there on time and absences without prior notification dropped from 30 per cent to just 10 per cent.

Another factor that can influence change is the style and delivery of the presenter. Many people like to hear strong arguments that can stand up to robust challenge. However, others will be influenced by a range of other signals that have nothing to do with the logic of the message, including the attractiveness of the speakers and the reaction of those around them to the delivery (Wood and Kallgen, 1988). The aim is to have motivators that can be logical, presentable and entertaining. This offers the audience the opportunity to be influenced by central and peripheral persuasion at the same time (Petty and Cacioppo, 1986).

Finally, and perhaps most important of all, is what is known as 'social comparison' factors. Wood (2000) explains that attitude change that occurs as a result of social pressure is not necessarily temporary or superficial. Cialdini (RSA, 2007) helps to illustrate this point with two more examples.

The first is an experiment that varied the signs in hotel bathrooms that asked guests to hang up their towels if they did not want them to be replaced. If they did want a fresh towel, they were instructed to leave the used one on the floor. Reusing their towels would, the guests were told, help the environment. Cialdini found that 38 per cent of guests responded to this and reused their towels. When the message was changed to say that 75 per cent of guests using this hotel reused their towels, the percentage went up. When the sign said the majority of guests using this room reused their towels, it went up even more.

In another example, he described a poll that asked 800 Californians to rate four different reasons why they might decide to save energy in the home. The reasons included benefits to the environment, benefits to society, saving money and because their neighbours might be doing it. The results showed the highest rated answer was to protect the environment, while the lowest was their neighbours' actions. Then the respondents were asked to rate the same reasons against their actual energy-saving activities. This time the top and bottom answer were reversed, with the actions of their neighbours being the highest rated influence on their actions.

All this evidence should empower business leaders to take the initiative and develop ways to persuade their employees to act in a sustainable manner. However, by taking up this challenge they will need to break out of some common behaviour of their own. Cialdini's (RSA, 2007) advice is that 'often, decision-makers focus too much on financial and economic factors when trying to motivate others'. This may be their comfort zone, but they would be well advised to concentrate instead on the social psychological factors affecting their business if they want to win over their staff to make significant sustainable changes. He says that

*the critical thing is to be able to go outside of the context in which we are working, to see what insights can be learned from traditions and knowledge bases that are more diverse than the ones in which we are currently working.*

These traditions and knowledge bases may seem other-worldly to some but, as we now describe, they not only work, but they work in a way that leads employees into a positive frame of mind, where better environmental and social justice choices seem more appealing and more rewarding.

## Art, science and sustainability

Over a decade ago, a residential course at a farm in the depths of the Kent countryside in Southern England was the setting for a meeting that would result in a
remarkable collaboration that has lasted right up to the present day. A dozen or
so people had gathered to learn about The Natural Step (TNS). At that time, in
1997, TNS was still a relatively new idea that had hitherto been practiced mainly
in Sweden. At that time no one really knew what type of organisation or person
would be best to spread a Swedish approach in Britain and so the small gathering
was a mixed bag to say the least. They varied from people interested in sustainability and wanting to change careers, right through to sustainable development
practitioners looking for the latest technique.

As ever, it was the gaps between the formal learning sessions that proved
to be highly productive, and the late night sessions were the perfect setting for
the National Centre for Business & Sustainability (NCBS) and Kandu Arts for
Sustainable Development to understand each other's perspective, and form a
lasting partnership. The NCBS was created by The Co-operative Bank (charged
by the personal determination of Terry Thomas as we saw in Chapter 3) to provide
credible and convincing science-based evidence for businesses. This evidence
showed both how environmental and social conditions were being altered by
man to the detriment of business, and how business could adapt to the new conditions for competitive advantage.

The bank formed an alliance with the universities of Greater Manchester
(UMIST, Manchester, Salford, and Manchester Metropoliton, to reinforce the
philosophy and the tactics of the Centre, which were based on a mix of serious
and thorough research, and the kind of economic pragmatism that even the
hardest nosed business leaders would find difficult to challenge. All the NCBS
technical staff were educated to Masters or PhD level and, while set up as a non-
profit company limited by guarantee, the NCBS was culturally more akin to a
mainstream commercial consultancy. This was important because the image that
both the bank and the Centre wanted to project was a commercially astute advisory body, offering the kind of message that had previously only emanated from
environmental pressure groups.

Kandu was founded by Ed Deedigan, former member of the band Blur, who
decided that it was better to follow his own path than to compromise his beliefs
in pursuit of rock stardom and the promise of personal wealth. In today's world,
where youngsters consider fame as a career destination, this certainly counts as a
decision against the tide. He knew that he wanted to use all forms of arts-based

media to give people a better understanding of themselves, and the world around them, but the exact means to do this took some time to come to him. Deedigan's search for the best way to do this took him on a ten-year journey.

After leading his own band, and a stint running comedy clubs, he became interested in the attempt by local authorities to engage ordinary people on issues of what we now call 'sustainable development'. His early work in this area was an inspired form of group facilitation, where he drew people into discussions with a combination of humour, role-play and an appeal to participants' emotional side. In Deedigan's world, it didn't matter that you were not an expert, or a leader, or a professional. You were there to say what you thought, listen to others, and at the end feel that you could make a difference with what you learned about the world and about yourself.

His mix of humour, empathy and intensity led to more and more invitations for Kandu to work with people that the authorities found difficult to reach. These were people on the periphery of society, including the homeless, prostitutes and, in particular, young people who were either in care, had been in trouble with the police, or both. Deedigan found that the people he was working with had been so disappointed or disaffected by the way their lives had turned out that they found it difficult to gain enough perspective to see a way out of their troubles. By this time he was well on the way to harnessing two vital antidotes to this problem. The first was an understanding of how the world works, and each person's value to that world. The second was the power of art, theatre, and film as the vehicle for self-awareness and confidence.

At the time of the meeting in Kent, the NCBS was doing very well co-ordinating large-scale sustainable business projects, using public monies and European funds in particular to improve environmental performance in companies. Smaller companies were often the subject of this activity, because the European Union has believed for some time that they are a neglected avenue to economic revival. Smaller organisations were also eager to make use of the free advice, and were at the beginning of the environmental awareness process which played to the strengths of the systematic approach employed by the NCBS. However, the Centre was having less success in attracting larger companies into its circle of influence. This was despite the interest that larger companies were taking in the Co-operative Bank's profitable yet sustainable and ethical approach to business.

Following the first few collaborations between Kandu and NCBS, it became clear where the problem lay, and it is as true today as it was in the late 1990s. Businesses that have taken an interest in improving their social and environmental performance are not stimulated to act on evidence alone. Other factors such as competitor activity, customer pressure, legislation, fiscal incentives and technological advances all play a part in the timing of a decision to invest in better performance. When there is a lack of clarity or evidence to support a decision, then the result is very often delay or paralysis. This is as true for a decision on whether to invest in energy conservation or to switch to a less resource intensive production process as it is for the next corporate acquisition, or a new product or service line.

When NCBS and Kandu compared notes it looked like they would be unlikely to work together. One based its delivery on hard science and painstaking research, and was directed toward business. The other was more emotionally and artistically rooted, and homed in on assistance for vulnerable members of society. But there were elements in each other's approaches that were attractive. After hearing about Kandu's use of Forum Theatre as a tool to explain sustainable development, the NCBS realised that its evidence-based approach could be packaged in ways that differed from the standard spiral-bound report or a structured workshop.

Kandu in turn saw that the power of credibility that went with rational fact-based arguments was just what it needed to reach a wider audience. Kandu was particularly interested in working with the corporate world, but thought that it lacked the technical gravitas to be attractive to that market. The affinity for each other's methods was cemented by the end of the Kent TNS sessions but, as ever, a partnership is never truly established until it is tested in earnest. That test was soon in coming.

## Can plastic ever be fantastic?

A few months later, Jonathon Porritt, co-founder of the UK's leading sustainability organisation Forum for the Future, came to the NCBS with a request. The major supermarkets in the country had been threatened with a boycott campaign by Greenpeace, unless they phased out PVC from their stores. Tesco, on behalf of a consortium of food retailers (the Retail Group), asked Porritt for help, and he advised that it would be sensible to find out if PVC was the dangerous toxic substance that Greenpeace claimed. The NCBS (with links to Terry Thomas and the Co-operative Bank and its university partners) provided an independent reputation and the ethical pedigree required to guarantee that the investigation into PVC could not be written off as an industry sponsored piece of greenwash.

Greenpeace maintained then, as it does now, that 'the production of PVC creates and releases one of the most toxic chemicals – dioxin' (from www.greenpeace.org/international/campaigns/toxics/polyvinyl-chloride). It goes on to assert that

*PVC products can leak harmful additives during use and disposal, when they are burned or buried. Burning creates and releases dioxins and compounds containing chlorine, which further contaminates the environment.*

The organisation goes on to claim that 'laboratory studies in animals show that some of these chemicals are linked to cancer and kidney damage and may interfere with the reproductive system and its development'.

At the time Greenpeace was concerned about three pollutants in particular: dioxins, chlorinated paraffins and heavy metals. The additives they talk about were primarily phthalates, the compounds which make PVC flexible. While there were many products, and plastics in particular, on the market that contained potentially toxic materials, the Greenpeace campaign formula picked out PVC because it was widely found in products that the public bought and used every day. Supermarkets were a smart target because they would inevitably be sensitive about linking food and toxins in the public's mind.

When the NCBS completed the research it found that

*on the balance of probabilities, the evidence reviewed provided no overriding scientific reason for the Retail Group to immediately abandon the use of PVC in food packaging or building/insulation materials.*

However, the NCBS said that this conclusion could only be justified if the Retail Group was able to conclusively show that the PVC it purchased was responsibly manufactured, and would be responsibly treated when the material had completed its function. In other words, that it would not have detrimental effects when it came to be discarded (www.thencbs.co.uk/index). While this was not the wholesale condemnation that the PVC industry had feared, neither was it a glowing endorsement. Greenpeace was similarly disappointed that the report did not confirm its claims that the product should be phased out. Greenpeace used the report to say that while it was theoretically possible to produce and dispose of PVC in a responsible manner, it was confident that the industry was either unwilling or unable to pull this off, and the supermarkets should disinvest until the unlikely time when the industry could produce a sustainable product.

The NCBS report might have produced a dead end – a message that neither side found to its liking – had it not been for two brief but significant events. The first enabled those directly in the firing line, the UK PVC manufacturers, to believe that they were not completely on their own. The second helped them to start a dialogue about the issues with the rest of the world.

A small meeting was arranged with the two UK PVC manufacturers and Greenpeace. Jonathon Porritt chaired the meeting. Jason Leadbitter, who had been representing Hydro Polymers (one of the manufacturers), later explained that this was his first meeting with Porritt, and he was dreading it. As a seasoned environmental campaigner, former leading figure in the British Green Party and former head of UK Friends of the Earth, Porritt had a formidable reputation. Leadbitter braced himself for a grilling. Instead, he was amazed to see Porritt round on Greenpeace with a barrage of questions about its publication *Building the Future: A Guide to Building Without PVC* (Greenpeace, 1996) that claimed cast iron and copper drains and guttering were a more sustainable alternative to PVC.

Greenpeace had based its campaign on the abolition of toxic substances. Its alternatives to PVC were materials which did not involve chlorine chemistry in their production. Greenpeace's mistake was to focus on one potentially unsustainable material, while ignoring another. The mining, smelting and manufacture of metals may not have involved chlorine, but it did emit large quantities of greenhouse gases, and caused environmental damage due to mining activities. While the phenomenon of global warming was known at this time, it was not the imminent threat that we now know it to be, and Greenpeace clearly considered carbon emissions to be the lesser evil.

Porritt was able to point out the scientific inconsistencies in the Greenpeace argument, and challenged them to come up with a working definition of sustainability. He also challenged them to put their aggressive campaign methods to one side, and join in the process to determine how PVC could be guaranteed to be sustainable. Greenpeace did neither, and were never to engage with the process again. However, their threat to the supermarkets receded, and they never went through with the mass boycott.

The PVC industry was not to know this at the time, and they accepted that there were elements of their industry that were environmentally damaging. Like many industries, and the oil industry in particular, they saw the environmental disbenefits of their product as a necessary price for society to pay in exchange for a vital material. Now they saw that a major UK environmentalist was at least willing to be objective about their industry, and they had found an organization in the NCBS that fought for sustainability based on the balance of evidence. However, they were not yet ready to open a dialogue with the wider world.

The NCBS report opened up a scientific route away from the industry's problems when it pointed toward responsible manufacture and disposal of the plastic. If the industry could prove that this was being done (there was precious little effort being made at the time the report was published), then it would have grounds to stand up to the Greenpeace accusations and to put the food retailer's fears to rest. However, none of this was likely to come to pass unless the industry was willing to accept that it had an issue to address, and that it was capable of engaging with both retailers and its detractors.

The PVC community and their suppliers (particularly the additives companies) were very angry people at this point in the story. They believed quite passionately that their product was not only safe but a genuine benefit for society. Their product was highly versatile, and was used in everything from packaging and plumbing to architectural and construction products. It could, with additions to the basic formula, be strong and ridged or soft and flexible. It could last decades without degrading and, although they really had not experimented much at this time, it could be recycled again and again without wrecking its structure. Later it was shown that adding a proportion of recycled PVC to virgin stock actually improved the product.

Disbelief that anyone could think that they were the enemy was not unique to the PVC industry. It was that same shock and confusion that Monsanto felt when, far from being hailed as the saviour of the planet and the answer to world famine, its genetically modified crops were vilified as Frankenstein food, an abomination that was to be opposed at all costs, in Asia and Europe. Shell was shocked and hurt by the reaction to its careful decision to deposit an oil service platform onto the floor of the North Sea.

But the PVC industry was also seething about the direct attacks it had suffered at the hands of Greenpeace. In 1996, there was a fire in an occupied terminal building at Rhine-Rhur airport in Düsseldorf. The fire killed 17 people and injured 62 more. Greenpeace, it was claimed by many in the industry, had inferred that the deaths were caused by toxic fumes given off by burning PVC cables and insulation material.

Supporters of the PVC industry made it known after the Düsseldorf Public Prosecutor gave his verdict that Greenpeace had got it very wrong (www.home.scarlet.be/chlorophiles). They quoted the *North Rhine Westphalia* press release on the day the official report was released as saying that the victims died from carbon-monoxide poisoning. They also reported the spokesman for the region as saying that PVC did not play the slightest role in the death of the people. This was cold comfort for some plastics executives who claimed that they and their families had been targeted by campaigners in their homes in the aftermath of the fire.

In 1999, the NCBS presented a summary of their work to date to the international PVC '99 Conference which was organised by The Institute of Materials. During its presentation, the NCBS asked the industry to be more open about their industry. This was somewhat undermined by another presentation that flashed up a portrait of Mark Strutt (the Greenpeace staffer in charge of the PVC campaign), which got the anticipated response: the audience booed and hissed even before they heard about the latest Greenpeace attack on the industry. To be fair, many in the room felt uncomfortable with the personalisation of the issues, but this was the prevailing view of an industry under attack, hurting and feeling totally embattled.

The future of the PVC project depended on bringing the PVC industry to the point where it would at least engage with the issues raised by the NCBS paper, if not by Greenpeace. The position of the retailers had not altered throughout this early part of the process. They did not want environmental protesters outside their doors, and needed the PVC industry to show some movement towards addressing the issues raised by Greenpeace. They were not hostile to the industry, but they also needed ammunition in the battle against the accusation that they had done nothing about making their stores more environmentally friendly. The supermarkets badly needed to explain how they were being responsible, and wanted help from the PVC companies to do this.

It was proposed that the industry gather together, discuss the NCBS findings, and agree on a way forward. The NCBS was given the job of organising the day, and the invitees included the two UK PVC manufacturers, a number of additive companies, British and European plastics representative bodies, plus people from The Natural Step UK and Jonathon Porritt. Greenpeace refused its invitation. The challenge for the NCBS was to bring the PVC industry out of its shell, and into a more creative and positive frame of mind. The industry had to be brought to a position where it wanted to show that its product was produced in a sustainable manner. Not only would this require a willingness to engage with those it had come to hate, but it had to come to terms with the fact that its product was not the golden gift that it thought it was – at least not in terms of the production and disposal methods that were being employed at the time.

It was clear to the NCBS team that the conventional methods of group presentations and facilitated workshops would probably not be very effective. The industry had been all through this, and it had not changed attitudes. It was then that the NCBS remembered its exchanges with Kandu Arts. Very quickly a plan emerged to use Forum Theatre as the means to transport the plastics executives into a place where they would realise that the solution was in their own hands. Kandu had trialled the method at a local authority event using kitchen table dialogue between parents and children to explore issues like organic food. The NCBS knew something different was needed and was prepared to see if 'theatre' would work in this context.

Forum Theatre was developed by Augusto Boal, a Brazilian who based his ideas on his experience of running theatre groups in China. The 'forum' part of Boal's concept invites the audience to intervene in the action they are watching, and come up with their own solutions to a storyline that highlights problems in society. It provides a creative space in which participants can bring their own questions. Typically the play would show a character who was feeling aggrieved in some way. This could be literal, such as an African being subjected to racial abuse by whites, or it could be self-inflicted, such as the youth that arms himself with a knife, drinks, takes drugs, gets into a fight and ends up in prison having stabbed someone.

At the conclusion of the first run of the play, the Forum Theatre players offer the audience a chance to change the outcome of the play. The actors begin the story again from the start, but this time the audience is invited to intervene at any time. They can suggest different dialogue, and different actions or reactions. If the audience thinks that the actors did not understand or execute the suggestions well enough, the cast might invite one or a number of them onto the stage to replace the actors and play out the alternative suggestions themselves.

The use of Forum Theatre enabled the NCBS and Kandu to build an event that was better than the sum of their skills. If NCBS gave technical information for actors to speak, it would have been very dry. If the actors were left to their own understanding of the issues, then they would have been challenged by the audience's own technical understanding.

The process of building the performance began with the NCBS compiling a briefing document that was written in plain non-technical language. It was not simplified, just written in a way that anyone could understand. Next, Kandu assembled a cast of four including Deedigan himself, and built the dramatic envelope around the information. Finally, the two groups got together to try out the material and hone it into a performance that did three things. First, it had to be entertaining with plenty of humour. Next, it had to be true, or at least have a story wrapped around kernels of truth. Finally, it had to invite the audience to come to their own conclusions while always knowing the answer.

The venue was a university conference suit in Manchester, England, and the bar the night before the meeting was filled with nervous people. Few of those that were invited had any idea what was about to happen, and the talk around the tables could have come from people preparing for a siege.

After a brief introduction to the day, the lights were dimmed, and after a pause the doors at the back of the room burst open and four screaming people came rushing up the centre aisle. Later it transpired that many thought that Greenpeace had found them and some were scared. The four actors started chanting 'Jerry! Jerry!' and 'Jerry Springer' duly emerged to introduce the day's 'show'. This would have 'the PVC industry' on stage and, it was explained, he was having a problem with his neighbour. To his surprise, from behind the curtain emerged his 'neighbour'. It was Greenpeace.

An ear splitting shouting match ensued, with the usual invitations to talk to the hands as neither face wanted to know. Almost as soon as the scene was constructed it dissolved, and was replaced by a pregnant woman seeking out the manager of her local supermarket. After exchanging pleasantries, the woman asked the manager whether he had seen the Jerry Springer show the day before, and whether he thought that the PVC in his store was likely to harm her unborn baby.

Clearly unqualified to answer the question, the manager promised to find out, thus concluding the initial part of the action. In a twist to the normal way that Forum Theatre works, rather than start the action all over again, the audience was invited to finish the story by supplying a reliable source of information for the supermarket manager to consult. Unknown to them, the NCBS had anticipated what they were likely to suggest, and this led to an hour of drama that would transform the project.

Again and again, the audience made suggestions about who the supermarket manager could approach to enable him to reassure his customer that PVC was completely safe and would not be any kind of threat to a pregnant woman. A scientist was suggested, and the actor's played out the discussion between the manager and a polymer researcher. The researcher could only say that, while many tests showed that the product was safe, some had shown that experiments on animals had resulted in endocrine abnormalities, possibly due to added plasticisers leaching out of the PVC.

The audience had another go, and somebody suggested that the manager ask someone at the environmental protection agency. The actors once again played this out, and once again there was no definitive defence for the industry. All the regulator was able to say was that the product complied with legislation, but this did not necessarily mean that it was risk-free.

Then Jonathon Porritt, by now trusted as a man willing to listen to the arguments, was suggested. In an improvisation that could not be resisted, Porritt was called out of the audience and into the action, playing himself. Understandably, he answered the manager by supporting the NCBS findings, and explained that the industry would need to show that their product had been produced and disposed of in a sustainable way before he was prepared to give out any assurances about its safety.

Eventually it dawned on the assembled executives that there was only one source that could reliably provide the facts about PVC, and put in place the necessary proofs and concessions that the public wanted to hear. It was the industry itself. They would of course need to rely on the independent verification of impartial commentators along the way, but all of those in the room realised that there would be no meeting of minds unless half of those minds were their own.

The 'futures' workshop that followed produced a wide range of ideas that could be used to better explain how PVC is manufactured, and how it might be produced and reused in sustainable ways in the future.

One of the most telling contributions of the day came from John Spillander, then head of the European Council of Vinyl Manufacturers (ECVM). The other European companies were quite hostile to the sustainable PVC initiative, and to the UK companies in particular, as they wanted the industry to pull together and resist change. Spilander, representing the whole community, could have holed the process below the water. Instead, he appreciated that change was necessary and started to say 'We have to tell…'. Then he paused and restarted the sentence saying 'We have to listen to what we are being told [about our environmental impact] before we decide what we should say'. Later John Spiers, then Managing Director of Norsk Hydro UK (owner of Hydro Polymers), would say until that day he never realised why people hated the industry.

This move from 'perplexed and hurt' to 'understanding and ready to talk' was certainly a movement away from the negative and toward the positive. To put this in motivational terms, it swung the industry from a starting point where it was stationary and defensive, to the next stage where it had resolved to move forward. This did not necessarily mean that the industry fully understood the work that lay ahead, and it would certainly have preferred the world to conform to the way that it saw itself – as a force for good in society. But the prospect of working to address the issues raised by the NCBS/Kandu team was certainly much better than the powerless and angry place they had occupied for many years.

The workshop generated enough of a consensus for the NCBS to be asked to put together an Environmental Charter. This committed signatories to:

- compliance with an Eco-efficiency Code of Practice for the manufacture of PVC;
- the examination of their operations in a broad social, environmental and economic context;
- participation in supply chain development and product stewardship initiatives; and
- contribution to research programmes on the environmental and health effects associated with PVC manufacture, use and disposal.

The charter was developed and agreed by the PVC Coordination Group, which was formed to engage a wider number of key players. The group included the UK food retailers Asda (now part of Wal-Mart), CWS (now the Co-operative Group), Tesco and Waitrose, as well as the Environment Agency and the two UK PVC manufacturers EVC and Hydro Polymers.

With Jonathon Porritt as its Chair, the group commissioned a string of reports by the NCBS (and later by The Natural Step UK) that examined, in finer detail, aspects of the PVC industry including the manufacture and use of additives, and the sustainable pros and cons of various disposal and recycling routes (NCBS, 2000; Everard et al., 2000; NCBS, 2003).

Jason Leadbitter later said that before the NCBS/Natural Step collaboration, his industry was living in a dark cave and stumbling into the walls of the challenge that was presented to them. When NCBS and Kandu came to analyse the whole process, which culminated in the attitudinal change of the PVC executives, they saw that it was a powerful vehicle with which to tackle the most difficult audiences. The pedigree of the team was right for the job, with Kandu used to working with cynical and untrusting people, and NCBS used to challenging a show-me fact-based corporate culture.

They would come to realise later that what they had done was to help the PVC industry make a choice that would lead them into a better situation. The reality was that this was the same choice that the industry had previously thought would put them in a worse situation. They had been highly resistant to open dialogue in the face of what they saw as blackmail, and were in no hurry to pointlessly expend effort defending a perfectly good product. Following the NCBS/Kandu session they embarked on exactly the same path, but this time feeling like they had something to look forward to. The food retailers were on board, Greenpeace had been challenged, and the future was in their own hands again.

There were of course those in the industry that continued to grumble, and later the European Union imposed bans on plasticisers in baby toys and a deadline to phase out heavy metals in PVC. However, the Forum Theatre session also allowed more progressive companies like Hydro Polymers to break ranks in the name of compliance with the new charter. Since then they have saved millions of euros in energy and materials, created a fast-track phase-out programme for lead, and have been one of the most profitable manufacturers in the European sector.

## Playing at a theatre near you

Encouraged by the success of the PVC work, the NCBS looked for another client that was willing to agree to this radical new approach. They found it in the construction company AMEC.

AMEC was at that time an international building and construction group, with particular strengths in a number of sectors, including oil and gas. In the autumn of 2000, AMEC was planning a large conference for about 130 Health, Safety and Environment personnel from across all of its divisions. Many had been given these responsibilities, as opposed to choosing them or training for them. Consequently, it was not the most enthusiastic audience assembled to hear why sustainable development was important to the company, and yet that was the NCBS brief. In an extraordinarily brave decision considering the audience, the head of Health, Safety and Environment, Jason Rowley, agreed to the NCBS suggestion that a Forum Theatre piece should be used to get the message across.

As before, the NCBS compiled a briefing document for Kandu about the construction industry in general, and a few stories about a number of projects where AMEC was either the lead contractor or was a primary sub-contractor. In particular, NCBS wanted to hear why jobs went wrong due to either environmental or social obstacles. This time around, the team thought that rather than a dramatic storyline, it would use the Forum Theatre tool to mimic a situation that was very familiar to the audience: a competitive bid for a building contract. However, in a twist that would be key to this event, the whole of the AMEC crowd were given a single role-play part; they were to play their own customer, a developer.

The reasoning behind this was simple. Even to this day, most construction companies bidding for work are confronted with a tender specification that is written in such a way that it invites variation and innovation. In other words, it can be a bit vague in places. This is good in theory, as it tests the market's ingenuity, as well as its ability to offer value for money. However, the system often works against contractors that want to introduce sustainable innovation. This is because many green building techniques, materials and technologies cost more at the construction phase, and only start to save money once the building is occupied. The developer's fixed budgets often means that they prefer to ignore the large sums they could save in lower maintenance and energy costs, in favour of a much smaller saving at the construction phase of the project.

Could the improved corporate reputation with new clients, or the attraction of environmentally-minded tenants and staff, sway their opinion? No, not at all. A bird in the hand is worth two in the bush.

Most contractors would never risk the loss of a job to a cheaper, less environmentally-minded competitor, and would avoid anything that pushed up front-end costs. The developer is then left with a number of cheap conservative bids and, because they comply with the broad specification, they have no choice but to award the contract to one of the bidders. Its quite neat for those that don't really care – they can blame it on the market. But for the ones that do care, the absence of specific tender clauses on sustainable energy and materials is close to negligence.

The current practice is to issue pre-qualification questionnaires, often festooned with sustainability queries such as 'will your design reduce the fear of crime?', or 'will your development encourage the take-up of public transport?'. This has not really helped. Contractors have quickly fingered the employee that has shown an interest in matters sustainable, and set them up as the one to ink in the right answers. Companies will happily fill out these pre-qualification questionnaires in the knowledge that they are unlikely to be challenged to explain what sustainable development really means.

The only thing that has made a significant difference in recent times, at least in the UK, is the Public/Private partnership that offers contractors a 'design build and operate' contract for between 10 and 25 years. If you are going to be responsible for maintaining the building that you build, and you want to make money, you better make sure the structure is durable and efficient.

Unfortunately, the Public/Private partnership model has been undermined by some very costly mistakes. The recent collapse of the company that took on the maintenance contract for the London Underground system is an example of this. After making very good profits for the first period of the contract, the shareholders withdrew their support from the private company, leaving the taxpayers of London to pick up the pieces. However, if this kind of deal is doomed, at least the lessons learned about durability and sustainable design should be incorporated into future public sector contracts.

Once the Kandu team understood these fundamental tensions in the construction sector, they were ready to put the Forum session together. This was important because the strategy for the event was based on a hunch that construction companies were beginning to lose its middle-aged, male, buffalo circle mentality towards sustainability. Many more women and younger people were joining the sector, and it was hoped that this might allow for some radical tactics on the day.

The audience was assembled in a large conference room in a new hotel next to a six-lane motorway. The attendees were told that they would hear the final presentations for two short-listed companies. The first company was the Eco-Build Corporation, or EBC. The other was Dinosaur Enterprises, or DiE. The proceedings were conducted by the 'chairman' of the petrochemical company interested in building a new plant, and played by a Kandu actor. Kandu staff also played the DiE team but, in a change from the PVC piece, it was NCBS staff (after some persuasion) that played the EBC team. This was done to ensure that all the protagonists were as convincing as possible.

The chairman asked each company a number of questions. An excerpt from the guiding notes (there was no fixed script as such) gives an idea of the tactic employed in the piece:

Chairman: Could you describe the general philosophy and approach you take to developing such a project as this?
DiE: We operate a competitive organisation offering cut-cost services to our clients. At the same time we place considerable emphasis on the development of partnership arrangements, which means we believe in the importance of forging long-term relationships in this area in order to foster interdependent learning to exploit mutually beneficial opportunities for improved quality and efficiency.
Chairman: I'm sorry, I didn't quite understand that, could you explain?
DiE: Not really, I was told to say that by our project manager, but I haven't a clue what it means.
Chairman: Right, um... EBC, could you outline your approach please?
EBC: We base our approach on leadership, sustainability, and a focus on the customer. We integrate the process and the team around the project, operate a quality driven agenda, and we are committed to our people. Most of all we are committed to sustainable development.

This time, when 'clarification' is requested, it is offered in plain terms that are based on competitiveness and value for money. As the piece unfolds the two 'companies' answer questions about risk assessment and managing problems, fair treatment of stakeholders, cost philosophy, and give examples of other projects.

In each case, Dinosaur Enterprises, modelled on a collection of all the worst practices in the industry, mock the idea of green building and assume the customer wants a cut-throat job that relies on at least one company in the supply chain going under, giving everyone else someone to blame when, inevitably, the budget is extended.

The eco-builders of course offer a textbook answer involving:

- sustainable and mutually dependent alliances along the whole supply chain;
- a range of energy-saving innovations;
- renewable technology and resource-efficient building and occupation ideas;
- a caring plan of action towards their own staff; and
- a community liaison scheme for those that live around the development site.

The theatrical setting gave plenty of opportunity for the injection of humour, and an emphasis that allowed the audience to be offered, very consciously, cartoon examples of the two extremes of their sector. At the conclusion of the presentations, the shareholders of the petrochemical company (the AMEC audience) were asked to vote on which company would get the job. Before voting, the chairman asked if anybody wanted to say anything about what they had seen and heard.

There was a longer than comfortable silence, and then a ruddy-faced man with a look of thunder in his eyes stood up and uncorked an angry tirade, aimed at the actors. He said they had wasted his time, because everyone knew that winning a construction project was all about the lowest bid. He resented the way that the actors had mocked the necessary measures that construction companies used to keep costs down, turning them into a cowboy's refuge. He thought that green building was a fad that was very unlikely to catch on, and he refused to vote for either of the choices on offer. He sat down, and there was another long pause. The next speaker agreed with the first, but in more conciliatory terms. The one after that said that nobody was against sustainability – it was just that clients would not buy it.

Contribution after contribution followed, each one a little closer to the sustainable construction company proposition. The last speaker, a woman, said that while she agreed that the company had to make money, there would be little profit in a world that has become so degraded that it ceased to function. She said that all AMEC workers that had families owed it to their children to change the company as soon as reasonably possible and place it on a more sustainable path.

Jason Rowley later said that before that session sustainable development was not on the radar of the company, nor was it in the vocabulary. Lindsey Forrester, now AMEC's sustainable development manager, was representing the civil engineering part of the company at the time of the event. She was interested in sustainability issues, but previously when she tried to raise them with her colleagues, their 'eyes glazed over'.

Of course, AMEC did not change overnight, but it wasn't far off. By March 2002, the company produced its first sustainability report, and in 2005 it was listed as sector leader in the Dow Jones Sustainability Index. This rapid rise started with a worldwide survey of the company that asked what environmental and social issues were most important to their business.

Next, a leadership team was set up to co-ordinate the information and feedback that was beginning to be generated. The sustainability report was based on the seven most prominent issues raised in the survey. Rarely, for a large multinational, AMEC took the United Nations Agenda 21 process as its guide. It allowed country and sector variations, but also produced some basic principles such as a commitment to human rights. This was vital for a company that operated in places such as East Timor during the conflict there.

The idea to allow variation across the company on the sustainability theme came from the NCBS/Kandu session. Lindsey Forrester recalls that many people took away different things from the session. For some it was a very practical desire to understand their impacts, while others wanted to organise more effectively, and went on to integrate sustainability into their existing health and safety, and quality systems. Some found that they wanted to be proud of their company, and to make sure that it avoided being cast as a pariah. Forrester said that

*none of us had ever seen anything like the NCBS/Kandu session before. Many thought that sustainable development was too big a subject and often got lost in the agenda. We never understood the power of feeling until that day. After the session, there was an overriding desire to be part of the solution, and not the problem.*

The PVC and AMEC experiences had confirmed to the NCBS/Kandu team that they had developed a method to unlock awareness in audiences that were certainly not predisposed to the message that they needed to change their behaviour. It was exciting work, and was both fun and risky. But most of all it was rewarding. Over the next seven years, the two organisations would collaborate to help very different organisations that had widely different challenges.

The continuous reworking of the technique revealed that it could be used as a common thread to link very different groups. One example of this was an event that sought to bring health practitioners together with regeneration workers and town planning professionals. Following the successful election promises made by the Labour Party in 1997, the National Health Service was in the process of planning for a massive injection of investment that would replace old buildings, and recruit and train many more staff.

Meanwhile, northern cities like Leeds, Manchester and Newcastle were experiencing rapid rates of regeneration, and schools were being completely rebuilt. The two worlds of health and regeneration rarely coincided in the midst of this rapid change, but they were struggling to find a common language in order to work together and combine their skills to better effect.

From the preliminary discussion, getting a meaningful dialogue between the two sets of professionals was not going to be easy. Their language, protocols and procedures, funding regimes and legal and political systems were all totally different. And yet a sustainable urban environment needed a health system that served the new environment, and the built environment had a direct effect on the heath of its inhabitants. They needed to talk.

This time the Forum piece set out a storyline that, on initial viewing, appeared to be a two-hander between a woman living in a sink estate (the term refers to underinvested housing developments where public authorities place the underprivileged) and her doctor. The woman complains about the lack of amenities, her problems accessing public transport, her housing conditions, her respiratory problems and her fear of crime. In response to every problem the doctor proscribes a government policy, a strategy document, or an investment promise.

Returning to a more classical Boal-type format, the action was then restarted and the audience invited to explain what the doctor should have said. Inevitably, the participant's more technical understanding leads to them being invited out of the audience, donning the white coat and mirrored headband and taking the stage in place of the actors. After the Forum session, the conversation flowed freely between the two sets of practitioners.

A session for the building construction and management firm Bucknall Austin started with a brief for NCBS to help them to ensure that the whole senior management team understood and believed in the company decision to specialise in sustainable construction and facility management. It ended in a raucous affair, with the chairman's impersonation of a man from Cape Verdi, using a tie wrapped around his head as a prop. Bucknall Austin had just undergone a difficult management buyout. Its core business was construction management, quantity and building surveying, and facilities management. It operated primarily in the retail, commercial, hotel and leisure sectors, and had managed to retain some high-profile clients, including the furniture retailer IKEA, during its change of ownership.

The new Board knew it wanted to build a unique selling point, and they were committed to advising their clients to build more sustainable structures. However, their staff had yet to accept that this was a sensible move, wishing instead to stick to the methods that they knew and understood. The NCBS was asked to help them to understand and embrace the proposed change of emphasis in the company.

The Forum piece for this event started as a more conventional role-play idea, but NCBS/Kandu wanted something more from the session. Their brief was to help resistant staff to willingly take on the sustainable advisor role, but there was a lack of confidence in many of the staff that hindered this transition. It was an unspoken feeling that going it alone (without a parent company) was scary enough, but to change marketing direction was beyond the pale. The session designer knew that if this wasn't tackled, the sustainability message would be lost.

The audience assembled in a Birmingham hotel and was divided into groups of five or six people. As usual they were taken through a few exercises that helped them to understand that they shared more personal values than they thought. This was something that the Kent TNS group had talked about, and both NCBS and Kandu continue to do this in both their joint and individual projects. Later, both would develop the idea of shared sustainable values in their own separate ways, a theme that is discussed further in Chapter 8.

Next, the groups were invited to play a giant board game. Based on snakes and ladders, the game required a die to be rolled, moving the team piece up the board. Then a separate card for each team was picked, which contained a task to explain an element of sustainable business practice. Each group then acted out their idea in front of their peers and the NCBS/Kandu judges. Bonus points were awarded for the best execution of the task.

The competitive nature of the participants ensured full commitment to the game, but it was the sheer ingenuity and creativity that ensured the game fizzed with enthusiasm. It was of course laced all the way through with a lot of leg-pulling and constant laughter. Each round ended with the positive reinforcement of the effort, but also the factual basis behind the tasks.

In this case, the NCBS/Kandu collaboration dispensed with the initial play, and gave vent to Boal's intention to remove the barriers between actor and audience. In effect, the Bucknall Austin team addressed their anxieties about sustainability by writing their own script, and conquered their concerns through laughter and teamwork. The insecurity that they were not up to the challenge of bringing sustainability into their company was eased by the obvious ability to give the right answers to the tasks in a creative, yet competitive manner.

Phil Higham, who was on the Board of the new company and commissioned the event, later said that it was probably the best team event the company had ever held. Not only did the managers get a clearer understanding about what the Board meant by sustainable construction, but it allowed the team to feel that the subject was 'exciting, and not a hair-shirt subject to be bolted onto their core business services'.

Finally, yet another variation on the NCBS/Kandu method was devised when NCBS was asked to give a speech on sustainable development to the entire staff of a Liverpool housing association as part of an away day. A large marquee (seating over 200 people) was set up in a Liverpool park.

The first question for the NCBS/Kandu team was whether it was possible to involve so many people in the Forum experience. The plan to ensure that happened was borrowed from the AMEC scenario, in that the whole of the audience was invited to be an interview panel for a new member of staff. The post holder would become the new regeneration officer for a former mining colony on another planet.

There were three candidates. Two were the normal cartoons, a man that just wanted to build new houses and fill them with paying tenants, and a woman that wanted to care for every tenet and use every green technology. A third candidate went just a little further than the housing association's existing sustainability initiatives. For this event the middle ground was important. Plus Housing's Chief Executive Ken Perry had done a good job in making sure that his vision for a new breed of housing association had been understood and accepted throughout the organisation. There was no need to challenge the audience into thinking about the issues. What Perry needed was reinforcement and refreshment of this policy from a new perspective.

Housing associations form the bulk of what are known as Registered Social Landlords, or RSLs in the UK. The associations have been around as philanthropic providers of housing since the mid-nineteenth century. They are run as businesses, but they do not trade for profit. Any surplus is ploughed back into the organisation to maintain existing homes, and to help finance new ones.

Generally, people housed by RSLs are those defined as being in 'housing need', but eligibility criteria differ. Some RSLs, for instance, specialise in providing housing for those who need special support such as people with mental illness or drug problems (www.direct.gov.uk). RSLs grew rapidly in the 1980s and 1990s after the Thatcher government made it financially difficult for local authorities to hold onto public housing stock. Many associations inherited public sector housing managers who considered that their responsibilities began and ended by providing cheap houses. Tenant welfare and the nature and standard of maintenance of that housing were often secondary considerations at this time.

More enlightened leaders of these associations, like Ken Perry, took the social mission more seriously, and considered that the reduction of their environmental impacts was part of this responsibility. Ken's aim for the away day was to help his staff see that they could contribute to this in a variety of ways, and that it was not the sole province of management to think about these issues.

A committee was 'volunteered' to sit in the middle of the tent and read out the questions to each of the candidates. Inevitably the audience chose the middle ground candidate, and the session ended with a whole-group discussion about what could be achieved in a sustainable company. In the afternoon staff were offered a range of environmental and social responsibility options thought up by Perry and his team.

## Positive movement and the creation of space

The lesson from the NCBS/Kandu Forum Theatre work is not that every leader of an organisation needs to contact their local drama group and prepare to throw off their inhibitions. Not only would that not work, but it is unrealistic to expect this to happen in the kind of numbers needed to make a significant dent in the current slow pace of sustainable change. For every leader of an organisation that agreed to the Forum Theatre approach, there were probably 10 that opted for a more conventional delivery, such as a speech or a workshop. For every one of those there are probably thousands that have never given a single thought to engaging their workforce in a meaningful discussion about sustainability and their role in making it happen. It is also fair to say that those that did agree to the Forum approach were probably not entirely aware of what they were getting themselves into.

The real lesson from the NCBS/Kandu experience is that employees always respond well to the cocktail of facts and feelings served up by this approach. The approach never diminished the facts; they are all there to be heard and assimilated. However, they are offered in a form that human beings prefer to receive.

The escapism of theatre allows the consideration of possibilities without the 'reality' of existing constraints. The use of humour, and the experience of laughter, bends the message from the earnest and obligatory to the interesting and provocative. Above all, the involvement of an audience in a drama, whether they are following a storyline or drawing reaction from each other in the ensuing debate, keys into the emotions. All of this has a positive effect on the audience. The kindling of emotion, experienced in a communal context and associated with a call to take action, is often what is missing in campaigns that are meant to lead us to more sustainable behaviour. The realisation that as individuals we can make a difference is a powerful positive feeling, and explains the success of the NCBS/Kandu approach.

It will take many more and braver business leaders to put this into effect, and is important to remember Ray Anderson's reading of the modern business leader as analytical objective, numbers orientated, factual, and result-driven people. This may be the reason why theatre-based initiatives are still fairly rare in the workplace. However, the positive aspects generated by the engagement of human emotion in the workplace is precisely why the new generation of sustainable motivation techniques are likely to be successful.

## Our common thread

There is an exercise that anyone can try. It can be done around a pub or a din-ner party table, or in a room full of employees. The audience is told that in a moment they will be asked to close their eyes and wait to hear a word from the facilitator. When they hear the word, they need to search for and hold onto the first image that comes into their head. They are then invited to close their eyes and the facilitator says the word. The word is sustainability. At this point, no dis-cussion has been conducted around the word sustainability. As it is a word that has come to be associated with an agenda, and not an object or a dictionary defi-nition, it is never completely obvious what people will see.

When the audience has had a while to conjure up the picture, the facilitator asks them to 'live' in their picture, to look around, take a deep breath. The audi-ence is then asked to open their eyes. When asked what they saw a remarkable pattern emerges. A very few, but there is always at least one, see a polluted or despoiled scene, such as the burning oil fields in the wake of the first Gulf War in Kuwait.

A few more see a technological solution, which is almost always wind tur-bines, but can be solar panels, or even a bicycle. Sometimes, particularly with audiences where women are in the majority, people see a scene with family and children. Well over 85 per cent see a pristine natural environment. Common visions are snow-capped mountains, rippling fields of wheat, sun-drenched river valleys, and lots and lots of trees and forests. This pattern is repeated over and over again. It does not matter if they are inner city kids, Bangladeshi business-men, large corporate executives or members of a food co-operative, it is always the same.

Some discount the exercise as mere word association – but association with what? Why should the interdependency and balance between social, environmen-tal and economic factors translate consistently into a big old pine tree? Regardless of why the association is so consistent, the exercise has two very important lessons for the audience. The first is that it is often a revelation, and then a huge comfort, for people to discover that they have more in common with their colleagues than they thought.

One of the most difficult negative emotions to overcome in the push to encourage people into better and more sustainable behaviour is their fear that acting differently will invite scorn or derision by others. It is often said that Britain is the only place where you actually can die of embarrassment. However, to varying degrees this is true in many countries, and the concern about the 'loss of face' is very strong in Middle and Far Eastern cultures. If you know that your neighbour is thinking what you are thinking, then this fear is diminished.

The second and more powerful lesson comes when the audience is asked how they felt when they were invited to dwell in their self-generated virtual natural environment. Most, without fail, say they felt secure, comforted, positive and happy. Producing those feelings of well-being in an audience is always useful for subsequent exercises, as the non-verbal and self-generated 'feeling' of sustainability is worth more than one hundred definitions.

There is another advantage in inviting people to close their eyes and think about sustainability. The majority of people later welcome the opportunity to close their eyes because they say it gives them the time and space, even if it was just a minute or two, to think about the issues around quality of life, and to experience that feeling of joy, coupled with an absence of anxiety or fear for the future. This is something we will come back to later in this chapter. It also explains to some degree why the transporting aspect of theatre works so well in this context.

Most people appreciate the opportunity to have a little time and space to contemplate and be reflective. They are often quite pleasantly surprised to find that they are experiencing positive emotions. Dread of listening to the usual depressing lecture by a sustainable development practitioner is quite common. Even those that support positive sustainable action would not volunteer to hear about the end of the world as we know it. The thing is, corporate gatherings on this topic are not full of volunteers. The audience is 'encouraged' or instructed to be at the meeting, which is an even harder sell for the speaker.

So the experience of being invited to feel good in one of these sessions, and maybe to laugh a little, is a good start. Why anyone should feel good about standing in the middle of a forest conjured up by their own imagination is an important question to answer. It turns out that it is something that business leaders should consider as a vital aspect in their search for ways to move their companies towards better sustainable performance.

## The rift between man and nature

The link to nature has been important in many of the positive examples of sustainable behaviour displayed by business leaders and cultures. Ray Anderson wept at the thought that mass extinctions caused by habitat loss were leading to 'the death of birth'. Yvon Chouinard was committed to protecting the natural world because of his exposure to the natural grandeur of Yosemite, and his later travels to other wilderness areas. The Swedes would think they had failed as parents if they did not regularly take their kids out into the countryside to pick berries. The trouble is, fewer and fewer people seem to allow themselves to be exposed to the natural world. Watching television programmes about vanishing tigers may lead to a donation to WWF, but it is no substitute for standing in the steaming jungles and watching as illegal logging companies carve away this majestic animal's home.

Of course, it is just not practical to plan for the whole population of the industrialised world to be transported to some beauty spot, and dwell there until they see the error of their unsustainable lives. This is particularly true as more and more people are living apart from nature. The Worldwatch Institute reported that in 2007, for the first time in human history, a majority of people will live in cities. Over 80 per cent of the G8 countries' populations live in urban environments. Every now and again someone does a survey that shows that the majority of urban kids think milk comes from a carton, and not a cow.

We are losing our grip on how the world works and what it should look like when it is healthy. This gap in understanding weakens our ability to connect the over-consumption of resources and the use of fossil fuel with the damage they cause. Well, so what. Would regular exposure to nature really help to convert more people to sustainable behaviour? Is there any evidence to say that nature has the ability to instil or restore the clarity of understanding that can link our actions to its destruction, and ultimately our own?

## Why the connection between our actions and nature's problems matters

Much has been written about man's relationship to nature. Almost every early religion held nature as the focus of spiritual support and worship. James Lovelock (1979, 2006) developed his Gaia theory based on the understanding that the multitude of complex natural interactions across the globe works as a single self-regulating organism. Biologists such as Elisabet Sahtouris (1997) talk about the importance of understanding how the natural processes of the Earth work, and then apply this to our own wayward lives. She says that

*when we humans, after all a very young species, drop our adolescent arrogance of thinking we know it all and read the wisdom in our parent planet's accumulated experience of living systems design, we too will mature as a species, to our own benefit and that of all other species, as well as the planet itself.*

Writing in the mid-eighteenth century Jean-Jacques Rousseau thought that people could never be happy in modern society unless they gave up their possessions, and modern way of life, and went back to living in the natural world.

The ability to rediscover or fall in love with nature has been covered by many writers, none more eloquently than Edward O Wilson (2002). In his book *The Future of Life*, Wilson describes a species-wide attraction to certain forms of nature as the acquisition of biophilia. While this is not so strong that we 'ambulate like robots to the nearest lakeside meadow' he describes how we do respond in remarkable ways to being exposed to natural scenes and surroundings. Wilson cites numerous studies where gazing upon nature leads to faster recovery for those experiencing both mental and physical health problems. Often this exposure is achieved simply by opening the curtains, but remarkably even a painting or a photograph can have a significant effect on the patient.

The effect is not universal. Famously, Woody Allen once said 'I am at two with nature'. Wilson (2002) explains that some avoid nature because of what lurks therein (spiders, snakes, bats and insects) and keep within the city limits. Wilson explains that most of these 'biophobias' occur before the age of 10, and are formed during an impressionable period of life. Wilson also observes that the clear felling of dense wood throughout human history cannot be explained by the need for arable land alone. He says that humans like to see where the predators are coming from, and are worried by landscapes that could provide cover for animals that might be a threat to their safety. This, however, does not detract from the fact that most humans have a desire to be out in nature.

Taking all this to its organised conclusion, the strong feelings of unity for the planet and the universe lead some to become pantheists. The website for some of these believers (www.pantheism.net) confirms that pantheism is 'an emotional response to the world around us' and has two elements. The first is 'a sense of awe, wonder, reverence and acceptance of the natural universe, based on its power and beauty and mystery'. The second is 'a sense of belonging, of community with the starry skies, with all living beings and with our own bodies. This sense is the basis for statements about the unity of all things, and about the unity of the individual with the whole'.

This will make sense to those who have come to feel a strong personal and spiritual union with the natural world, but will leave those who haven't more than a little cold. Thinking again about our cynical and sarcastic construction sector workers, there would need to be a huge jump in perception even to convince these people that the pantheists were serious, never mind getting them to consider the substance of their argument. However, even the hardest nut in the bag would probably be able to relate at least one story from their own experience when they gazed out onto a natural scene and felt moved in some way. Midgley (1979) says that 'though we have been educated to detach ourselves from the physical matter of our planet as something alien to us, this detachment is still not a natural or necessary attitude to us'.

## We are not in Kansas anymore

A strategy to use nature as a sustainable change persuader must start from an acceptance that the current parlous state of the world has reached a point at which it is becoming visible to ordinary citizens. If people can't see it, they can't react to its destruction. But many commentators and practitioners are now saying that big changes are starting to take place in the global population. Hawken (2007) thinks that

*the world is fast reaching a 'we-are-not-in-Kansas-anymore' moment whether it realises it or not. Although the scale of the environmental and social breakdown is so vast it isn't possible for any individual or institution to be fully informed about it, the warning signs are omnipresent.*

Most of the awareness is due to regular media reports of impending disaster as a result of climate change, natural resource depletion (such as forests and fisheries), and the implications of an unplanned release of genetically modified organisms. However, even if it were possible to give everyone first-hand experience of this loss, and convince them that the damage was (in part) their fault, it is highly unlikely that the experience would have a permanent effect on behaviour.

Consider the farming community. While they understand how nature affects the land better than anyone, they have not been in the forefront of demands to reduce the burning of fossil fuels. No doubt some rural dwellers are calling for these changes, but they are certainly not a dominant force in any society. Simple exposure may have a calming, inspiring, and even healing effect on people, but there clearly need to be a few more ingredients before the recipe is complete. One ingredient may be the requirement to move from appreciation and concern to something that generates a more compelling need to protect.

## Awe of nature as a motivator

The sense of awe and wonder about the Earth should, intuitively, help people to put their own lives, businesses, and decisions into perspective. If that awe is converted into feelings of stewardship and a personal sense of responsibility, then this could generate a compelling desire to protect. If there is a clear link between an individual's own actions, and the effect that these have on the natural world, then this would be a positive incentive to act in a sustainable manner. Admittedly, there are a number of leaps in that cascade of logic.

To start at the top again, it is possible to find very persuasive arguments that can link the natural world to our daily lives. A compelling example of this can be found in Robert Macfarlane's (2003) explanation of why mountains have such a profound effect on our psyche. He says that

*mountains seem to answer an increasing imaginative need in the West. More and more people are discovering a desire for them, and a powerful solace in them. At bottom, mountains, like all wildernesses, challenge our complacent conviction – so easy to lapse into – that the world has been made for humans by humans. Most of us exist for most of the time in a world which is humanly arranged, themed and controlled. One forgets that there are environments which do not respond to the flick of a switch or the twist of a dial, and which have their own rhythms and orders of existence. Mountains correct this amnesia. By speaking of greater forces than we can possibly invoke, and by confronting us with a greater span of time than we can possible envisage, mountains refute our excessive trust in the man-made. They pose profound questions about our durability and the importance of our schemes. They induce, I suppose, modesty in us.*

Reading Macfarlane's account makes it easy to see where Yvon Chouinard's passion comes from. It also points to an interesting clue about the ease with which humans deny environmental destruction. The immodesty or arrogance that comes from the belief that human beings are the undisputed champions of nature could easily block out the question of durability that Macfarlane mentions. Experiencing the awe of nature could have the ability to benevolently take human kind down a proverbial peg or two, allowing the reflection needed for a change of direction to take place. As Macfarlane suggests, the impact of mountains can instil a 'priceless capacity for wonder which can so insensibly be leached away by modern existence ...'.

Paul Hawken, Karl-Henrick Robèrt, Ray Anderson, Jonathon Porritt and many others have, for some time, used astounding and counter-intuitive facts about life on Earth to influence their audiences. At the very least this makes it impossible for the listener to take the world for granted, at least for a while. At best it helps them to change their attitudes about the way they treat it forever.

A selection of facts that you might see in their speeches, writings and courses include:

- there is more biomass below the soil surface of the Earth than above it;
- one quadrillion cells make up a human being, and 90 per cent of them are bacteria, fungi, yeasts, and other microbes;
- some desert tortoises have allegiances to small habitat ranges that have lasted upward of 40 000 years, dwarfing any dynasty in China;
- if the history of the Earth was compressed into a six-day period, man moves from hunter–gatherer to farmer at 1.2 seconds to midnight on the last day;
- 35 per cent of the Earth's land vertebrates and 44 per cent of its plant species are limited to 1.4 per cent of its land surface (about the land mass of Alaska and Texas put together). These are contained within about 25 sites, and have now been reduced to 10 per cent of their pre-human levels;
- if the Earth were a basketball, the biosphere – the part of the Earth (land, water and air) within which life occurs – would be about as thick as the paint on the outside of the ball;
- every animal cell simultaneously conducts millions of molecular processes involving trillions of atoms, far outstripping the capabilities of any man-made microprocessor;
- extinction rates are 1000 higher than they were during pre-human times. While 1.4 million species have been described, the number thought to be living on the planet is somewhere between 10 and 100 million.

## Valuing nature

Why do some people appreciate being in nature so much, and respond so strongly when it is under threat? Work by Shultz and Tabanico (2007) shows that for many people the primary motivation is to further their own egocentric interests. However, they say that some people feel a concern for other living things, a condition they call 'ecocentric'. This concern could be for other people, but it could be for other animals or plants. They do this because they feel an inclusive sense of self and identify with the natural environment.

The socio-environmental organisation ValuingNature (www.valuingnature. org), responding to a presentation that Tom Shultz gave to WWF-UK, commented that few environmentalists would take this tack to lead a campaign, probably because they would be worried that the message would sound like soft, hippy philosophy, and could be open to ridicule. However, if an environmental campaign did try to appeal to people's affinity for nature, then it would be a strategy that any advertising executive would immediately recognise. This is the strategy of getting people to identify with the goods they want them to buy.

With this egocentric vs. ecocentric division in mind, ValuingNature.org explored how best to motivate people to behave in a more sustainable manner. Three choices are suggested. First, you could ignore the ecocentric minority and try a range of incentives and disincentives that are targeted at the self-interested. This could range from money-saving opportunities through to increases in tax and pricing on unsustainable goods and services. Some may be targeted on self-esteem where unsustainable products are demonised and ridiculed to the extent that they are traded in for a more sustainable alternative.

The second option is to use ecocentric reasoning on the egocentric. This will only be effective if the target of the campaign is made to feel very guilty. This must be a gamble at best, as it would be difficult to pick out the issues that are sufficiently morally loaded to stop the self-interested in their tracks. As values and morals differ from person to person, this approach would always affect some, but would be unlikely to result in a significant change in behaviour for the majority.

The third option involves the belief that almost everybody has either an unconscious or conscious but unarticulated bond with nature. If this could be made more explicit, then environmental campaigns could appeal to the majority and not the minority. While it is unclear how this might be achieved, it infers that environmental campaigns to date are trying to beat the retailer at their own game by appealing to the self-interested on a product-by-product basis. If Shultz is right (and he admits in a later communication to ValuingNature.org that he is continuing to research this point), then consumers can be reached through their in-built empathy with the environment. If buying green gets personal, then concern for nature becomes an extension of the self.

## Awe, empathy and the workplace

Companies have a fairly traditional view of how to use nature to improve the productivity of their workforce. Corporate retreats, or away-day trips, generally fall into two categories. The most common is the team-building event, where a group of people that are associated with a business or a department are encouraged to solve challenging problems in a challenging environment.

The countryside surroundings may appeal to some, but the general idea is to remove the group from their comfortable and familiar environment, and to offer them a problem to solve that is often physically as well as mentally demanding. They might have to cover long distances, operate in uncomfortable conditions, and overcome physical obstacles. The course designers would hope that the stress and endurance that the experience generates will draw out leadership qualities in some, trust between all, and bond the group together in the face of adversity. While this may or may not have the desired effect, the role of nature in these circumstances is mostly to test and not to savour.

The other type of trip uses natural surroundings as the context for broader thinking and planning, or to reward employees who have performed well. These are designed to put employees at ease and to relax them into the right state of mind. For decision-makers, the role of the remote setting is to remove them from the day-to-day distractions of the office, so they can focus on what they came there to do. A little pampering is generally the order of the day, and opportunities to fish, run or play golf are often available, as well as some very pleasant settings. While very relaxing, the venues are more like luxury hotels than a place to experience nature. Some may argue that a little of the grandeur will rub off on the employees sent to these destinations, but this would be a passive, not an active, influence.

However, there are some organisations that employ nature in a much more influential manner. The John Muir Trust (a UK-wide organisation with its base in Scotland) runs an award scheme for both individuals and employees. An 'enhanced environmental awareness within organisations' is listed among the benefits for companies that put their employees through the programme (www.jmt.org). While organisations arrange for groups of employees to do the John Muir Award, each individual participant engages in four 'challenges' including: 'discover a wild place; explore its wilderness; conserve a wild place; and share your experiences.'

Many elements of the award reflect John Muir's own experiences. For example, he was not only keen to explore new areas, but he also wanted to see familiar places in a new light. This means that it is not necessary to travel for days to a desolate point. A park or garden would also suffice provided that the experience allows the participant to 'tune in …, understand, and appreciate more about it' (www.jmt.org). The conservation element could involve physical clean-up, but might also involve a campaign, research, or fundraising. The award handbook reinforces this point by quoting Muir's belief that

*it is not enough for people to be in sympathy with the plight of the natural world, they must become 'active conservationists', as campaigners, as practical project workers, as scientists, as artists, as writers.*

The last element – 'sharing your experiences' – has proved to be one of the more powerful parts of the award. It is one thing to do something for a personal impression, but quite another to try to express that to others. The award scheme allows participants to do this in any media they want, from photographs and drawings to guided walks and drama or poetry. Each expression is personal, and it leads the participant to draw a direct line between themselves and the world around them.

The award takes its inspiration from John Muir's passion to get people out into nature, but its structure comes from an educational model developed by Patrick Geddes. Geddes (1854–1932), another Scot, was a botanist and an educator who also took a keen interest in the formation of successful communities. He is also widely acknowledged as the father of town planning. He was firmly of the opinion that the tightly controlled teaching methods of the Victorian era were hindering the learning process. His views on learning were grounded in the belief that in order to truly understand something it had to be experienced, and that education should therefore be based on the three Hs: 'head, heart, and hand'.

The John Muir Award has adopted this idea, and expresses it by saying that the 'heart' develops 'strong feelings about nature, or about a particular place – people will care about it, want to know more, and want to do something to protect it'. The 'head' leads people to

*understand and develop knowledge about nature and wilderness, the interdependence of living systems, and the threats to wild places – this will encourage a sense of responsibility and stronger feelings.*

Finally, the 'hand' enables people to 'get actively involved and take practical action for a place or issue – a sense of "putting something back" helps people to enjoy and value the experience more'.

The John Muir Trust will appeal to companies that want to offer employees the option of an active environmental protection experience. The award will inevitably offer the same 'challenge' in an outdoor setting, but in a more supportive context, compared to the classic tough task methods of the team-building event. The award also centres on the individual first, and then the organisation, rather than a more overt attempt to bond disparate members of a group.

It is therefore possible to build teams for competitive advantage using nature as a backdrop, and equally possible to find good nature programmes to help companies invest in the environment. However, it is harder to find programmes that directly link nature to competitive advantage. It is rare to find a company that combines exposure to nature with a discussion about what it would mean to run a truly sustainable business.

One company that is rapidly moving towards this position is Impact International. Founded by David Williams, for over 20 years the company has offered training and development courses to the corporate world. Williams was originally influenced by an Outward Bound course that he said changed his life, because it made him re-evaluate his priorities, his job and his outlook.

While Williams always had a great respect and love for the environment, the issue of the 'sustainable enterprise' did not really start to impinge on the core business until corporate social responsibility prompted Impact's clients to divulge their environmental and social policies. Like many businesses, the commitment to being a responsible organisation was implicit in the Founder's mind and behaviour, but not explicit enough to prove how this was done on a day-to-day basis. The company soon put this right, and Impact's current literature now says that it works with organisations to become 'sustainable enterprises'.

The process involves 'organisational change leading to new innovative business propositions'. The reality of their offer ranges from leading sessions in the middle of the English Lake District to bringing groups out to countries in Africa and Asia, and helping them work with local communities. They pride themselves on leading their clients by example, and have won many prizes for best small company including a 'Great Place to Work' (a Financial Times award) in the UK and Europe.

Recently, Impact has worked with Sharon Jackson of Carlton CSR to show clients both the stunning beauty and the aftermath of mining and clear-felling on the island of Tasmania. Programmes with the financial institutions Deutche Bank and Swiss Re have also raised the issues of sustainable development and its consequences for financial institutions in ways that go much further than previous programmes.

Andy Dickson, Head of UK and European Customer Solutions, explains that for a long time Impact was aware of nature and used its power to add emphasis to their training, but may not have thought all that deeply about precisely what part it played in the learning and enlightenment process. Now he has a theory influenced partly by a strand of neuro-linguistic programming (NLP), and partly by observing one of his own exercises.

Dickson had come across the concept of 'Neurological Levels' developed by Robert Dilts (2003). Dilt's model looks like a pyramid, with environment as the base followed by layers of behaviour, skills and knowledge, values and beliefs and identity. His contention is that everything from day-to-day behaviour, through to the perception of who we think we are, is informed by our environment. When Dilts talked about 'environment' he did not mean nature. He was talking about a person's immediate surroundings, at work, at home, in church, etc. Dilts explains that environmental influences shape experience and that 'the decisions that people make, and the resources that they choose to mobilise, are often the result of the environment in which people perceive or assume they are acting'. However, Dickson considers that an identification with nature as the ultimate 'environment' context could have as profound an effect on identity.

Dickson took this theoretic explanation and applied it to an exercise that Impact does with senior company leaders. The leaders are taken individually to the top of a hill with a beautiful view. They are given a canvass shelter, and the means to brew tea, and nothing else. Then they are left there for three or four hours. Dickson says that when they come to collect these captains of industry, it is not uncommon to see that the experience has had a profound effect on them, and some of them are in tears.

It would be tempting, but a stretch, to say that those executives were shocked into re-evaluating their priorities because they felt humble in the presence of the grandeur of nature. Dickson thinks that something else is going on here; it has more to do with the combination of being alone with yourself, beginning to throw off the familiar environmental contexts and starting to assimilate a new and more powerful context, based on the natural world. Take a person who is under constant pressure to perform at work, while simultaneously maintaining a successful and fulfilling private life and plunge him into nature, and it is hardly surprising that the opportunity to reflect in humbling surroundings causes an emotional response.

While this is valid, and very good to know and understand, particularly for personal development professionals, it does not move the argument towards a definitive conclusion about the role of nature in shifting human behaviour and, ultimately, identity. Conceivably, it would be possible to immerse someone in any non-distracting alien environment, give them the time and space to reconnect with themselves, and expect this to have the same effect as perching them on the top of a hill. Anyone that has experienced an emotional response to meditation would understand this.

Equally, if people's life changing and confidence-building experiences are more to do with problem-solving in a different and challenging environment, then they could be meeting that challenge almost anywhere as long as it was away from a familiar setting. This is supported by one of Impact's projects that sought to unlock self-belief in a group of farmers. The group was taken out of the countryside and challenged to make designer T-shirts. The farmer's initial reaction to the challenge was hostility and fear. But this turned to delight as they learned to master a new skill, and create something new. It would not be difficult to imagine that if they took a group of T-shirt designers to a farm and challenged them to shear sheep, then exactly the same result would have been achieved in reverse.

However, if a permanent shift is to be achieved, then it would seem to be essential that a different way of thinking about the world would have to occur to every individual. This would lead to living and working in a sustainable manner, with a clear understanding of the effect every decision had on the wider world. We are talking here about a specific empathy for environmental and social conditions, or ecocentricity as Schultz puts it. Intuitively this makes sense, and yet the precise role that nature can play in this process is hard to find. The key may be in looking at nature, not as an active influence, but as a potent passive force on the human mind.

## Nature as context

There is obviously evidence that some people feel a natural affinity to nature, and that bringing employees out into nature has had some beneficial effects on both their productivity and their loyalty to the company. However, the belief that we can make this minority affinity to nature more explicit for the majority has to be more in hope than expectation. Sure, everyone likes a good day out, but that is very different to deciding that your nice new 4 × 4 is a crime against your inner self. Even if the key to nature's door could be found, it would probably take too long to get humanity to file through the threshold, only to find they were too late to save what was inside.

It would be a terrible mistake, given this reluctant but realistic conclusion, to give up on nature as a tool to positively influence people to become more sustainable. Its lure and power probably can't work on its own, but without it the direct link is lost. One of the things that we have learned from looking at how business leaders have become more sustainable is that they, and by inference everybody else, need first-hand experiences.

And so we have a paradox. We could bring everyone in the world out to gaze upon a mountain or a wilderness scene, but even if this were possible, most might enjoy the experience but would not necessary make the connection between their lives and what they see. They would be unlikely to be permanently moved to change their ways. But without nature in the equation, the task of showing people what they are damaging makes the explanation of why sustainability is so important that bit harder to achieve, and it is pretty difficult as it is.

The answer to this conundrum may lie in Malcolm Gladwell's (2000) book *The Tipping Point*, and what he calls 'context' in particular. Gladwell's proposition is that far from thinking that major changes in perception and achievement are hard to influence, it really only takes the conjunction of a few elements, working together, to tip the balance and change the situation. He explains that there are three main ingredients in his recipe for success. First, you need particular kinds of people that are good at starting what he calls 'word-of-mouth epidemics'. The people he identifies are well connected, or have a vast store of knowledge, or are excellent communicators. Some may have a combination of these abilities.

The second is the 'easy to say, harder to do' task of making an idea memorable. Gladwell calls this the 'stickiness factor'. In the context of sustainable change, a sticky idea would ensure that manufacturers designing a product would remember that some of the materials and methods of production would be more damaging than others. Shoppers would remember that different products would have arrived on the shelf in different ways, depending on the manner in which they were grown or fabricated, how far they had come from the point of production, and how they were packaged. They might even recall how they could be recycled once they had come to the end of their function.

Nature comes into the third factor; the 'power of context'. He gives two examples illustrating how context influences change. The first is the effectiveness of new ideas when they are shared within groups of up to, but not beyond, 150 people. He argues that beyond this number it is difficult to gain enough of the personal experience that comes with the familiarity of people involved in the idea. With less familiarity comes less trust, and trust is a vital part of accepting and adopting new ideas.

Gladwell's other type of context relates to reinforcing conditions in which different kinds of behaviour can develop and take hold. He illustrates this with the 'broken windows' strategy used to bring New York's crime epidemic from record levels in the 1980s and early 1990s, to the significant decline in violent crime by the mid-1990s.

The broken windows strategy was the idea of criminologists George Kelling and James Q Wilson. It was based on the observation that if a window was broken and left un-repaired, then anyone who was passing and noticed this would assume that nobody cared about the property. This would lead to vandalism that could spread to other buildings, leading to the assumption that any bad behaviour will go unpunished. Extrapolated to a whole city, minor transgressions such as graffiti on public property, aggressive begging, and littering represented the broken window, and violent crime and murder is the most extreme product of the assumption that nobody cares about bad behaviour.

The strategy adopted by the city reversed the trend by starting with the assumption that all bad behaviour should be unpunished, thus starving the more extreme bad behaviour of the oxygen of neglect. Creating an environment that says, 'we (society) all care about where and how we live', sends a powerful signal to those that may not share all of the values that shun bad behaviour, but makes it clear that acting differently is not an acceptable choice. This supports Dilts' (2003) idea that the immediate environment can ultimately influence how individuals sees themselves.

Nature has the potential to be the mended window for those people who have not really thought about the effect that their actions could have on the wider world. If nature can inspire in the ways that we have already seen, then it also has the potential to overturn some of the defeatism about the ability of humans to exhibit sustainable behaviour. Gladwell, talking about the pessimism expressed about reducing crime, says that 'once you understand that context matters, and that specific and relatively small elements in the environment can serve as Tipping Points, that defeatism is turned upside down'.

Using nature as a context for sustainable change is particularly relevant when helping those who need an explanation about their role in reversing the environmental and social ills of the world. Those that are already aware, but carry on regardless, are more likely to respond to egocentric forms of influencing. However, there are many who are not committed to sustainable change right now, but could be, given the right information. Explaining sustainability to a crowd of people in a soulless city-centre hotel room is better than not explaining it at all. But as we have seen, both in the reaction of leaders like Yvon Chouinard, and the employees working with the John Muir Trust and Impact, if you are in the middle of nature and you come to understand how the world works, surrounded and positively inspired by its grandeur and its vulnerability, it tends to stay with you for the rest of your life.

# 9

# It's values and emotions, stupid!

## Two Formula 1 racing car drivers stood at the gates of heaven

A room full of people wait for the speaker to be introduced. They know they are going to hear something about sustainability. They may all be from the same company, or public sector body, or they may be an invited audience working for a range of different organisations. Some will be looking forward to the presentation while others may be thinking 'here we go again', and dreading sitting through the grim message from another prophet of doom.

The speaker starts by addressing those people that were expecting to be thoroughly depressed by what they were about to hear. He says that he would be happy to fulfil their expectations, and launches into a catalogue of environmental and social crisis facing the world today. He talks about the three or four planets that would be needed if every person in the world consumes resources at the same rate as the Europeans or the Americans. He explains that just 2 per cent of the world's military budget is required to give every person on the planet basic healthcare and education, that greenhouse gases have increased by 70 per cent since 1970, and that Alpine glaciers have been reduced by 50 per cent in the last 150 years.

He goes on to point out that one in four mammals on the planet are now endangered, and that less than 300 people have the same aggregate wealth of the poorest 2.5 billion people on the planet. He tells them that over 1000 man-made chemicals have been found in polar bear milk, and that in 2003 the US power generation industry spent less on research and development as a proportion of turnover than the country's pet food industry. He finishes by saying that every man, woman and child in the UK throws away an average of £420 worth of food that was bought but never consumed, and that it is likely that money markets and the insurance industry will be increasingly destabilised by the severe conditions brought on by climate chaos.

He pauses and looks at the audience. They don't look happy. He asks how they all feel, and whether their mood has darkened in the last few minutes as a result of what they heard. Most raise their hands. He then asks whether what they have just heard will now result in them changing their work, or personal habits, to make the world more sustainable. Very few put their hands up, although it takes longer for people to decide whether they should. They look like they want to, but honesty keeps their hands in their laps.

The speaker asks them to consider why these facts have not sent them on a headlong dash for the door, and the dynamic action they know is necessary to save the planet. Could it be that they think market forces will ride to the rescue?

He explains that Sir Nicholas Stern, the former World Bank economist, says that dangerous climate change is the result of the worst market failure that has ever been. He asks if they think that technology will save them. He points out that the time lag between the installation of low carbon and renewable energy solutions, and the need to cut greenhouse gas emissions, means that technological solutions alone are not going to be enough to avert disaster. He asks if they worry about spending money on something that they are not sure will happen.

He returns to Stern's *Economics of Climate Change* (2007) which says that it will only cost 1 per cent of global GDP per year to lower carbon emissions enough to solve the problem. The alternative is to keep doing what we are doing, and watch as 5–20 per cent of consumption is wiped off the global economic slate, causing a massive destabilisation of global finances.

He appears to sympathise with an increasingly uncomfortable audience, and says that it is never easy to react to the 'effect' (your house gets flooded) if there is no clear link to the 'cause' (heating your home with fossil fuel). There is no evidence that anyone else is running off to act in a decisive manner, and there are arguments between scientists and politicians about what should be done almost every day, which makes feeling decisive a very difficult thing to achieve.

While the audience is mulling over the fact that this speaker may well have trashed their favourite reasons for not acting sooner in support of radical sustainable change, he asks them if they had considered why other people (not them) have had trouble in coming to terms with the current unsustainable situation. He runs through the cascades of denial including the dialogue between the Native American and the white man, illustrating each excuse with a recent event. When the issue of shooting the messenger comes up, he reminds people of what happened to the NASA scientist Dr Jim Hansen when he dared to say that dangerous climate change was upon us.

At this point he pauses again, and acknowledges that he has not given the audience much cause for hope or optimism, but promises that he will remedy this now. He does the 'close your eyes' exercise with them. Most experience the good feelings associated with what they see in their heads, and are generally surprised to find that most of the people around them saw and felt similar things. He explains that humans (most of them) also have the same taste in tree shapes and landscapes (Wilson, 2002).

He then does another quick poll, and asks them to imagine that they are negotiating with a client or a supplier. They vote on which of the following motivations are uppermost in the other persons mind: environmental factors, social factors, economic factors, or an equal mix of all three. Unanimously they pick the economic factors. Now he asks them what motivates the audience as individuals, and gives them the same four options. The majority vote for a combination of all three. He then asks them what those same clients or suppliers would have said about them in response to the same two questions. He asks them if they recognise the fact that they hold a number of views and values outside work but, once they enter the workplace, these personal values are replaced by corporate ones that seem to favour economic prudence above everything else.

He asks the audience to look at the cards they were asked to fill out before he started to speak. The question on the card reads: 'What was the last thing that made you feel happy?'. He asks if any of their answers had anything to do with money. Only a few put their hands up. He says that while the creation of wealth, and having enough money is obviously important, and particularly so if you are struggling to make a living, what is the point of wealth and profit if it does not bring happiness?

He switches to the story about the two rival Formula 1 racing car drivers. They are standing at the gates of heaven. One has a big grin on his face, and the other turns to him, incredulous, and says, 'we have just driven into a solid wall at 250 km an hour, a wall that many people told us would be there, but we did not listen. What do you have to be happy about?'. The smiling driver replies, 'I was winning when we crashed'.

He moves into the last phase of his talk by asking if they are now agreed that there were few reasons for delaying action to avert what the Intergovernmental Panel on Climate Change calls the 'looming abrupt and irreversible impacts on the world'. Do they accept that if they did take action, they would be supported by many others that share the same values? He suggests the need for them to see the world's problems at first hand, like Lee Scott of Wal-Mart and Rupert Murdoch of News International. He concedes that the short-term political and economic cycles are a big problem, and points out that the choices for sustainable change are numerous, and the advice on the best path is conflicting and confusing.

He then suggests that, while all these things are understandably daunting and apparently insurmountable, really all that is needed is to give the process a nudge. The nudge is in the form of a 'positive incentive'; something that will bring a smile and a sense of positive momentum to their colleagues. It could be a prize, a pay award, a share in savings or profits, or just peer recognition of a job well done. He gives a number of examples of things that other companies have done, and then asks the audience to look at the other questions on their card which read: 'What do you think that you can do to be more sustainable?' and 'Will you do it tomorrow?'. He asks them to consider whether they would feel better if they acted on their idea by the end of the following day, and then he sits down.

# The role of emotion in sustainable change

It seems inconceivable that the engagement of human emotion is so often marginalised in the battle to change people from unsustainable to sustainable behaviour. Both the environmental movement and the business world are reliant on the use of facts and figures to bring the message home that we must act now to protect the environment, and dispense social justice. But people are just not built that way.

We are living in an age where there are many different ways in which humans can extinguish themselves forever. The possibility of nuclear holocaust has been with us for over half a century. An escape of genetically modified organisms and nanotechnology into the biosphere are newer threats, and global warming is the clear and present danger. Anyone thinking about these issues in a meaningful way would be lying to themselves if they were not emotionally engaged with the consequences.

Boal (1979), who understood about motivating an audience, said that 'The important thing about emotion is what it signifies. We cannot talk about emotion without reason or, conversely, about reason without emotion; the former is chaos, the latter pure abstraction'.

Practitioners like Penny Walker (2006), who have been working with small groups to understand sustainable development for many years, have come to understand how emotional responses to the threat of environmental and social catastrophe affect people. She finds that

*broadly, people either feel something, or nothing. The ones who feel something are either energised (they feel courage, curiosity, excitement, motivation) or engaged but disempowered (they feel grief, sadness, fear, impotent anger). The ones who feel nothing seem to be somehow in denial; they have apparently accepted the evidence and the arguments, but they do not believe them. There is a mismatch between intellectual acceptance, emotional response and behaviour change – it's as if people's brains and guts are on different planets.*

When confronted with these emotional participants, her first reaction was to try to calm them with 'trite reassurances'. Later she realised that she needed to recognise them and work with them. She did this by trying to understand why people were reacting in an emotional manner.

She found the research and opinions of Elizabeth Kübler-Ross and George Marshal helpful. Kübler-Ross (1975), working with the terminally ill, described a cascade of five reactions to calamity starting with denial and then moving through anger, bargaining, depression and acceptance. Marshall (2001) wrote about denial and climate change, and said that 'emotional responses are bound to be generated by the subject matter of sustainability, and are important in motivating people to change in the face of dominant trends'.

Using these and other research materials, Walker reviewed her own experience, and concluded that

*the evidence of the crisis can overwhelm some participants with grief, anger or fear. For others, the evidence of the need for change is both too terrifying, and not immediate enough to their own experience, leading to denial phenomena.*

She adds that the need to change behaviour often appears onerous for the individual, but it also occurs to them that their effort will not make a significant difference if they are the only ones that act.

She also makes some interesting observations about what happens when employees leave a workshop on sustainability and return to normal work conditions. She observes that an emotional investment by an employee will be complemented by an organisation that already has a context for sustainable change. However, if this context does not exist, then she concludes that

*in the absence of strong leadership, legislative push and customer pull, then personal motivation (i.e. emotional engagement) is pre-eminent in determining whether change occurs.*

However, Walker warns that where personal motivation meets corporate apathy then a sophisticated understanding of the problems can lead to dissatisfaction with superficial behavioural changes in one's colleagues, and an uncertainty that can generate strong negative emotions.

Walker's experiences with emotion explain what happens when sustainable issues are discussed in an open way with groups of employees. The emotional response is a by-product of learning about, and coming to terms with, the changes that everyone will need to make, both at work and in their private lives. However, it is also important to get employees to articulate, and then to acknowledge their emotional responses to environmental and social threats. To many, this will be an alien concept. The workplace is where we see and act out professional, rational, and cool-headed behaviour. It is a place where decisions are made based on the facts, and businesses are geared to respond to the needs of the customer and to reward the investor shareholders.

This may be the way business managers want to run a business, but it is simply unnatural, and will never overcome the 'denying' and 'deflecting' behaviours associated with unsustainable habits and procedures. Until every employee meets the issues head on, including their emotional response to the possibility of big changes in their way of life due to climate change and other impacts, then it will be very hard to bring teams together to work for a common sustainable purpose. Facts have their place but, as we have already seen, by themselves they don't work for the majority. Similarly, exposure to nature will not work on its own for the majority; and emotional manipulation on its own is more likely to lead to entrenched resentment, rather than real change.

Instead, the approach adopted by the speaker at the start of this chapter may be the way forward. A mixture of fact, emotion, and invited self-reflection, always injected with an element of humour, seems to be right for today's professional audiences. Shock tactics have their place, but the poor level of awareness or acceptance about the range of arguments associated with the sustainability agenda makes it easy for many to discount the thrust of this approach. The question remains whether business leaders will allow emotion, theatre and open discussion into the workplace. The trend to talk about corporate values suggests that there may be a glimmer of hope in this direction.

## The fuzzy world of values

For over 10 years the National Centre for Business & Sustainability (NCBS) has trained professionals in the science and art of social and ethical accounting, auditing and reporting. The five-day course is promoted and overseen by the international organisation AccountAbility that devised AA1000 (www.acountability21.net), the process standard for social accounting. AA1000 was designed to resemble a classic quality cycle, and helps users to

*establish a systematic stakeholder engagement process that generates indicators, targets and reporting systems needed to ensure greater transparency, effective responsiveness and improved overall organisational performance.*

The NCBS method of teaching the course has always been heavily dependent on active learning workshops and role-play. In the final exercise, small groups run through the whole process and devise their own system. Against a company brief, the attendees are required to identify their stakeholders, define their values, identify issues and indicators, explain how information is collected, and explain how stakeholders will be encouraged to participate in the process. Normally a dependable way to summarise the learning from the whole course, the NCBS was surprised to find that this exercise was not going according to plan.

The attendees quickly identified their stakeholders, and then took far too much time on the values. Some never came to a consensus, and a few fell out with each other. The course was amended, and the creation of values was taken out of the list of final tasks and given its own exercise earlier in the week. What the NCBS had discovered was that given an unfamiliar company scenario, a group of people who didn't know each other very well, and the pressure to complete an exercise in a tight time-frame, it was almost impossible to agree on the charged and highly personal businesses of establishing a set of agreed corporate values.

Corporate or business values have attracted a lot of attention over the past 10 to 15 years, and particularly since corporate social responsibility became something that established itself in the lexicon of the business world. The link between values and positively motivating employees to achieve them is vital, but the importance and consistency of the application of corporate values is still very patchy.

An attempt to find a definitive explanation of corporate values, and what they should be, will always lead to an array of different answers. A common and trusted definition of values can be found in the Collins and Porras (1997) book *Built to Last*, which helped to inspire Terry Thomas. This definition states that

*values are the organisation's essential and enduring tenets – a small set of general guiding principles, not to be compromised for short-term financial gain or expediency.*

Values in the corporate context tend to describe the way a company would like to conduct its affairs, how it treats people and how it would like to be regarded by the wider world. These descriptors relate to a company, but they could also relate to an individual.

Many turn to an internationally respected figure such as John Elkington (1997) for guidance on values. In his book *Cannibals with Forks*, he voices the questions about corporate values that most business leaders will have asked at some stage. These include the acceptance that values are important, '... but are they crucial to the long-term future of capitalism? Are they little more than flies in the economic ointment, and can business afford to leave this area to public affairs professionals and industry chaplains?'

He answers these questions by referring to *The Seven Cultures of Capitalism* by Charles Hampden-Turner and Fons Trompenaars (1993). They explain that economists, and by inference many business leaders, understand how wealth is created, but don't stop to ask why people should be interested in making money, or what motivates them to spend it. The Seven Cultures authors say that ' behind every economic transaction are people making choices, acting on their values, giving one thing high priority, another one low'. While it may be counter-intuitive to say it, it is 'values' and 'human relationships' that are most important to the decisions that human beings make, not the economy.

Values, then, should lie at the heart of any organisation that says it is committed to improving the deteriorating environmental and social conditions of its market place. Mark Goyder (1998), founder of the 'responsible business' organisation Tomorrow's Company, says that

*the most successful will have found new ways of doing business that simultaneously create shareholder and social [and environmental] value – demonstrating afresh that business success is only ultimately sustainable where the company is meeting human needs, and that values are inextricably linked with the creation of value.*

The ability to positively incentivise employees to think and perform in a sustainable manner is entirely dependent on the ability of senior managers and the leader of the company. It is rare to find more than half of middle managers, or a quarter of shop-floor workers, that can name any of their company's values, assuming that they have been articulated at all. Many employees would say that they can ensure that environmental problems do not occur because of the procedures and processes put in place by the company. Few would be able to explain how the company contributes to society beyond the staff volunteering and charity schemes.

Many large companies (though not all) publish their values in annual corporate responsibility reports. These reports are a mixed bag, and some of the stated values are not values at all. Picking out a number of typical examples, you can read the British Nuclear Fuel's (BNFL, 2006) report that sets out five values including acting with integrity and respect for others, being safe and environmentally responsible, a commitment to achieve success for their customers, delivering value and profit, and excelling in their operations.

Williams-Sonoma (www.williams-sonomainc.com) has corporate values including 'people first, customers, quality shareholders and ethical sourcing'. Within these headings are other values such as motivating high performance, pride in what we do, integrity, and honesty. The company also talks about superior returns to the shareholder. Boeing has 'leadership, integrity, quality, customer satisfaction, people working together, a diverse and involved team, good corporate citizenship and enhancing shareholder value'.

A review of hundreds of others would show that many of these 'values' are repeated again and again. There are no rules that apply to the values a company can choose, but to include shareholder value and profit is questionable in that it can easily conflict with any of the others. Quality, safety and customer satisfaction are all things you would look for in a company, but they too are not very good values, as an inattention to these elements would be commercial suicide.

Mark Goyder (1998) highlights the values of three companies explored by Shell as part of a debate about business diversification. Shell wanted to analyse companies that had been around for a long time. The three companies that were chosen were DuPont, Mitsui and StoraEnso, the Swedish paper products company.

StoraEnso's values are not so different from other companies, and include customer focus, performance, responsibility (to sustainability development), an emphasis on people, and a commitment to pioneering innovation. Expressing innovation as 'we take the first step' shows a good understanding of how to word a value so that it resonates with the people that it intends to draw in and bind to the company.

DuPont has just four values, which are safety and health, environmental stewardship, ethical behaviour and respect for people. Here DuPont's use of words like ethical and stewardship is designed to ensure that there is no misunderstanding; the company is bound to these values and will not simply try to do their best by them.

Finally, the values expressed by Mitsui show how the generation and expression of corporate values can be used to their full effect. They are:

- Making it a principle to be fair and humble, we, with sincerity and in good faith, will strive to be worthy of the trust society places in us.
- With lofty aspirations and from an honest perspective, we will pursue business that benefits society.
- Always taking on the challenge of new fields, we will dynamically create business that can lead the times.
- Making the most of our corporate culture that fosters 'Freedom and Open-mindedness', we will fully demonstrate our abilities as a corporation as well as individuals.
- In order to nurture human resources full of creativity and a superior sense of balance, we will provide our people with a workplace for self-development as well as self-realization.

Goyder, Terry Thomas, AccountAbility and others would say that the most successful companies live and trade by the same values that any individual would subscribe to. If you are employing people, and selling to people, why would you adopt values that are alien to people?

## What does a values-driven business mean in practice?

The acid test of the value of 'values' as part of a sustainable strategy is whether a company can use them to create a self-motivating culture as opposed to one that has to rely on megaphone messaging and real or veiled threats. The experience of a social enterprise based in Liverpool could show the way forward for many other organisations that aspire to positive motivation through values (Bichard, 2008).

The Furniture Resource Centre, now known as the FRC Group, was originally founded in 1988 as a charity. Its primary purpose was to collect and distribute unwanted furniture to people in poverty who did not have the means to secure furniture for themselves. In 1993, it worked with the poverty charity Crisis to launch a one-stop service that linked the securing of a tenancy with good quality furniture. This allowed a widening of the FRC social objectives to provide work and training opportunities to the long-term unemployed, and included both the manufacturing and remanufacturing of furniture. The company is now considered one of the jewels in the crown of UK social enterprise.

There are many definitions of social enterprise. The UK government's Office of the Third Sector defines social enterprise as

*businesses with primarily social objectives whose surpluses are reinvested for that purpose in the business community rather than being driven by the need to maximise profit for shareholders and owners [www.cabinetoffice.gov.uk/third_sector/social_enterprise].*

The value for local authorities in the North West of England, including the city of Liverpool, is that they are able to procure a service that offers the added value of employing people that had previously cost them money in the form of social services, training and healthcare. The better jobs that FRC trainees get on leaving the company brings in higher taxes for the local authority, and helps the city to portray an entrepreneurial environment as opposed to an area of economic deprivation.

FRC found that 30–40 per cent of the volume of bulky items that were collected as waste from people's homes were not merely salvageable – they could actually be reconditioned and sold in FRC's own retail stores to people on low income as 'pre-loved' furniture. Later, the company found that the volume of non-recyclable material could be reduced to just 30 per cent by deconstructing items that could not be sold in the store. This has been achieved through a process of deconstruction, sorting, and cleaning of recyclable materials.

The next stage for FRC is to become more sophisticated and specialised in its recycling efforts. One example of the new opportunities opening up for the company comes from new European laws that ban the landfilling of waste electrical and electronic equipment. Social enterprises like FRC that have a close link to their communities and local authorities, and have the skills to recycle household items, will be well placed to serve society's needs in a way that addresses both environmental and social problems. But crucially, they also have the ability to generate wealth that can be invested back into the business and the community.

The success of the collection service, charmingly and memorably named 'Bulky Bob's', grew and became attractive to other local authorities. Today, Bulky Bob's serves five councils in the North West of England, and has attracted interest from dozens of others across the country. FRC still provides furniture to social landlords, but it now sources its new stock from companies that have an affinity for their aims and ethos. Their main supplier, Dove Designs, is also a social enterprise.

The group has very clear charitable objects which they have translated into four succinct objectives. The company aims to be:

- great to do business with;
- a great place to work;
- great for people; and
- great for the planet.

In the group's 2005/06 sustainability report (www.frcgroup.co.uk) explains how the company tries to put these objectives into place by saying:

*We aim to deliver on our triple bottom line all of the time throughout the year. Our objectives enable us to articulate how we do this. Being great to do business with means acting on customers' and suppliers' feedback. Being a great place to work means we take seriously what our employees think about working for FRC. Being great for people means offering training and job opportunities for the long-term unemployed and getting low cost furniture to low income families through our Revive stores. All this is carried out whilst working to be great for the planet and accounting*

*for and improving on our environmental impacts. And we can never forget that we . . .*
*have to be commercially minded and always deliver on our financial bottom line.*

While this is beginning to be the kind of communications message that most
large companies are aspiring towards, it is still very rare in a company that
employs less than 100 people. However, it is the way that FRC works with its
staff that is particularly noteworthy. A list of just some of the methods that they
employ includes:

- regular feedback through face-to-face interviews, questionnaires, focus
  groups and telephone interviews from our stakeholders.
- a report on performance in an independently audited annual sustainability
  report.
- the maintenance of a virtual University for the People that provides job
  related training through the day, and hobby and cultural activities for
  employees to develop their interests outside of work. The University delivered
  366 courses equating to 1682 hours worth of training in 2005–06.
- an employee feedback scheme called 'How's it going' where, in 2006, 100
  per cent thought that it was a fair opportunity to discuss: their progress
  at work; how they felt about their jobs; their relationship with their team
  leader; and their training needs and aspirations.
- monthly and annual meetings of the whole company to give out employee
  awards and discuss the direction and performance of the company.
- an open governance system at Board level where Board members and the
  Chair of the company are periodically required to asses their performance
  and value to the company.
- a values set that is the core of the employee motivation and management
  system.

It is the FRC 'values set', and how it is employed, that tends to be noticed by those
conferring prizes on the company. It is an exemplar for companies that aspire to
sustainability, and want to work with their staff in order to ensure that this message is fully accepted and enthusiastically disseminated.

When asked to sum up the application of their values, the company said that:

*Values are our beliefs in action. We acknowledge and reward behaviour and com-*
*mitment where employees are brave, creative, passionate and professional. We give*
*on-the-spot values awards; celebrate Employee of the Month; and have annual*

*awards voted for by all staff. We gave out 309 values awards in 2005/06 and pin up details of all values awards on notice boards and in our newsletter.*

(Extract from a funding application, 2007)

Alison Ball, one of the three directors that lead the company, argues that while company strategy, experiences, and ideas vary with the business environment, the 'company values' remain constant, and are about the way in which everyone works. She says that the values 'keep us on the straight and narrow' and the directors work hard to encourage all of their employees to champion them, and they in turn are rewarded when they demonstrate them.

FRC runs 'values days' during the recruitment process for certain jobs, and the company believes that this process helps it to see the beliefs and passions of applicants, so that they can identify the people that will contribute positively to the culture of the company. Ball explains that 'this is a key issue for certain posts such as managers and team leaders who must not only agree with our values, but also lead by example so that they can embed behaviours within their teams'. This effort is noteworthy because it goes beyond the managerial ambition to achieve sustainability in a commercial company. The FRC culture is also designed to engage staff in this goal, and the appreciation and acceptance of this is reflected in the attitudes of staff in the annual surveys.

However, the best way to show how a values-based culture benefits FRC is explained through the individual accounts and testimonies of the individuals that have been employed by the company. The story of John Hopkins is one of many that could be told.

John was born in Scotland and suffered abuse from his stepfather. By the age of 14 he had an alcohol problem, and was frequently drunk at school. He drifted in and out of employment, often losing jobs because he was either unreliable or unsafe at work. Alcoholism and an anti-depressant dependency eventually led to a homeless and jobless existence, first in Manchester and then in Liverpool. At the age of 34 he came to realise that he would not live much longer without accepting help, first from a charity and then from an alcohol dependency agency.

Once he had broken his drink and drug dependencies, his efforts to find a job proved to be difficult and demoralising. Even though he had case workers and staff at his local employment agency working on his behalf, employers would not take on someone who had not worked in a regular capacity for most of his life. He found that the rejection reinforced his lack of confidence and low levels of self-worth.

He accepted an offer for an interview at FRC with enthusiasm, but low expectations. FRC expressly targets people who are hard to reach, have been out of the labour market for a long time, and need a second chance. Trainees would be employed in the bulky household waste business, Bulky Bob's. While they worked for the business, they would also receive other life and certified training. It did not matter to John that he was unsure about what exactly he would be doing or what qualifications he might get, the prospect of regular work was enough. When John was called by FRC and told he had been accepted, he was ecstatic and promptly hung up the phone, only realising later that he had failed to ask when he was expected to report for work.

In the following 12 months that John worked for FRC, he passed certificated courses in First Aid, Manual Handling, and Forklift Truck operation. He also passed his driving test after one week of intensive lessons. John was Employee of the Month four months in a row during this period. From visiting his doctor at least twice a month, John has not needed to seek medical help since he started work at FRC. His levels of general anxiety and self-doubt have diminished to such a degree that he is revelling in his own self-assertiveness now. On leaving FRC John was recruited by another social enterprise in the city (the Eldonians) where he first worked as a driver and a contract cleaner and later become a supervisor.

John puts his success story down to two things. The first is that his belief in the sincerity of FRC to help him put his life back together was rooted in his understanding that the company stood for social and environmental justice. There was a credibility there that convinced him that these people really meant what they said. The other factor which is related to this is the role of his fellow workers, trainees and management. He repeatedly refers to the support and congratulations that he received each time he met with a personal success. At first he was amazed and then came to accept their refusal to entertain any other belief except that he would sail through each of his challenges. He talked as though the people at FRC knew him better than he knew himself.

While John is not a typical story of employee/employer relations, the story exemplifies the power of a successful 'sustainable organisation' to communicate its beliefs throughout the workforce. There has to be a genuine and close to unanimous feeling within the company that its commitment to sustainability is sincere, and directly relevant to all workers. Policing this commitment would be an almost impossible task for management. The FRC example shows that while the regular efforts to bring all employees and trainees into the circle may appear excessive to some commercial or industrial cultures, it has paid dividends for FRC.

The concern for all companies and organisations wishing to emulate FRC is whether its methods can be transferred and made relevant to their own organisational culture. There will inevitably be doubts about whether their corporate culture would be able to carry off these exemplary efforts. The answer is that it is generally a bad idea to import any method or approach unless it fits with the existing culture of the company. Every organisation has its own corporate personality. However, the dividend that comes from developing, reinforcing and rewarding a company's own brand of value-driven sustainable performance should be clear to any business manager.

There is a piece of advice that the sustainable communications company Futerra (2005) offers climate change campaigners. It says:

*forget the value-action gap and stop searching for the sparky magic bridge that simply leads from values to action or from attitudes to behaviour. People's behaviours, attitudes and awarenesses are all different and linked in complicated ways – if they are linked at all.*

This may be true for the public at large, but it is not true for a company that has invested in its corporate culture to the extent that values and actions are fused. This not only means that there is little need to ram home the importance of environment and society to the employees, but it leads to self-support and innovation within the workforce, freeing up management to concentrate on other pressing matters. Its all good.

# 10

# You shall be rewarded

## The unattractively paternalistic world of happiness

The achievement of sustainability, whether it is at the individual or the corporate level, will inevitably mean change. It will certainly lead to a change in the perception of what it means to be successful and prosperous, and it will also require changes to the way we use and value the possessions and pursuits that we associate with success. It does not mean a diminution of quality of life, levels of satisfaction, or happiness, but at present there are very few that would accept this. Right now there are not that many rewards associated with a life or a business that does not consume more resources than is globally fair, doesn't use energy that contributes to global warming, or moves forward in such a way that does not disadvantage or exploit others. Suggest this to almost anyone, and ask if they would be better or worse off if they tried it, and they would say worse off without any hesitation.

It would be very tempting, yet fanciful, to imagine that some magic bullet of an argument will lead humanity to accept that the sustainable path is not only the right path, but one on which they will gladly tread. It is equally fanciful to think that they would take the path thinking that making this decision was reward enough for their actions. But why is this so fanciful? There is a mountain of evidence that can be waved in front of the doubters and the disbelievers that says you will be happier in a sustainable society. Somehow most people just don't believe that this will be the case.

The index of Sustainable Economic Welfare, and other indices, consistently show very persuasive data that plots relative happiness (as defined in survey returns) against economic growth (GDP), public expenditure and other parameters. In every case the happiness line of the graph stays more or less flat, while increases in wealth and spending climb. New Economic Foundation's Happy Planet Index (www.happyplanet.org) calculates the efficiency with which countries convert the Earth's finite resources into well-being experienced by their citizens. This work shows why resource consumption should never be linked to well-being. For example, while Germany and the USA have almost identical life satisfaction and life expectancy levels, Germany's carbon footprint is one half that of the USA. These facts show that Germany is twice as efficient as America at generating long and happy lives, based on the amount of carbon they consume.

Jonathon Porritt (2006a) sums this work up when he says that

*ever since the groundbreaking work of Abraham Maslow who identified the 'hierarchy of human needs', psychologists and alternative economists have set out to demonstrate that far from there being any automatic increase in well-being in response to consumption, much of our current consumption is turning out to be a very inadequate surrogate for meeting human needs in a more satisfying, durable way.*

Humans needs, from the basic physical elements of enough food, shelter and health, through to the more advanced needs of financial security, the support of loved ones, feeling useful, and the belief that it is possible to fulfil personal aspirations, have very little to do with the possessions and pursuits that many would argue they could not bear to be without. Braun (2000), using the example of lottery winners, shows that less than one-quarter stop working after they win. Like many others, he does not believe that money has much to do with happiness. His list of things that make people happy includes:

*strong social connections, long-term loving relationships, a sense of optimism and openness to new experiences, the opportunity to pursue meaningful work, and spiritual belief or identification with an issue or idea that is larger than oneself.*

However, Braun does add a note of caution when he says that it is not clear whether these things 'make for happy people, or whether happy people are simply more likely to be optimistic, enjoy their work, and form long-term relationships'.

But while the broad arguments about happiness continue, the consensus is that once a human is past the point where basic physical needs are met, and the worry about survival is not a regular factor in their lives, most authorities think that piling on the products does not make us any happier. This invites a discussion about whether it has any effect at all. There are arguments on all sides about this. Some say that the misguided belief that buying things makes us feel happy is harmless, while other contend that the compelling need to keep up with the Joneses is actually damaging our mental health and making us feel much worse (Layard, 2005; Oswald, 1997; Johns and Ormerod, 2007; James, 2007).

In the end, the most important point for those arguing for sustainable change is that no amount of fine, rich statistical discourse is going to convince an ardent 'petrol head' that buying the new Land Rover Discovery is going to do anything other than cheer him up to the gunnels. It won't even convince the guiltily aware but harassed parent who is once again late for the kids' school run and opts to drive instead of walk.

Of course, politicians know all this, which is why they are always going to struggle to limit personal choice to fly or drive. And the business world knows it too. The current anger at the way supermarkets are squeezing the farming industry is having very little effect on their pricing regime or their product specifications. The supermarkets keep turning the screw on their suppliers, because they are safe in the knowledge that their customers will always demand cheap food. This argument is completely spurious because customers would also prefer cheaper petrol, cigarettes and alcohol. They don't get it, but the world keeps turning.

The argument against buying too much stuff, or travelling at dizzying frequencies, may eventually transfer from academics and health professionals to policy wonks and politicians, but it will wean no one off the consumption conveyer. Meanwhile, Johns and Ormerod (2007) say that the experts that seek to tell people they are wrong to seek solace in shopping are both 'undemocratic and unattractively paternalistic'. You can guess what those same experts would be told if they tried to argue with shoppers at the Trafford Centre in Manchester on a busy Saturday that they should curb their consumption for the good of the world. Consumers will only stop buying the planet to death when they believe that modifying their behaviour will make them feel better than they feel now when they rush home and start pulling their new acquisitions out of the bag.

## I'm so sorry, let me buy you another

This mass personal enlightenment may well come to pass, one day, but probably not in the time-frame that we have to correct the acute wrongs in the world today. Stepping down from this glorious yet unrealisable image of success, we are left with the daunting prospect of motivating humanity to change in some other way.

The South Pacific Tikopians that Diamond (2005) described saw that they could move away from a way of life that had endured for centuries, and they did this twice. The three business leaders we highlighted all found ways to introduce radical sustainability measures without sacrificing long-term profitability.

The Swedes and Germans can hardy be said to have failing societies, and yet the majority of their populations embrace sustainability as a life strategy. There must have been a period before they all chose to act more sustainably when they suspected their current way of life was not going to work out, but continued regardless. Later, when the realisation hit them, they may have had a number of discussions, or possibly full blown battles about who was to blame, before it became obvious to them that their current path was not going to be beneficial either to them or their surrounding world. Later still, they must have had to consider a number of options to realise their conviction before deciding on what they thought was the best solution.

Coming up with a solution to an acute problem, say a burst pipe, is fairly easy to envisage. A problem that has yet to happen, and one that has uncertain consequences, is not so easy to solve. Investment in potential disasters (emergency planning) is a good example. How much money do cash-strapped town and city authorities invest in flood defences for floods that may never happen, or at least not in the politicians' term of office? It is not easy to put a price or even a level of urgency on an uncertain risk. Nobody is going to thank public officials for spending large sums on something that was not needed. In these situations, the negative voice in the ear of leaders will whisper that the higher pay deal, or the new school or hospital, is a better bet if you want the praise and gratitude of your electorate. Businesses leaders face the same kinds of choices, but with shareholders and staff as their constituency.

The positive voice that counter-balances this will say 'you would be a hero if you anticipated a disaster, and invested in the means that saved the day. The lives, or businesses and homes that were protected would vindicate your decisions and draw sympathy for the criticism you had to endure'.

This tussle is the nub of the argument about positive influences. The positive push for change needs to be stronger than the negative pull to maintain the status quo. In order for the true tug-of-sustainability to commence, a few obstacles need to be cleared off the field.

## An end to the blame game

The first is the excising of 'blame' from the equation. It is easy when things go wrong to point the finger at others, usually a minority group, when in reality the problem is caused by the majority. We have seen how deniers can do this, and history is strewn with the most vicious persecution of people that were easy to blame. Of course, once the retribution is meted out to these victims, it solves nothing and often delays the time when the real solution can be discovered and put into effect.

The comfort for those blaming large corporations, or the Chinese and Indians and Americans, or people that subscribe to certain religious beliefs or political ideologies, is the certainty that these people are evil and bent on destruction for their own selfish end. But this is almost never borne out on closer examination. Midgley (2005) explains that people seek some kind of concrete or positive explanation that they always fail to find. She says

*if we ask whether exploiters and oppressors know what they are doing, the right answer seems to be that they do not know, because they carefully avoid thinking about it – but that they could know and therefore their deliberate avoidance is a responsible act'.*

This may sound perverse to some but, as Aristotle knew and others have been saying for thousands of years, humans fool themselves all the time.

The more positive way forward is to understand that the damage that the Earth has sustained has been caused more out of ignorance than wilful negligence. In the business context, the situation is akin to the actions of the corporate host who is looking after a visiting delegation from an important prospective customer. The host moves quickly through the tables of a pub to place an order for his visitors' drinks at the bar. In his haste he knocks over someone's glass of wine. The negligent act (or the display of rational bad behaviour as Diamond [2005] would put it) would be to ignore this as collateral damage in order to further the greater good of the company. If he gets the drinks quickly, and the visitors feel valued, they will be in the right frame of mind to place a large order with his company. This in turn will boost the economy. The person that had their drink knocked over may later benefit from a better job, or more and better buses, or a better cancer treatment service, as a result of the higher profits made by the company, which in turn could result in higher levels of investment and more taxes for the State. His small sacrifice will eventually be repaid.

But the host does not rush on the bar. He stops, possibly irritated by the delay, but he stops. He may or may not apologise, and he may be stopping because of a fear of negative consequences if he doesn't. This could be immediate if a scene is created by the offended party, or it could be delayed if the pub-goers and their friends and family boycott the host's company for his bad behaviour.

While these thoughts may be swirling around at the back of his mind, he immediately turns and instinctively offers to buy the person another drink because it was an accident. The host did not mean to do it. The negative act may have been perpetrated in the pursuit of a positive one; however, in the interests of harmony, and a general sense of doing the right thing, the offer is made to replace the drink. Very little thought goes into this and while there certainly is a guilty party and mess that needs to be cleared up, the whole thing generally gets sorted out very quickly. This is the position the world needs to get to before solutions can be found; that is to say, we need to come to the instinctive understanding that we are repairing the damage without recriminations on one side, or excuses on the other. Would that sustainable development could be as simple as buying the Earth another drink.

The Tikopians clearly got over the blame stage, and were able to make the changes that ensured that their society was able to continue into the future.

They must have agreed at some point that the first part of acting responsibly is for the majority to work together without recrimination. It is a prerequisite for the later decisions concerning what to do and how to get all the people to do it.

The Swedes do this in modern times. James Lovelock (Midgley, 2005) is clear that 'it would be wrong to ignore our awesome responsibility as Earth's first socially intelligent species'. Lovelock believes that this social intelligence allows us to realise that 'we are not stewards of the Earth, nor its owners or even its tenants; we are an integral part of it'. The requirement is, therefore, to generate an understanding and belief that we are all part of the solution and that only by working together can we overcome adversity.

## I can't wait for you

The next obstacle to overcome, to guarantee that positive push wins over the negative pull, is the suspicion that if one company acts, and its competitors do not then the proactive party will be disadvantaged. This is exactly the argument that the GW Bush administration used for inaction on climate change. In this case, the competitors are not companies but countries like China, Brazil, India and Indonesia.

There is a negative pull that is strong when feelings of injustice or futility reign. This is confirmed in a report by the Sustainable Consumption Roundtable (2006), which was a joint initiative between the UK Sustainable Development Commission and the National Consumer Council. The Rountable concluded that

*a critical mass of citizens and businesses is ready and waiting to act on the challenge of sustainable consumption. But to act they will need the confidence that they will not be acting alone, against the grain and to no purpose.*

The report adds that

*both the business world and citizens are increasingly willing to embrace key aspects of smarter, more sustainable lifestyles, but on one reassurance: that others, whether your neighbour at home or your competitor in business, act likewise – the simple idea of 'I will if you will'.*

The Roundtable suggests that it is government that should co-ordinate a joint approach for society to follow, and this may well be the case. However, placing faith in government plays right into the hands of those that would displace their own responsibility into the hands of others. A better and less intensive method is to provide enough of a positive push so that proactive actions offer an advantage. That way it really does not matter what anyone else is doing.

There have always been some companies that saw a competitive advantage in selling environmental, ethical and social values. Ben & Jerry's, the Co-operative Bank, the Body Shop, Patagonia, Interface, Timberland and Rabobank have all been consistent in their commitment to sustainable business practices. They did this well before the current crop of sustainability statements from bigger and better known companies. More recently companies like Marks & Spencer, GE, Honda and many others have begun to gain public trust for their sustainability convictions. However, it is still too easy for the great majority of less active businesses to discount the efforts of others. Large companies have deep pockets, and exemplar companies are firms to admire, but are either 'not like us', or have specialised to the degree that to emulate them would be irrelevant.

More business owners and leaders need to be exposed to the arguments, both economic and values-based, before the tide will turn. Personal conviction, as we saw in Chapter 3 waits for no one. The business politics of 'I will if you will' is a slow game, focused on the lower common denominators. We just don't have time for this to work.

Programmes such as the Prince of Wales's Business & the Environment Programme at the University of Cambridge regularly produce senior leaders that have been encouraged to argue out their doubts, and emerge as people of sustainable conviction. Sadly, there are not enough of these programmes to make a big difference. If governments want to make a difference, they could do much worse than to provide the resources to ensure that every business leader, political decision-maker and major fundholder is exposed to the positive aspects of sustainable development through peer-attended programmes that allow them the time and space to listen, talk and think their way into a more sustainable frame of mind.

## An end to inaction

The final obstacle is the paralysis caused by uncertainty. This is commonly seen in the reaction to economic conditions. Alan Greenspan (1992), former chairman of the US Federal Reserve, observed that

*faced with mounting financial problems and uncertainty about the future, people's natural reaction is to withdraw from commitments when possible, and to conserve and even build up savings and capital.'*

The same behaviour was displayed by many when the early evidence was presented about the possibility that global warming, caused (primarily) by the burning of fossil fuel, was going to create a major global upheaval. Now that the majority of people have accepted that the threat is real, there is another reason for uncertainly, although the effect (a reluctance to invest in a significant lowering of carbon emissions) is the same. This is the uncertainty of what to do about it.

Part of this problem lies in the current choice of technology, and the differing levels of investment and payback associated with low carbon or renewable energy solutions. These problems will diminish fairly soon as energy experts and efficiency reviews catch up with what works, and what needs more research and development. However, there is a step before companies get that far – one they have leaped over in their haste for a solution – that needs to be tackled next. This is the question of how much is enough. The uncertainty about what proportion of profit is prudent to plough back into securing sustainable operations is holding many back from spending anything at all. Climate scientists would say that this is potentially disastrous, and any delay now could mean that future investment will be too late.

This problem can be easily overcome with the help of Sir Nicholas Stern's *Economics of Climate Change* (Stern, 2007). While the journalists were writing about Stern's dire warning that climate change represented a bigger market failure than the combined cost of both World Wars and the Wall Street crash, many will have missed the practical advice he offers to companies. He said that by investing 1 per cent of GDP now (and then year-on-year) the world can avoid a loss in consumption of between 5–20 per cent as a result of climate disruption. The citing of GDP is often misinterpreted as something that the government controls, but of course GDP is a measure of added value, and it is almost exclusively business that adds this value. This fact is the key that can unlock the uncertainty of how much is enough (Bichard, 2007).

As GDP is a national figure, businesses first need to calculate their own value added. This is a simple matter of adding operating profit to labour costs, plus minor adjustments for depreciation and amortisation. This figure for any business is considerable, particularly if salaries make up the bulk of overheads. If businesses spent 1 per cent of this figure on lowering carbon emissions, then they would comply with Stern's remedy for the planet. Very few companies can say that this level of expenditure is being directed towards global warming strategies at present. Those that are devoting funds to the problem think they are doing well, even though they are nowhere near the Stern spending target.

However, anecdotal evidence shows that business managers are immediately relieved to understand the Stern formula, and are eager to determine how close they come to the target. Not only does this solve the uncertainty about how much is enough, but it also gets around the uncertainly about when to invest because Stern talks about annual expenditure. This clears business to spend a defined and universally determined budget wisely, and enables action against a 12 month assessment of how best to reduce carbon emissions. Efforts to produce this level competitive field would cure the 'I won't if you won't' logjam.

## Dangling the prize

Once the three main obstacles are understood and navigated, the next step is to gravitate to the fastest part of the track. Here the strategy is to use positive incentives in a manner that will encourage sustainable behaviour, without the need to spend time and resources exhorting people to be better human beings or to do the right thing. There are many examples, from both the corporate and the domestic world, that show how people can be incentivised to be more sustainable. Almost all of them have relied on cash or cash equivalents in return for the required behaviour change or purchase. That is not necessarily a bad thing. However, there is a difference between a bribe that leads to a temporary shift, and an incentive that leads to a more permanent way of thinking. The additional challenge today is to understand which incentive can be adapted, and in what context, to produce maximum effect in the shortest period of time.

Incentives are not to be confused with disincentives. There have been many tax-based disincentive ideas. Disincentives are problematic as a mechanism to change behaviour as they represent a negative influence on a prefered action. The message behind disincentives can also be missed because of minimal or poor communication. This results in the taxpayer (the public or business) being unaware that they are paying more to enhance environmental or social conditions. Not only is this a missed opportunity, but it sets up a dangerous pre-conception for future policies.

Ineffective taxes have been imposed in Europe on waste, air travel, virgin aggregate and fuel, to name a few. The 'pay-as-you drive' schemes such as London's successful congestion charge appears to be the exception. However, as we have already discussed, the London congestion charge would not have gained popular approval if it depended solely on a negative financial disincentive. The majority of the citizens of the city decided that they preferred the conditions that the charge had produced and moved from opposition to support as a result.

The problem is that few people would ever be aware of the diminished threat of climate change, the land saved from mining, or the slower rate of landfill deposits as a result of paying more for petrol, houses or garbage disposal. What actually results in these cases is a smouldering resentment among business and the general population that the government is using the flimsy argument that there is 'something wrong with the environment' to hose them for more money. If any change in behaviour is achieved, it reverts right back again as soon as the disincentive is removed, giving governments very little room for manoeuvre in any future economic plan.

If disincentives are such a problem, then we should be seeing both government and business grasping positive incentives with both hands, but this is not the case. A quick trawl of current ideas in the UK and the USA reveals a range of interesting yet modest ideas. The UK Department of Transport scheme for employees to purchase tax-free bicycles through their employers (Rogers, 2007). Google is offering cash incentives to their employees to purchase hybrid cars. The London congestion charge exempts low emission and renewable fuel vehicles. The think tank IPPR suggests that employers located at the edge of cities or on industrial parks should be given money to provide shuttle buses for staff (Retallack et al., 2007).

Public authorities have always tried to entice developers into their area with fast-track and grant-based incentives. Recently this has extended to climate change incentives. In the UK, these still have a negative emphasis where developers are asked to incorporate anything from 10 to over 30 per cent energy from renewable sources into their proposals. Santa Monica in California has a 'sustainable city plan' effective since 1994. In 2005, the city announced that it would speed up or 'expedite' planning approvals, and offer financial incentives of up to $35 000 for developers that registered their building for LEED certification. San Jose, Sacramento, and other Californian cities offer free parking for hybrid cars. Many US cities have high occupancy lanes that reward drivers that carry multiple passengers, and California also allows single occupants of hybrid or alternative fuel cars in these lanes.

Other positive incentives are simple economic interventions in the market, and are designed to place sustainable goods on a competitive footing. One example is the purchasing of energy-efficient fridge-freezers in the European Union. The most efficient 'A' rated models increased from 3 per cent of market share in 2001 to 70 per cent just three years later (Sustainable Consumption Roundtable, 2006). This was achieved by 'price support' (effectively a subsidy from the energy producers), which made efficient models competitive with less efficient ones. This allowed price editing by the retailers, some of whom would not stock anything less than 'C' rated units. Finally, the manufacturers saw what was going on, and voluntarily increased the efficiency of their ranges.

Another example of a positive incentive are feed-in tariffs that allow microgenerators of renewable energy to sell their excess power into the national grid at higher than market values. This dramatically cuts the time between initial investment in the hardware, and the point where the investor begins to make money. The preferential tariffs were introduced in Germany in 1999. Since then most European countries have adopted them. Anyone in Germany who wants to generate electricity from solar, hydro and wind sources gets a guaranteed price, which is four times the market rate for a 20-year period. This can ensure a payback period of less than 10 years, and a return on investment of more than 8 per cent. Germany has 200 times more solar energy than the UK, which, up to 2007, had no plans to introduce the green tariff.

Beyond these market interventions, there are many reward-based ideas that have been dreamed up to incentivise consumers to make sustainable choices. Incentives to reduce energy consumption in homes could involve rebates on annual local taxes, or tax breaks for householders investing in micro-generation. In the UK, drivers already pay less road tax if they drive fuel-efficient cars, but they also pay more if they drive inefficient models. Incentives in the future could roll together payment for environmental pollution and carbon damage, physical (road) damage, accident cover and congestion charging into a single addition at the pump, in the ultimate pay-as-you-drive charge.

Even air travel could benefit from incentivising the passenger. Air travel is the thorniest of problems for governments seeking to limit greenhouse gas emissions. Taxes have been imposed in a number of European countries, but with no real expectation that this will dissuade travellers.

The air industry is putting great store on the fuel efficiencies of new planes, packing in more passengers, and considering ways to reduce time spent taxiing and circling airports waiting to land. While all these things are to be welcomed, the problem with efficiencies is that they only pay off in a static economy. If increases in air travel continue, on their present trajectory, then efficiencies will be overtaken by growth. However, there is no reason why passengers should not be incentivised to limit the weight that they bring onto planes. Rather than charging for extra bags, the carriers should also reward passengers for travelling light. The pricing structure between short-haul and high-speed trains could also benefit from the same approach that led to the phasing out of inefficient refrigerators.

There are also existing schemes and new ideas associated with energy efficiency incentives. The Mayor of London has offered £100 to people who accept an offer of subsidised insulation material for their homes. Public sector bodies such as the Energy Savings Trust (2005) have argued that a rebate on local taxes could be paid to those that invest in energy-efficient materials such as loft and wall insulation. In addition, a rebate on the tax imposed on a new house could be available if it was an energy-efficient building.

Perhaps a better idea would be to reward those that reduce the overall use of energy, or invest in renewable sources. Some business and public sector bodies in the UK have benefited from the Climate Change Levy. Imposed in 2001, the scheme adds about 15 per cent to gas and electricity bills. However, there is up to an 80 per cent rebate on this charge in return for meeting energy or carbon savings targets. There are very few such incentives available for the domestic sector.

There is no reason why householders could not be similarly rewarded if their quarterly energy bill is less than it was during the comparable period the previous year. The difference could result in a cash equivalent reward that does not necessarily need to be associated with an environmental gain. For example, local supermarkets could issue vouchers for certain brands that are locally produced, effectively choice editing the prize without evangelising about the product. If customers like the product, then there is a better chance they will choose it without voucher support on their next visit. Of course, they could just claim a rebate from their annual income tax bill, but where is the fun in that.

Waste minimisation and recycling are fertile areas for incentive ideas. The Japanese national and regional governments have collaborated with local business and academic institutions to create over two dozen 'eco-towns'. Often located in or near ports, these are aggregations of recycling businesses that gain added benefits from co-location. The reason why they are there is because of incentives which were offered in a variety of forms. Some businesses were offered very low interest loans to relocate and build state-of-the-art recycling facilities. Others were given large rent and service discounts. The public sector benefits from having the recycling industries all in one place, which aids logistics, planning, and gives them positive notoriety and a sense of civic pride.

In the past, there was a culture of claiming money back on empty containers, mainly for thicker glass bottles and aluminium cans. While this has died out in some countries, such as the UK, it persists in much of northern Europe and many other parts of the world. The financial incentive to recycle in richer countries is not very strong, and citizens are more likely to claim their small change out of civic duty rather than for the cash reward. More innovative container return ideas can be found in isolated examples including vending machines adapted to reward recyclers with supermarket vouchers, or coupons for schools to collect and spend on computer equipment or sports gear.

The difficulty with incentive schemes that offer relatively small sums for individuals is that they don't have a strong enough push to get over the inconvenience pull in places where there is no cultural affinity for this behaviour. British MPs (House of Commons, 2007) found that, from an average bill of £75, an ardent recycler could expect an annual rebate of up to £30, whereas someone that ignores their recycling bin would pay an extra £30. They concluded that this sum was unlikely to represent much of an incentive, and would encourage poor recyclers to complain about more taxation rather than modify their behaviour.

This leads to the question of why incentive schemes are not geared to amassing larger sums by targeting larger numbers of people. One idea is to combine the interest in communities or neighbourhoods to improve local conditions, with the ability to increase local democracy and recycling rates (Bichard, 2004). This type of incentive is based on the fact that most waste has a value.

According to the House of Commons' (2007) figures, a 500-strong neighbourhood could collectively recycle up to £15 000 a year. This sum is large enough to incentivise individual action, but only if people can see that the aggregate sum would directly benefit their own situation as part of a community initiative; this benefit might be better street lighting or cleansing, security patrols, or an extra carer at the local nursery. The benefit would need to be something that was over and above the provision offered by the authority from taxes, and there would be collective (neighbourhood or organisation-wide) decisions on how the money should be spent. This incentivised experience (that happens naturally in Sweden) could lead to a wider community discourse about sustainable behaviour.

Some of these incentives may appear stealthy and underhand, but the outcome is that short-term and medium-term gains are made in reducing greenhouse gas emissions and sustainable consumption. Fooling people into sustainable behaviour is probably too strong a criticism for this tactic, as the incentives benefit the individual, without the risk of potentially negative reactions to messages that exhort people to be better citizens.

Beyond single issue incentives, there have been some ambitious attempts to draw in the consumer across the whole of their purchasing interests. Many of these ideas fall under the general category of 'complementary currencies'. Seyfang (2007) explains that complementary currencies

*refers to a wide range of new exchange systems which are designed to address specific economic, social and environmental needs which conventional money neglects, and which complement 'ordinary' monetary exchange.*

She points out that 'the movement has been growing rapidly since the 1990s, and includes a diverse range of systems in developed and developing countries.' These countries include Brazil, Mexico, Uruguay, Senegal, Thailand and Japan. In Argentina, where they were conceived as a 'solidarity economy', Seyfang says that complementary currencies became a lifeline to those people who were excluded by the mainstream financial system during the national economic crisis in 2001/02.

An initiative to explore the possibility of a nationwide complementary currency to incentivise sustainable behaviour was championed by the National Consumer Council and the New Economics Foundation (Holdsworth and Boyle, 2004). Their work highlighted a number of large-scale initiatives that showed that the idea is not just limited to the community level. One example is in the city of Curitiba, Brazil, which is more widely known for its impressive public transport system. The city operates a points scheme to citizens for recycling any waste they find. The points can be spent on the bus system during off-peak hours, resulting in one of the cleanest cities in Latin America, paid for out of cash-equivalent spare capacity on the city transport service.

Another example is the NU-Spaarpas scheme in the Netherlands (van Sambeek and Kampers, 2004). Launched in Rotterdam, the initial pilot ran from May 2002 to October 2003, and was devised as an incentive-based sustainable purchasing scheme. At its peak, there were over 100 commercial participants and just under 10 000 card holders. The NU-card shoppers could collect points by separating waste and buying sustainable products. Sustainable products included organic energy-efficient and fairtrade goods, bicycles, green financial products, renewable energy, rental, repairs and second-hand goods. They could spend their points in a range of places including an art library, several museums and a public swimming pool.

The Nu-card scheme did well considering that it was a time-limited pilot that underwent a number of adjustments in response to commercial and customer issues along the way. However, its main problem was the amount of effort it took to sign up participants, and the competing efforts of large supermarkets to keep loyalty points within their own control. It did have an appreciable effect on the recycling rates of Rotterdam, and its backers are now looking for new areas to launch a revamped scheme.

## Incentives in the workplace

The Curitiba and Rotterdam case studies are examples of how surplus public service capacity can be used as a reward for people's behaviour. Other schemes have used surplus or donated goods as rewards. The main problem for consumer-based reward schemes is that the consumer has to want both the green option, and the rewards that are on offer for buying them. If you never go near an organic vegetable, and ride around in your own car all the time, then these schemes will probably be unattractive to you. However, this is not the case in the company context.

The key to 'company rewards' for sustainable behaviour lies in the ability to recognise and draw attention to good behaviour in a way that is much more difficult in open society. This is recognised in the 'carrots not sticks' report by Holdsworth and Boyle (2004), which explains that

*the problem is that people's efforts are not rewarded in any way. Quite the reverse; they take time and are often inconvenient. Nor are they recognised. They are taken for granted by the local authorities that hope that, either because it is ethical or because people want to be rid of their own rubbish, people will take whatever action they are asked to. Good behaviour that is inconvenient, unnoticed and unrewarded is unlikely to be successfully reinforced simply by rhetoric.*

A company that has values and can stitch sustainable behaviour to the fabric of its culture will find it very easy to use incentives to keep sustainable performance and innovation moving forward. Good behaviour is not reinforced by rhetoric. Good behaviour is reinforced by reinforcement, and incentives are very good at doing just that. This was seen to be true in the FRC story, where company values are regularly reinforced by regular awards that the whole company comes together to celebrate.

One company that wanted to find a way of getting employees to turn off their monitors when they went to lunch explained that they would tie balloons to the chairs of transgressing staff. Another company liked the principle, but turned it into a positive incentive by leaving a cake for the retuning employees that had switched off. No explanation was given, and it took a few weeks for everyone to figure out what the reward was for. The debate, and the realisation, was enough to make the sustainable habit unanimous and permanent. In another example of surprise tactics, BSkyB employees came in one day to find that each of them had been given a 'carbon credit card'. Each one had a unique number, and staff found that they could log on to a register and claim credits for low carbon activities such as cycling into work. The incentive to join the scheme was a prize draw every quarter.

Examples of company incentives are very varied. Over a decade ago, Lovins (1996) was arguing that understanding how to save energy was not enough, and that incentivising employees was key to the rapid achievement of targets. He said while it was right for utilities companies to be rewarded for cutting customers' bills, and not for selling more energy, their staff members should also be rewarded for helping customers to use electricity more productively. Incentives work. Lovins explained that the 'result was that the volume of savings achieved (verified by ex post audit) went up and their costs went down – both by an order of magnitude'.

This policy depends on the principle of decoupling, which shifts utility company profitability from an increase in sales to a decrease in consumption. While there are small gains to be made in improving customer efficiency, the core business of energy companies around the world is still sell, sell, sell. In addition, energy companies have a credibility problem on the doorstep as customers think that there has to be a catch if someone is trying to sell you less of what they supply and not more. Utility companies would do better investing in independent parties to do the fuel efficiency work, and pool the gains.

Incentives in a workplace environment do not just depend on the nature of the scheme, but also on who is behind it. An incentive scheme that originates from junior management but is blocked by senior management, generally does not have much hope of success. However, if middle management is not keen on the leader's idea, it may not succeed either. Occasionally a good idea catches on, and is successful because of the sheer will and positive personality of a single employee.

There is a story in *Factor Four* (von Weizacker, 1997) about Ken Nelson, an engineer in the Dow Chemical Company's Louisiana Division, who set out to galvanise his 2400 co-workers into a collective action to cut energy consumption. He did this by organising a competition between teams of staff. The reward for winning was 'peer respect'.

Between 1981 and his retirement in 1993, Nelson helped Dow Louisiana to save millions of dollars. Close to 1000 separate projects netted the company well over $100 million in savings. These savings came off the bottom line in the year they were first achieved, and every subsequent year. Compared to the effort in generating profit through new sales, this is the kind of return on investment that would please any CEO. All this was achieved without any fancy change management or empowerment processes, nor was it embedded in the vision and mission of the company at the time. He goes as far to say that it probably succeeded because the CEO didn't know about it, and couldn't get in the way.

The point is that the ability to motivate has its root in individual drive and innovation, not seniority. This is brought home by what happened when Nelson retired. Dow decided to disband Nelson's organising committee in a restructuring move and further progress was not systematically reported. While it might have been the most obvious thing for other divisions to make their own savings by copying Nelson's lead, even the neighbouring Texas Division failed to follow suit. In a classic case of 'not-invented-here', the managers in Texas decided to do things their own way.

Present day performance suggests that Dow has taken energy savings and de-intensification to its corporate heart. In May 2007, Dow Chemical joined the US Climate Action Partnership (USCAP), a business and NGO partnership whose goal is to pressure the US Government to enact laws to significantly reduce greenhouse gas emissions over the next 40 years. This, the Partnership says, is to be achieved by a combination of fair tax disincentives, economic incentives, and a cap and trade scheme among others.

Meanwhile Dow was named winner of the 2006 American Chemistry Council (ACC) Responsible Care Energy Efficiency Award. Dow received an Exceptional Merit award in recognition of its longstanding energy efficiency and conservation efforts. This included an energy intensity improvement of 22 per cent from 1995 to 2005. All this was achieved while production increased by 32 per cent over the same period.

Not satisfied with this, the company announced that it intends to further reduce energy intensity by 25 per cent from 2005 to 2015. Energy intensity (Dow normalises this as $CO_2$ equivalents per pound of production) is not the same as greenhouse gas emissions. Dow's $CO_2$ emissions actually rose by more than 11 per cent between 1994 and 1999 (www.dow.com/commitments/stewardship). However, measured between 1994 and 2005, emissions dropped by 24.8 million tones, or about 20 per cent. It's Dow's recent performance since 2001, therefore, that has caught the eye. Prior to that, the Nelson effect does not seem to have infected the whole of the company.

The Dow figures reinforce the point about the value of inspired individuals, as Dow went backwards in the years after Nelson retired. However, the company has now moved forward, clearly with a different management team and a changing business imperative, driven by global climate scientists. It is interesting to speculate how profitable Dow would have been today if it had worked the Nelson magic throughout the whole company instead of for a few golden years in Louisiana.

## Looking in the right place for the right incentive

As polls and surveys have shown, the level of awareness and concern about the deterioration of environmental and social conditions around the world has been growing steadily since the turn of the twenty-first century. But these sources also show that there has not been a headlong rush through the sustainability door, for all the reasons that we have already explored. This drag on decisive action may come from the 'I won't if you won't' syndrome, or the wait for a legislative or economic lead from government, or the faith in a white knight technological fix, or the uncertainty over how to act. However, they all result in the same outcome: inaction leading to a worsening situation for the planet.

Many sustainability practitioners believe that there will, eventually, be an awakening and that sustainable change is inevitable. But they also worry that the change may come too late to avert chaotic market upheaval, and societal and ecological devastation. In order to avoid despair, the positive move forward for them would be to get together with those business leaders that are beyond doubt, but still ponder on the way forward. These leaders may have already thought about the implications of climate change on their business. They may have even made some investment decisions to off-set the implications of climate change on future markets. However, many will still welcome an approach to engage their workforce in a discussion about a more holistic approach to the issue.

The golden rule for any change of strategy for a business is to ask three questions: can we afford it, will our customers understand it, and will our employees support it? The initial answer to the first question is almost always 'no', but when longer-term accounting considerations are factored in, then the discussion often becomes more balanced. Customer understanding comes with a good organised programme of social accounting and accountability practice. In simple terms, if there is sufficient investment in customer dialogue enabling the company position to be understood, and the reaction of the customer heard and given due respect, then generally buyers will not undermine change.

The most underinvested part of this triumvirate is communication with the staff. Employers looking at all those surveys into public attitudes and behaviours to sustainability issues would do well to remember that most members of the public are also employees. A few memos and a poster saying that 1000 cups of tea could have been made, if only someone had turned off the photocopier last night, are not going to be enough. Work with employee groups is always rewarded when three positive factors are woven into the approach: know your audience, make room for sustainable change both now and later, and encourage disruptive innovation.

### *Know your audience – motivation and values count*

The first of these three positive elements is a requirement for employers to have confidence in employees understanding the company's intention to be more sustainable. In order to do this, business leaders and their advisors really need to know what kind of motivations or incentives they will embrace. The idea that one approach fits all, reinforced by anecdotal evidence that it worked elsewhere, is still widely held and is almost certainly doomed to failure. Rose (2007), describing efforts to persuade people to make sustainable changes, says that 'many of these well-intentioned efforts are naively conceived and executed, and stand little chance of being effective'.

This is hardly surprising given that the workplace has never been a comfortable place for raising issues of wider societal importance, or for talking about individual emotions. However, as we have seen, the future of the planet is an intensely emotional issue, which explains why previous tactics have failed. The presentation of more and more information, and the explanation of planetary trends that get more and more detailed, have been shown to miss that mark as Rose (2007) explains. He cites work by the Robert Gordon University (Anable, 2006) and points to energy-saving websites like the Energy Saving Trust (www. energysavingtrust.org) to illustrate why information alone is not effective.

Explanation, he says, creates uncertainty and demotivation leading to inaction. However, it is his point about the messenger, and not the message, that may be the most important to those in business that want to ensure a positive outcome for their sustainability programmes. Rose says that many leaders assume that 'what worked for them in terms of motivation, will work for other people'. This is not the case, and in order to understand what will work with a diverse set of employees, some understanding of values sets is required.

Cultural Dynamics (www.cultdyn.co.uk) is a strategy and marketing company that has a core business that advises organisations on the implications of changing cultural and individual values on policies, processes and procedures. While he was with Greenpeace, Chris Rose became very interested in the techniques that Cultural Design used to ensure that people understood the issues that were being put to them. Rose was worried to see that the old 'shock tactic' ways of bringing sustainability issues to the public were not working any more. In the twenty-first century, he observed, the

*environment is now colonised by groups with very different needs and motivations. What worked in its formative days, or even in the early 1990s, will not work now, not at least if you speak to and expect action from a wide range of people. Until campaigners and politicians adapt their motivational strategies accordingly, environmental action will remain thoroughly bogged down.*

Rose was attracted to the way that the Cultural Dynamic team developed a system that segments people according to their psychological needs, as opposed to the usual lifestyle or shopping behaviour, or class and wealth demographics. As sustainability is likely to depend on 'motivation' rather than 'knowledge', then this would appear to be a much smarter way to approach an employee group. Rose warns against the adoption of a growing array of 'rules' and guidance without a clearer understanding of the motivations that drive behaviour. He is also critical of work that the UK government has done on sustainable behaviour change, because it concentrates on what people may be directed to do, as opposed to why they would want to do it.

The approach that Rose favours is founded on the Maslow-based research into the hierarchy of human needs. The segmentations falls into three main types of people: inner directed 'pioneers', outer directed 'prospectors', and security-driven 'settlers'. Settlers like to meet people like themselves and people they know. They connect through clubs and family, and like to be associated with tradition. Their reaction to a problem is to look for somebody to do something about it, and they search for brands that make them feel secure.

'Prospectors' like to meet important people, and connect through big brands and organisations. They like to be associated with success, and don't like threats to the things that they have worked for. Their reaction to threats is to organise, and they search for brands that make them feel good. 'Pioneers' like to meet challenging and intriguing people, and connect through their own networks. They like to be associated with good causes where they can put their values into practice. Their reaction to threats is to do something about it themselves, and they search for brands that bring new possibilities. Rose et al. (2007) explain that these three segments can be sub-divided further into four grades or 'value modes' for each segment.

Faced with a suggestion to get involved in a programme to improve the sustainable performance of the company, Rose (2005) suggests that the employee audience is likely to react in one of five ways.

The 'champions' are likely to be ahead of the message, and will be impatient to run with the idea. There are not many of these, but they will often speak out. These people are Pioneers. The 'chasers' will understand the advantages of the change and will move early but are often reluctant to talk about what they are going to do. These people are on the Pioneer/Prospector border. Converts need evidence to act. They are also quiet, and will reject the proposal if they come across more compelling counter-evidence. These people are on the Prospector/ Settler border. The 'challengers' will resist, but only because they see that the outcome is important to them. These people are Prospectors. If they are won over then they can be important to the success of the project. Challengers can be very vociferous. Finally, 'change-phobics' will never be convinced. There are not many of these actors but, like the champions, they can be very vocal in their rejection of the idea. These people are Settlers.

Many business leaders, faced with undertaking a values-based analysis of their staff, will probably find the prospect both interesting and problematic. A typical reaction may be for them to either hand it to a colleague (probably in Human Resources) to figure out, or they will convince themselves that they know their people well enough not to bother with this complicated, and expensive-sounding approach.

The problem with many systematic marketing and decision-making tools is that they do get very complicated very quickly. This is not the tool designer's fault; human beings are complex creatures. It would be risky to leave the vital task of devising a sustainable change programme to the gut instinct of its leaders. But it is equally unreasonable to expect the high levels of commitment and faith in a complex conceptual tool to deliver this for businesses.

It should be sufficient for leaders to understand that change is linked to motivation, and that different people are motivated by different things. The simple answer is to design sustainable change programmes that have multiple voices. To some the programme will say 'this sustainable change thing is new, exiting and morally the right thing to do'. To others it will be saying 'if you participate in the programme then you will be held in very high esteem by colleagues and management'. Yet others will understand that 'your contribution will ensure the company survives into the future'. If some leaders want to get more technical then that is their decision. The main thing is to make sure that they appreciate the diversity of their audience.

## A brief word about time

The second positive factor that should form part of an employee sustainability programme is the appreciation of the significance of time. Much has been written about the way that time, or specifically the lack of it, is destroying the physical and mental health of people living in richer countries (James, 2007). The expectations of individuals about their lives, and the technologies they use to support them (including the internet, e-mail etc.) conspire to quicken the pace of living. Added to this, there is the current business emphasis on efficiency, low inventories, flexible working arrangements and outsourcing, which adds complexity and shortens the time anyone expects to wait for what they want. Packing more into communicating, and delivering on expectations, means less time for family, leisure, sleep and recovery pursuits that require time and space to clear the mind and relax the body.

Porritt (2004) asks

*how in a genuinely sustainable society will we simultaneously nurture those aspects of human nature that make us uniquely powerful in evolutionary terms, such as a hunger for change, our insatiable curiosity, our pioneering spirit, our ability to manipulate nature, and so on, and those aspects of human nature which depend on a different rhythm – cultural continuity, stable communities, time for reflection and spiritual devotion, an enduring symbiotic relationship with the natural world, with its very different cycles, seasons and time-frames?*

This tension is likely to remain for the foreseeable future. The truth is that humans are complex creatures, and they need both the fast and the slow. In the same way that we need food and drink, nobody advocating a more sustainable way of life is going to persuade the majority of people to calm their lives down. While some would not even listen to anyone telling them how they should run their lives, most would probably agree that it is easy advice to give, but almost impossible to follow.

The lack of time occurs in almost everyone's life almost every day, but it becomes even more threatening to sustainability when it is institutionalised into the rhythm of society. Alan Greenspan (2007) explained that it was very difficult to contain the US economy within the boundary between 'over activity' due to exuberance, and 'under activity' due to fear, because short-term electoral cycles never gave politicians sufficient time to consider any solution other than lower interest rates.

The same short-term cycles affect the world of business, which marches to the annual rhythm of the financial year. Accountants see a drop in profits due to an investment in energy-efficient machinery and ask whether the company is a going concern. No business leader wants to deal with that question on their watch. Lack of time to research how to source more sustainable raw materials and supplies leads to the placement of orders for the same old unsustainable stuff.

Then there is the time taken to plan strategic moves, and the time-frame that is considered to be strategic. Three to five years is normal, but still far too short to justify the investments needed to adapt to climate change over the next 25 years.

There is also the time required to properly train people, and to sit down with business partners, suppliers and staff to discuss their expectations and requirements.

Most of the unsustainable activities that happen in a business context are not done out of spite, but out of ignorance, miscommunication, or an assumption borne out of a lack of time to find the better way forward. The common answer to the request for more time is that time is money, and a company cannot afford to be talking when it needs to be generating wealth. The counter to this is the Formula 1 racing driver story; there is little point in accelerating around the track, if you are not equipped to drive around the obstacles.

## Disruptive innovation

The third and final positive element is about encouraging employees to question the way things have been done, both inside the organisation and beyond in the wider world. The fastest way back to an unsustainable base-camp is a statement that begins, 'we can't do that because …'. The 'because' could be something to do with internal rules about what is allowed to be bought, or what people think the customer would or would not tolerate. Sometimes the 'because' is pinned on really big things like the economic realities of the world, which would not support a decision designed to move towards a sustainable goal. The 'because' might be a perception that there are too many bad people out there, or just too many people out there.

These are the fears of a proportion of employees that are worried about change, or do not like the possibility of confrontation, or the prospect of the need for them to persuade others to change. The best way to work with these worries is to create the understanding that the old ways will not work, and that their job security lies in innovating away from the old solutions. One way of expressing this is to talk about, and later to reward, 'disruptive innovation'. This is a term that was used by a research report published by NESTA (National Endowment for Science, Technology and the Arts), the rational for which was that 'talk of wind farms, carbon offsets and hybrid cars often drowned out the bigger issues' (NESTA, 2007). The report said that what was needed was the development of 'entirely different ways of building, travelling, shopping and even eating'.

But while this sounds like a preamble for a proposal for a new world order, the intention is much less grandiose and more subversive. The report explains that

*disruptive innovations are typically cheaper, easier-to-use versions of, or alternatives to, existing products or services that target 'low-end' or new (previously ignored) customers. They upset, supersede and transform established business models and user expectations, and often come from non-traditional players.*

There are many innovative and entrepreneurial people, both within and outside organisations, that have simple ideas that are thwarted and discouraged because of the inertia of the system, and the 'we've always done it this way' brigade. The NESTA report gives examples of ideas that are disruptive, not because they upset the system, but because they are surprising in the way they run counter to assumptions about how things need to change. A good example of this is the inventor that thought up a way to harness the energy generated by the pressure inside gas mains.

There have been other ideas like this, such as ways to generate energy from the flow in sewers or drinking water pipes. This thinking could conceivably be applied to any system that maintains a flow, such as air conditioning systems inside buildings, or micro-currents flowing around large buildings. Another idea in the NESTA report is a way to ensure that all large windows are shielded from the sun to reduce solar gain inside buildings. There is nothing new in that, but the idea goes further and incorporates photovoltaic cells in the shutters. New glass technology is advancing so fast that in the future we might even have glass houses that generate enough energy to heat and cool themselves.

Shell runs a programme called Springboard that offers awards of up to £40 000 to businesses that have commercially viable ideas for products and services that contribute to combating climate change. In the first three years that it ran the competition (between 2005 and 2008), many disruptive ideas have won the money. Examples include a bodywork design team that could produce polymer panels for vehicles that are both safe and fully recyclable. There was a design to adapt a fitting for the energy-saving T5 fluorescent tube, which allowed landlords to replace the inefficient T8 tubes without having to change all of the existing T8 fittings. Another team devised a way to convert fallen leaves into an efficient heat log, and there have been many efficient heat generation ideas including one that uses existing materials to make domestic ovens into low carbon devices.

All of these ideas are relatively simple and, with the occasional need for some expert help, could have been generated by an employee group tasked with reducing the company contribution to climate change. As most of the ideas are based on observation and common sense and anyone of any ability could and should be encouraged to participate.

The NESTA report rightly states that

*this division between technology and behaviour is artificial, and unhelpful. We need to look at how the two interact: how new technologies can help to change our patterns of behaviour, and how new systems, structures and policies may be necessary to allow new technologies to flourish.*

The blind faith that technology alone will be the saviour of human kind is a very dangerous gamble. It may well be that we are just around the corner from a techno-fix that will allow everyone to continue to consume and trade in exactly the same way as before the climate change crisis hit. The question for those that believe this is: how sensible is it to put all your chips on that square? Would it not be more sensible to at least cover the bet, and invest in changing patterns of behaviour?

The search for a technological solution to our current planetary difficulties is similar to the attempts to remove Al Capone from society by finding proof that he was directly responsible for a spectacular and bloody murder. In the end this strategy failed, although the authorities felt sure that the proof was out there somewhere. The spectacular discovery that solves the crime of climate change could be nuclear fusion, super-efficient heat exchangers, solar power generation, or the ability to store energy in convenient and powerful packages. But solution to Al Capone turned out to be tax evasion. This was hardly spectacular or eye-catching, but it was just as effective as a conviction for murder, and Capone never regained his authority on release from prison years later.

The investment in sustainable solutions by small things is the tax-evasion equivalent of the Al Capone story. Every procurement officer that favours sustainable products, every cancelled trip in favour of a virtual meeting, every decision taken based on a longer time horizon than six months or a year will make a difference. These will not make the news bulletins, but every one will make a difference. These small decisions will not be taken without the investment to ensure that those who take them feel that they are doing the right thing, that they are not alone, that they are recognised and incentivised to make them, and that they, and those that are affected by their efforts, are better off as a result.

## Positive responsibility and habits

The UK Sustainable Development policy, 'Securing the Future' (HM Government, 2005), contains a model that shows how four different approaches can be used to change public attitudes and bring about sustainable behaviour. The model includes 'enabling' people through the supply of information, the provision of facilities and viable alternatives, and the capacity to make room for change. It also includes 'engagement' (a whole range of ways to draw people into a discussion about the issues) and 'exemplification' through leading by example. The fourth approach in the final document was 'encouragement'. Here, the examples include taxation, grants, rewards, penalties and fines, and social recognition or pressure through public identification of good and poor practice. However, in an earlier draft of the policy this approach was not called 'encouragement' – it was called 'incentivisation'.

This seemingly insignificant change lies at the heart of why business and government policy is not working. All of the evidence we have presented in this book suggests that humans will not be encouraged out of unsustainable behaviour. A positive incentive, providing it is strong enough, that draws people away from existing behaviour despite their beliefs, is always going to be more effective. These incentives need to appeal to decision-makers as they make the quick calculation on the consequences of their policies, and find that the outcome will provide obvious advantages to everyone, including themselves.

The tactic of encouragement respects the position of the individual and invites them, all things considered, to do the right thing. This may be a gentle, safe and non-threatening approach, and is certain to preserve the politician's or the business leader's popularity, but it is a disaster for the kind of decisive action that needs to be taken right now. An incentive bypasses this and says, 'you would be foolish not to take up this opportunity'. That crucial difference short-circuits almost all of the obstacles we have discussed. You can still be a disbeliever, a doubter or a sceptic, but you would be plain stupid to pass up a good opportunity.

If the incentive results in the establishment of a habit, then the need for further incentives diminishes. If by chance the incentive results in the realisation that the sustainable path makes you happier, or at the very least does not make you feel worse, then the incentive will have done its job, regardless of the original motivation of the beneficiary.

It is hard to establish a habit without stimulating change through motivation. Positive incentives, whether material or emotional, are more powerful and stay longer in the psyche than negative ones. The habit of sustainable thinking and working still needs to be embedded and reinforced but, if the seed does not take root, it will be carried away on the unsustainable gust of the next task or challenge.

**11**

The next positive steps forward

*We are now faced with the fact that tomorrow is today. We are confronted
with the fierce urgency of now. In this unfolding conundrum of life and history
there is such a thing as being too late. Procrastination is still the thief of time.
Life often leaves us standing bare, naked and dejected with a lost opportunity.
The 'tide in the affairs of men' does not remain at the flood; it ebbs. We may
cry out desperately for time to pause in her passage, but time is deaf to
every plea and rushes on. Over the bleached bones and jumbled residue of
numerous civilizations are written the pathetic words: 'Too late'.*

**Reverend Dr Martin Luther King, Jr.**

## Life in the freezer

Karl-Henrik Robèrt, founder of The Natural Step, is fond of telling a story of a
transforming moment in the life of a company. The company was the Swedish
electrical goods manufacturer Electrolux, and the story started when it was con-
tacted by the Nordic food retailer ICA. ICA had come under pressure from its
customers who were concerned about the ozone layer. They wanted to know when
the supermarket chain was going to phase out the use of ozone depleting gases.

The biggest concentration of these gases was in refrigerators and freezers,
and this led them to Electrolux's door. Electrolux came back to ICA a short time
later and said that they would consider replacing the refrigerant CFC gases with
less potent HCFCs. ICA informed Electrolux that this solution did not comply
with The Natural Step. Robèrt got a call from an annoyed Electrolux and went to
see them. He explained to them that while they had produced an answer for the
short term, HCFC was still an ozone depleter, and would not be sustainable in
the medium and long term. Companies like ICA were not interested in a quick
fix, they wanted to solve the problem once and for all.

Electrolux, after a bit of an argument, went away again, and this time came up
with a solution that ICA could accept. The company became the first white goods
manufacturers to market ozone friendly refrigerators. They did this by using the
gas R134a, accepting that this was a greenhouse gas, and began researching how
to use another refrigerant (isobutane) so that it complied with safety regulations.
Isobutane had a lower environmental impact, but it was explosive and could not
be used in certain circumstances.

While the refrigeration engineers were trying to find the right sustainable refrigerant, the whole experience sparked a deeper debate inside Electrolux. Why, someone asked, was the company making a product that was based on a box made of non-renewable metal, relied on man-made substances for the refrigerant and the manufacture of the insulation materials, and needed electricity that came (primarily) from fossil fuel to make it work?

This led to a back-to-basics discussion about the purpose of the refrigerator. At some point during the discussion there was a realisation that the company was not really in the business of making a cold space in the middle of a box. Instead, they realised that the primary purpose of their product was to extend storage and transport time, and to reduce shopping frequency by extending the shelf-life of perishable goods. Their function was, therefore, to facilitate a different (some would say better) way of life for its customers.

The Electrolux strategists accepted, once they deconstructed their product, that metal boxes that were reliant on damaging man-made substances, and fitted with inefficient heat exchangers, were not fundamental to the service that they were offering. They needed no sophisticated future predictive model to tell them that these materials were destined to become scarce, expensive, or unlawful to use very soon. At the time of this revelation, the company had not figured out how to make a refrigerator that worked without some kind of impact on either the ozone layer or the climate. But the medium to long-term strategy shifted attention away from the worrying, fog-bound path to the future, and onto a clearer route that would lead them to where they wanted to go.

Robèrt's Electrolux story contains many of the elements of a positively responsible business strategy. It cleared away uncertainly, made go-it-alone investment exciting and competitive instead of unfair, and did not rely on the need to pin the blame on anyone, or anything, before it got going. The decision was sparked by a challenge, involved some fairly spirited debate, and ended with an answer founded in collaboration, both between sectors (retail and manufacturing) and within Electrolux.

## Positive change is possible

One of the lessons that Electrolux, InterfaceFLOR, the Co-operative Bank and many others have learned is that sustainable change is not only possible, but desirable. They were not deflected by arguments that others were to blame, or that the government needed to fix the problem, or that it would only be prudent to act once something else happened, like the USA, China and India all having a change of heart about binding greenhouse gas emission targets. They saw that these were negative reasons for inaction, and made positive decisions that accorded with their own internal sustainable pathfinders.

The evidence for positive sustainable change is all around us, from the philosophical writings of Mary Midgley, to the socio-psychological evidence of Robert Cialdini, and through to the historical record set out by authors like Jared Diamond. The steadfast belief by business leaders that corporate sustainability is a societal obligation is becoming too commonplace to be written off as the province of a few misguided souls.

Of course, business leaders still have demons to fight. The unrelenting call for growth and short-term returns will not go away just because thousands more Bangladeshis die in the latest record-breaking cyclone. It is far easier to avoid lower profits by putting off the investment in low carbon technology, than it is to pay up and look forward to the absence of climatic disruption. Leaders can easily find themselves in the negative position of being conflicted and condemned whichever way they choose to turn. The positive way forward is to ensure that the internal compass is calibrated to point in the right direction, and to make decisions that are in the long-term interests of the company.

## Comfort in numbers

One element that recurs in many of the stories we have told is that sustainable change is facilitated by collective discussion. Whole cultures, like the Swedes, trust each other to come to the right decision. The absence of consensus leads to extreme behaviour such as boycotts, but collective action is a lifeline for people who want to make a difference. The social influence to act in concert with fellow citizens is part of the winning formula for sustainable behaviour. Robert Cialdini's notices about hotel towels and other research bears this out. The collective workings of the construction company AMEC over a one-hour period is another example of the power of a whole group to figure out how to walk themselves over to the sustainable path.

There is also evidence about how trust can be fostered in organisations, including an understanding of the upper limit (150) for the number of people that can easily reach a consensus (Gladwell, 2000). Offering the facility of group discussion among employees is vital to the process of sustainable change. Without it, the doubts, anxieties and expectations that everyone harbours are left to be negatively reinforced, and enthusiasm will whither on the vine. At the very least, organisa-tions should be gauging the feelings of their people on a regular basis. Making the time for people to talk pays dividends when collective decisions lead to positive outcomes.

## I, human

The fear tactics used by pressure groups to jolt or shame companies into more sustainable performance will not work. This is understandable, and can be partly explained by the defensive reaction to threats, and the discounting of inconveni-ent information and bad news. However, this still leaves the nagging worry and resulting anxiety in some (and probably many) that we may well be heading for disaster, and it is all our fault. Sustainable change will not be able to take place if this is not addressed. It needs to be converted into energy of a more positive kind. While the future cannot be predicted with any certainty, we have shown that it is possible to clear a path through the enclosing forest of worry.

Exercises like 'close your eyes', the 'spaceship', and sustainable visioning can all help to clarify an individual's understanding of humanity's role in the coming dec-ades. These exercises offer both emotional and logical freedom, without the cloy-ing and distracting constraints of everyday life. However, far from being escapist, they offer the escape route from the unsustainable practices of the present day. Experiencing the awe and solitude of nature can have profound effects on busy people as the organisation Impact found. However, nature has another use: the ability to humble and to define the individual's relationship with the rest of the world. Regrettably, some individuals have fallen into the trap of thinking that humans can fix anything, and can manipulate any situation to their advantage. Exposure to the grandeur of nature slows up, and forces them to think again.

Finally, the human dimension can be a positive force within companies, pro-viding it is allowed to thrive. Subjugation of natural human values in favour of an overriding emphasis on economic progress, while minimising the importance of the social and environmental issues, not only hurts the long-term interests of the company, but undermines the spirit of its employees. Shell, Tomorrow's Company and Terry Thomas's Co-operative Bank understood this very well.

And leaders should not feel that they are immune to their own needs. Personal experiences create a bridge between duty and the need to make a difference, be appreciated, and create a lasting legacy that will be well regarded by poster-ity. Personal experiences mattered to John Muir (the Black Locust tree), Rupert

Murdoch (the parched landscape of his homeland), Ray Anderson (the vision of dying caribou), Yvon Chouinard (the polluted Siberian countryside) and Lee Scott (devastated Louisiana in the wake of Hurricane Katrina). Most of them seem to have had an emotional reaction to their experiences. All business leaders should give themselves the opportunity to have their own experiences.

## Rewarding cultures

The evidence for positive incentives, offered in a culture based on rewards instead of punishments, is emotionally attractive. However, their worth is probably measured more in terms of a dislike for sanctions, rather than a belief that rewards actually work. But this view is based on a mistaken pessimism about human nature.

When the potential for innovation is taken into account, incentives begin to make much more sense. The Dow energy-savers came up with ideas because they wanted to win the competition. The Co-operative Bank adopted sustainable practices because it wanted to turn the business around. Interface devised leasable carpet tiles because it wanted to please its customer. Sweden wanted to be the first country to be free of oil dependency because it was culturally rewarding, but also because it was a route to promote its environmental technology sector.

The role of employees in the reward culture is vital. Many ideas, such as lease instead of sale, any number of energy efficiency schemes, logistics improvements and improvements in customer relations, regularly come from the employees of those companies that encourage participation.

A culture that favours bravery and initiative, such as FRC Group in Liverpool, will perpetuate a positive environment for its staff. There is no reason why every company can't encourage this by offering generous incentives and peer praise. Manchester Rusk gave all of the money saved in a waste minimisation drive back to its employees. Some, like Dow, will be motivated for the sheer fun of it. Any number of things can excite and motivate employees. If managers are not sure what their staff would like to work towards, why not ask them?

Positive responsibility can be engineered in the short term by incentives, supportive working contexts, and allowing the time and space to form a consensus on the way forward. But ultimately companies need to sit down and work out how they are going to survive into the future given the looming constraints on the horizon.

There needs to be a corporate 'close-your-eyes' exercise where everyone finds the place that looks and feels safe, prosperous and comfortable. Once this has been found it is never forgotten. The factors that shape that place need to be understood, so that when, regrettably, the imaginer returns to reality, there is a tangible end-point to aim for. It may not be reached for some time, but it is always there. That sustainable future needs to be embedded into every organisation, because the positive push will always triumph over the negative pull.

## Don't worry, but do hurry

Martin Luther King, speaking in 1967, was talking about the urgency needed to end the Vietnam War when he described the 'bleached bones' of civilisations that hesitated too long over crucial decisions, and then were lost. He could so easily have been talking about the urgency that is now needed to address dangerous climate change and resource depletion in the early part of the twenty-first century. Jared Diamond's (2005) book *Collapse* lays out the civilisations that failed to live within their means like so many corpses on the slab. Those that are gambling that it is all a panic over nothing may be right, but if we listen to them and do nothing we risk everything. Anyone that understands risk management can see that a potential terminal threat to the company has to be met with an effective contingency plan.

In order to put that plan in place, the world needs to have the majority of its people behind it. That is why there needs to be an understanding of the price of failure, but only as a spur to create an alternative future that is truly sustainable. Positive incentives, leading to a willingness to change and a belief that combined action will prevail, have to be the key to survival over the coming decades.

At the end of *The Tipping Point*, Malcolm Gladwell (2000) invites the reader to

*look at the world around you. It may seem like an immovable, implacable place. It is not. With the slightest push – in the right place – it can be tipped.*

There is enough evidence to suggest that this 'push' should not be a dig in the small of the back. Rather, positive responsibility requires the push to be an arm around the shoulder, drawing every organisation willingly towards a better and more prosperous future.

# References

Accountability. (2007). *The State of Responsible Competitiveness.* Accountability.

Ajzen, I. and Fishbein, M. (1980). *Understanding Attitudes and Predicting Social Behavior.* New Jersey: Prentice Hall.

Ajzen, I. and Madden, J.T. (1986). Prediction of goal directed behavior. *Journal of Experimental Social Psychology,* **22**, 453–474.

Anable, J. (2006). *An Evidence Base Review of Public Attitudes to Climate Change and Transport Behaviour.* Department of Transport.

Anderson, R.C. (1998). *Mid-Course Correction.* White River Junction, VT: Chelsea Green.

Armstrong, M. (2006). Climate change produces little shift in corporate attitudes. *The Guardian,* 6 November.

Arnold, J., Robertson, I.T. and Cooper, C.L. (2005). *Work Psychology: Understanding human behaviour in the workplace.* Fourth Edition. London: FT/Prentice Hall.

Barton, R. (2007). At the Peak of his ethical powers. *The Observer,* 25 February.

Bichard, E. (2004). *Sustainable Governance in England's Northwest.* Sustainability Northwest.

Bichard, E. (2007). Turning environmental pressure into business opportunities. *International Energy Review.* International Chambers of Commerce.

Bichard, E. (2008). Creating a sustainable and healthy work environment – future challenges. In *The Oxford Handbook of Organizational Well Being* (S. Cartwright and C.L. Cooper, eds), Oxford University Press.

Birchall, J. (1994). *Co-op, the People's Business.* Manchester: Manchester University Press.

BNFL. (2006). *CSR Report.* BNFL.

Boal, A. (1979). *Theatre of the Oppressed.* London: Pluto Press.

Braun, S. (2000). *The Science of Happiness.* Wiley.

Brook Lyndhurst. (2004). *Bad Habits and Hard Choices*. Brook Lyndhurst.

Bryman, A. (1992). *Charisma and Leadership in Organizations*. London: Sage.

Chouinard, Y. (2005). *Let My People Go Surfing: the education of a reluctant businessman*. London: Penguin.

Christian Aid. (2007). *Coming Clean: Revealing the UK's True Carbon Footprint*. Christian Aid.

Clout, L. (2007). Green guilt causing neighbors to fib. *The Telegraph*, 24 May.

Collins, J.C. and Porras, J.I. (1997). *Built to Last: Successful Habits of Visionary Companies*. Harper Business.

Co-operative Group. (2004). *Shopping with Attitude*. Co-op Group.

Coopersmith, S. (1967). *The Antecedents of Self-Esteem*. W.H. Freeman.

Cowell, A. (2006). Sweden and U.S. Agree About the Oil Dependency Problem, but for Different Reasons. *New York Times*, 5 February.

Crichton, D. (2006). *Climate Change and its Effects on Small Business in the UK*. AXA Insurance UK plc. September.

Dahl, G. (1998). Wildflowers, Nationalism and the Swedish Law of the Commons. *Worldview: Environment, Culture Religion*, **2**, 281–302.

Dawkins, R. (1976). *The Selfish Gene*. Oxford: Oxford University Press.

Denny, C. (2002). Retreat by Nestlé on Ethiopia's $6 m debt. *The Guardian*, 20 December.

Diamond, J. (2005). *Collapse – How societies choose to fail or survive*. London: Penguin Books.

Dilts, R. (2003). *From Coach to Awakener*. Meta Publications.

Downing, P. and Ballantyne, J. (2007). *Tipping Point or Turing Point? Social Marketing & Climate Change*. Ipsos MORI.

Eagly, A.H., Wood, W. and Chaiken, S. (1978). Causal inferences about communicators and their effect on opinion change. *Journal of Personality and Social Psychology*, **36**, 424–435.

Elkington, J. (1997). *Cannibals with Forks*. Capstone.

Energy Savings Trust. (2005). *Changing climate, changing behaviour: Delivering household energy saving through fiscal incentives*. EST.

European Commission. (2005). *Special Eurobarometer – Social Values, Science and Technology*. European Commission.

Everard, M., Monaghan, M.M. and Ray, D. (2000). *2020 Vision Series No. 2: PVC and Sustainability*. The Environment Agency/The Natural Step (TNS).

Festinger, F. (1957). *A Theory of Cognitive Dissonance*. Stamford University Press.

Finch, J. (2006). Asda hits back as Tesco takes the train to show its green credentials. *The Guardian*, 27 May.

Futerra. (2005). *New Rules: New Game.* Futerra.

Gemmill, G. and Oakley, J. (1992). Leadership: an alienating social myth. *Human Relations,* **45**, 113–129.

Ghosh, P. (2007). Climate messages are 'off target'. *BBC News 24,* online 15 May 2007, www.bbc.co.uk.

Ginsborg, A. (2005). *The Politics of Everyday Life: Making Choices, Changing Lives.* London: Yale University Press.

Gladwell, M. (2000). *The Tipping Point.* Abacus.

Goyder, M. (1998). *Living Tomorrow's Company.* Gower.

Grayson, D. and Hodges, A. (2001). *Everybody's Business.* London: Dorling Kindersley.

Greenpeace. (1996). *Building the Future: A Guide to Building Without PVC.* Greenpeace.

Greenspan, A. (1992). Statement to Congress – Alan Greenspan's presentation of the Federal Reserve's Monetary Policy Report – Transcript. *Federal Reserve Bulletin,* April.

Greenspan, A. (2007). Interview on BBC2 Newsnight, 1 October.

Grist (2005). Bulletin posted on www.grist.org, 22 November, viewed 15 September 2007.

Gunther, M. (2007). Rupert Murdoch's climate crusade. CCNMoney.com, 27 August 2007.

Hampden-Turner, C. and Trompenaars, F. (1993). *The Seven Cultures of Capitalism.* Doubleday.

Hawken, P. (1994). *The Ecology of Commerce: A Declaration of Sustainability.* Harper.

Hawken, P. (2007). *Blessed Unrest – How the largest movement in the world came into being and why no one saw it coming.* New York: Viking Penguin.

HeadLand. (2007). *Has the debate on climate change affected institutional investment behaviour?.* HeadLand.

HM Government. (2005). *Securing the Future, Delivering UK sustainable development strategy.* TSO.

Holdsworth, M. and Boyle, D. (2004). *Carrots not sticks: the possibilities of a sustainable consumption reward card for the UK.* Report of seminar jointly organized by NCC and NEF. NCC.

Houlder, V. (2007). One third of biggest businesses pays no tax. *Financial Times,* 28 August.

House of Commons. (2006). *High Street Britain: 2015.* All Party Parliamentary Small Shops Group.

House of Commons. (2007). *Refuse Collection, Fifth Report of Session 2006–07.* The Stationery Office Ltd.

Hovland, C. and Weiss, W. (1951). The influence of source credibility on communication effectiveness. *Public Opinion Quarterly,* **15**, 635–650.

Hovland, C., Lumsdaine, A. and Sheffield, F. (1949). *Experiments on Mass Communications.* New Jersey: Princeton University Press.

Human Rights Watch. (2007). *Discounting Rights – Wal-Mart's Violation of US Worker's Right to Freedom of Association.* HRW.

Interface. (2002). *Interface Evergreen Lease Programme: Vision, Progress and Learning.* Interface.

Intergovernmental Panel on Climate Change. (2007). *Climate Change 2007 (AR4) – The Synthesis Report.* IPCC.

James, O. (2007). *Affluenza.* Vermillion.

Jensen, D. (2006). *Endgame Volume 2: Resistance.* New York: Seven Stories Press.

Jepson, C. and Chaiken, S. (1990). Chronic issue specific fear inhibits systematic processing of persuasive communications. *Journal of Social Behavior and Personality,* **5**, 61–84.

Johns, H. and Ormerod, P. (2007). *Happiness, Economics and Public Policy.* The Institute for Economic Affairs, Research Monograph 62.

Kiesler, C. (1971). *The Psychology of Commitment.* New York: Academic Press.

Kingsnorth, P. (2003). *One No Many Yeses.* The Free Press.

Kübler-Ross, E. (1975). *On Death and Dying: What the Dying Have to Teach Doctors, Nurses, Clergy, and Their Own Families.* New York: Macmillan.

Laurance, J. (2006). 4 × 4 debate: Enemy of the People. *The Independent,* 23 June.

Layard, R. (2005). *Happiness.* London: Penguin.

Llewellyn, J. (2007). In a confusing climate, I think the scientists are probably right. *The Observer,* 2 September.

Lloyd, R. (2007). *What Assures Consumers on Climate Change: Switching on Citizen Power.* Accountability (in partnership with Consumer International).

Lovelock, J. (1979). *Gaia: A New Look at Life on Earth.* Oxford: Oxford University Press.

Lovelock, J. (2006). *The Revenge of Gaia.* Penguin Books.

Lovins, A. (1996). *Negawatts: Twelve Transitions, Eight Improvements, and One Distraction.* Invited Commentary for Energy Policy, April 1996 special issue on the future of DSM, 19.VIII.95 revision.

Lowe, T. D. (2006). Is this Climate Porn? How does climate change communication affect our perceptions and behaviour? Tyndall Centre Working Paper 98, December 2006.

Lynas, M. (2007). *Six Degrees: Our Future on a Hotter Planet*. London: Fourth Estate.

Macalister, T. (2007). Consumers distrust business on climate change. *The Guardian*, 19 June.

Macfarlane, R. (2003). *Mountains of the Mind*. London: Granta.

Marshall, G. (2001). The Psychology of Denial: Our Failure to Act against Climate Change. *The Ecologist*, 22 September.

Mathiason, N. (2007). Tesco faces attack over carbon footprint. *The Observer*, 9 September.

Meadows, D., Meadows, D. and Randers, J. (2005). *Limits to Growth. The 30 Year Update*. London: Earthscan.

Mendick, R. (2007). Exposed: I'm not an ethical bag. *London Evening Standard*, 27 April.

Midgley, M. (1979). *Beast and Man*. Routledge Classics, 2002 edition.

Midgley, D. (ed.) (2005). *The Essential Mary Midgley*. London and New York: Routledge.

Mitchell, D. (2006). Wal-Mart Flirts With Being Green. *The New York Times*, 22 April.

NCBS. (1999). *An Environmental Charter for UK PVC Manufacturers*. National Centre for Business & Sustainability.

NCBS. (2000). *Eco-efficiency Code of Practice for the Manufacture of PVC*. National Centre for Business & Sustainability.

NCBS. (2003). *Recycling end-of-life PVC packaging*. National Centre for Business & Sustainability.

NESTA. (2007). *The Disrupters; Lessons for low-carbon innovation from the new wave of environmental pioneers*. NESTA.

Organic Exchange (2007). *Organic Cotton Update Meeting*, Istanbul, Turkey, 2 July, 2007. Viewed on-line at www.organicexchange.org, 1 November, 2007.

Oswald, A. (1997). Happiness and Economic Performance. *Economic Journal*, **107**(445), 1815–1831.

Pan, Y. (2007). *Green China and Young China*. Accessed on-line at www.chinadialogue.net, 12 September.

Patagonia (2007). *Environmental Initiatives*. Accessed on-line at www.patagonia.com, 15 June.

Petty, R.E. and Cacioppo, J.T. (1986). The elaboration likelihood model of persuasion. In *Advances in Experimental Social Psychology* (L. Berkowitz, ed.), Volume 19, pp. 123–205. New York: Academic Press.

Porritt, J. (2004). Seduced by Speed. *Resurgence*, No. (222). Jan/Feb.

Porritt, J. (2006a). *Capitalism as if the World Mattered.* Earthscan.

Porritt, J. (2006b). Sustainability is Central to Survival. *The Guardian,* 6 November.

Retallack, S., Lawrence, T. and Lockwood, M. (2007). *Positive Energy.* IPPR.

Reuters (2007). China Blames Climate Change for Extreme Weather, 2 August. Accessed on-line from www.planetark.com/dailynewsstory, 30 September, 2007.

Robèrt, K.-H., Daly, H., Hawken, P. and Holmberg, J. (1995). *A Compass for Sustainable Development.* Stockholm: TNS.

Rogers, L. (2007). *Climate Change: why we won't believe it. New Statesman,* 23 April.

Rose, C. (2005). *How to Win Campaigns.* London: Earthscan.

Rose, C. (2007). *Sustaining Disbelief: Media Pollism and Climate Change.* Accessed from www.campaignstrategy.org, 15 August 2007.

Rose, C., Dade, P. and Scott, J. (2007). Research Into Motivating Prospectors, Settlers and Pioneers to Change Behaviours That Affect Climate Emissions. Accessed from www.campaignstrategy.org, viewed 29 August 2007.

RSA (2007). *Which messages spur citizens to protect the environment? The secret impact of social norms.* Speech to the RSA, 25 January 2007, London: RSA.

Sahtouris, E. (1997). *The Biology of Globalization,* Perspectives on Business and Social Change, September; viewed on-line at www.ratical.org/Lifeweb/Articles on 2 July 2007.

Save the Children. (2007). *State of the World's Mothers 2007.* Save the Children.

Secord, P.F. and Backman, C.W. (1969). *Social Psychology.* New York: McGraw Hill.

Seyfang, G. (2007). Personal Carbon Trading: Lessons from Complementary Currencies. *CSERGE Working Paper,* ECM 07–01.

Schultz, L., Folke, C. and Olsson, P. (2007). Enhancing ecosystem management through social-ecological inventories: lessons from Kristianstads Vattenrike. *Sweden Environmental Conservation,* **34**(2), 140–152.

Shultz, P.W. and Tabanico, J. (2007). Self-identity and the Natural Environment: Exploring Implicit Connection with Nature. *Journal of Applied Social Psychology,* **37**, 1219–1247.

Soil Association. (2007). *The Organic Market Report.* Soil Association.

Stanford Graduate School of Business (2004). *MBA Graduates Want to Work for Caring and Ethical Employers.* January, accessed from www.gsb.stanford.edu/news/research/hr_mbajobchoice.shtml, 8 November 2007.

Starkey, R. and Anderson, K. (2005). *Domestic Tradeable Quotas; A policy instrument for reducing greenhouse gas emissions from energy use.* Tyndall Centre for Climate Change Research, Technical Report 39, December.

Steedman, P. (2005). *Desperately Seeking Sustainability.* National Consumer Council.

Stern, N. (2007). *The Economics of Climate Change.* Cambridge: Cambridge University Press.

Surowiecki, J. (2005). *The Wisdom of Crowds: Why the many are smarter than the few and how collective wisdom shapes business, economics, societies and nations.* New York: Anchor.

Sustainable Consumption Roundtable. (2006). *I will if you will: Towards Sustainable Consumption.* SDR.

Teather, D. (2007). Wal-Mart proclaims its conversion to a caring, sharing firm. *The Guardian,* 26 October.

Temko, N. (2007). Firms pay 'lip service' to cutting pollutions. *The Observer,* 23 September.

The CarbonNeutral Company. (2006). *Climate Change: followers and leaders.* June.

Turner, L. and Lu, Z. (2006). *State of the World 2006: Special Focus on China and India.* Worldwatch Institute. January.

van Sambeek, P. and Kampers, E. (2004). *NU-Spaarpas: The sustainable incentive card scheme.* Stitching Points/Stuurgroep NU-spaarpas.

Vidal, J. (2007). Climate change to force mass migration. *The Guardian,* 14 May.

von Weizsacker, E., Lovins, A.B. and Lovins, L.H. (1997). *Factor Four: Doubling Wealth, Halving Resource Use.* Earthscan.

Wackernagel, M., Niels, B., Deumling, D., Linares, A.C., Jenkins, M., Kapos, V., Monfreda, C., Loh, J., Myers, N., Norgaard, R. and Randers, J. (2002). Tracking the ecological overshoot of the human economy. *Proceedings of the National Academy of the United States (PNAS),* **99**(14), 9266, 9 July.

Walker, P. (2006). Different Planets: Belief, Denial and Courage. The Role of Emotion in Turning Learning into Action. *Greener Management International,* (Issue 48).

Wilson, E.O. (2002). *The Future of Life.* Abacus.

Wood, W. (2000). Attitude change. *Annual Review of Psychology,* **51**, 539–570.

Wood, W. and Kallgen, C.A. (1988). Communicator attributes and persuasion. *Personality and Social Psychology Bulletin,* **14**, 172–182.

WWF-UK. (2006). *Counting Consumption.* Godalming, Surrey: WWF-UK.

Zeldin, T. (1994). *An Intimate History of Humanity.* London: Vintage in 1998.

# Index